PERSONALIZED LEARNING IN THE MIDDLE GRADES

PERSONALIZED LEARNING IN THE MIDDLE GRADES

A GUIDE FOR CLASSROOM TEACHERS
AND SCHOOL LEADERS

Penny A. Bishop

John M. Downes

Katy Farber

HARVARD EDUCATION PRESS

Cambridge, Massachusetts

Paperback ISBN 978-1-68253-317-8
Library Edition ISBN 978-1-68253-318-5

Library of Congress Cataloging-in-Publication Data is on file.

Published by Harvard Education Press,
an imprint of the Harvard Education Publishing Group

Harvard Education Press
8 Story Street
Cambridge, MA 02138

Cover Design: Wilcox Design
Cover Photo: iStock.com/Rawpixel

The typefaces used in this book are Rogliano, Myriad Pro, and Humanist 531 BT.

CONTENTS

ACKNOWLEDGMENTS

This work would not have been possible without the support of many people who are committed to engaging young adolescents in powerful learning.

We would like to thank the Richard E. and Deborah L. Tarrant Foundation for the establishment of the Tarrant Institute of Innovative Education (TIIE) through their generous grant to the University of Vermont. Without Rich's initial vision of the power of technology to engage young learners, the many partnerships, projects and stories shared in this book would never have been possible. Over a decade ago, Rich and Deb spearheaded one of Vermont's very first technology-rich, middle grades classrooms and the journey toward increasing student engagement has been rewarding and robust ever since. We are grateful to all members of the foundation's board for their belief in our work, and to the foundation's executive director, Lauren Curry, for her unyielding support along the way.

We extend enormous gratitude to our team of professional development coordinators at TIIE. The many examples and resources in this book are the direct result of their hard work, dedication, and passion as they work daily with middle grades educators to improve the learning lives of young adolescents. The professional development coordinators are truly co-authors of this book, as their work, writing, and vision are threaded throughout. Without them, the book would not possess the depth and detail that it does now. We are forever grateful for their contributions: Susan Hennessey, Emily Hoyler, Life LeGeros, Rachel Mark, Jeanie Phillips, and Scott Thompson.

Thanks are due to the University of Vermont (UVM), and the College of Education and Social Services (CESS) in particular, for supporting our vision for partnering with Vermont schools. CESS has supported the institute in many ways over the years, not the least of which has been in advancing a robust research collaboration between and among UVM faculty, CESS doctoral students, and TIIE staff. Mark Olofson, Steven Netcoh, Jessica DeMink-Carthew, Tricia Stokes and Meredith Swallow all played important roles in the ongoing research endeavor that informed this book.

We are deeply thankful for Audrey Homan at TIIE, who has been listening to students and teachers and telling their stories through blog posts, podcasts, vodcasts and various other forms of social media for years. She supplied us with rich examples from the field that we most certainly would not have found without her. And the richness of her voice is embedded in many of these.

Robin Merritt at TIIE helped us with myriad details for this project, and there are too many to name. We offer her our sincerest thanks for keeping us—and the many figures and images in this text—on track. It surely was like herding cats and, true to her nature, she shepherded cheerfully.

James Nagle, co-director of the Middle Grades Collaborative, has been an especially important intellectual collaborator in this work of personalizing learning for young adolescents. Our work is undeniably better for his involvement. Similarly, the highly skilled faculty team at the Middle Grades Institute has continually pushed and deepened our thinking.

We greatly appreciate the assistance of our editor, Nancy Walser, at Harvard Education Press, for her initial vision for this book and her continued encouragement and support throughout the process.

Finally, we wish to acknowledge the many Vermont educators and students and thank them for their bravery, openness, vulnerability, skill, and effort in making learning personal and powerful. While we could not possibly capture all of their great work here, they nonetheless inspired and informed this book. It is an honor to work with them and to share their stories.

INTRODUCTION

Miles pulls up the hood of his sweatshirt in the dark morning and hoists his backpack onto his shoulder. The cool late fall air nips his face as he walks to the end of his driveway on the dirt road where he lives. He thinks about the kids in his sixth-grade inquiry group with whom he texted last night. They are so close to completing their big project to establish a nature trail on school grounds and they're excited and nervous about presenting their proposal to the school board. He's still a little stunned that they'll be assessed on their presentation, rather than taking a test or writing a report. He remembers that he still has a few things to finish on the slide deck but he's feeling good about the argument he's written, the budget tables and cost projections they've developed, and their compliance with trail safety and accessibility standards. The bus lumbers along the icy roads, rattling as it climbs the hill to where he stands and gasping puffs of air as it stops. As Miles climbs the stairs, he wonders if his friends will be already sitting together, and if there will be room for him.

While Miles has a sleepy and uneventful bus ride, his advisory teacher, Ms. Phillips, is already at school, preparing for the day. She sips her quickly cooling coffee as she reads her students' latest entries in their personalized learning plans (PLPs) on her laptop. She tries to spot patterns in their personal communication goals so she can group them for peer practice and critique as they prepare for their upcoming project presentations. In 20 minutes, she needs to be standing by the door and even a quick glance at the PLPs usually leaves her ready to greet her students, with something specific to say about each.

Miles disembarks from the bus, is greeted cheerfully by the school principal, and walks through the door down the hallway toward his advisory period. On his way he sees the colorful self-portraits created in art class on the walls. His face, in an art deco style with cartoon eyes, stares back at him, one of only a handful of students of color in his class. He liked being able to choose a different medium for his self-portrait than many of his friends, thanks to the choices available in his teacher's art studio. He keeps walking, thinking that his portrait might be a good thing to upload to his digital PLP. After all, the PLP is his own personal website, his story.

At the door, Ms. Phillips, now up from her desk, greets him. "Hey, Miles. How's it going? How did the soccer game go this weekend? I know that was a tough team you were facing."

"We lost. They played really rough," Miles says.

"Sorry to hear that, bud," she says.

He nods, hangs up his pack and says hello to his friends, who are hanging out in a group by the fish tank. Miles walks to his desk and sees the choices on the board: check the class blog, upload identity work to PLP, meet with a PLP partner, work on a project of interest, read a book, or check in with the teacher. Miles has already made plans to meet with Maria, the fifth grader who is his PLP partner, this morning.

Miles heads to his table and smiles as he greets Maria, who is already seated. As the more experienced PLP partner, Miles is helping Maria prepare for the student-led conference she will hold with her family later in the month. This morning he plans to walk her through a few of the items in his own PLP to show her one way she could do it.

He snaps open his netbook and sees the last window still open—his PLP stares back. There is his name. He's happier with the look of the webpage since he changed its overall appearance, including the font and colors. He clicks on his identity page and smiles. There I am, he thinks. His favorite PLP entry is the video at the top of his identity page. In it, each member of his advisory holds up a sign that states something about them that most people don't know. This had been his friend Emma's idea, and it was created by a team of kids who are into film and video. Each sign tells a different story. Miles waits for his to go by. It reads: I know three languages. He's pretty proud of that. Miles then scrolls through his current goals, talking to Maria about each and informally assessing them as he does: playing forward in soccer (check), expanding the genres of books he reads this year (slow but steady progress on that one), and learning to write computer code (still working on figuring that one out). He scrolls through some recent PLP entries. He points out a learning profile he completed in science class that explains how he prefers active, hands-on learning. He clicks into a coat of arms he drew in literacy block featuring the important people in his life, a special place, and his favorite hobby. He shows Maria a photo of work on the Lego robotics team that he hopes will help him toward his coding goal. And he sees the picture he uploaded last night of himself playing soccer at the clinic he attended this summer, along with the accompanying reflection on teamwork skills that he recorded on VoiceThread. He plays that for Maria as an example, since he knows that she has a hard time with writing but has plenty to say. She is inspired by this idea, sees that the classroom's homemade podcasting booth is available, and retreats to try out audio-reflecting for herself.

Miles suddenly remembers walking by his self-portrait and he asks Ms. Phillips if he can go take a picture of it to add to his PLP.

She nods, "Miles, that is a great idea! Sure, head down there now. Got a camera?"

His cheeks burn a bit at the sudden compliment from his teacher. He smiles, holding up the iPad he grabbed from the class tech station as he heads down the hall. He checked the iPad out from Sarah. Every student in the class has a job and Sarah is the technology manager because she simply loves the gear. It seems like she can fix anything: a broken camera, a locked iPad, or Chromebook that won't start. Miles's job is to make sure that the class transitions from one space to the other on time, and this is no small task. He is learning to keep track of time for the class.

Snap! His self-portrait is now captured on the iPad. He tags the image to two indicators in his Creating Visual Art proficiencies and uploads it to his PLP. He ponders for a moment how he needs to capture and tag all the learning he's done for the trail project, like graphing the budget projections and learning about the Americans with Disabilities Act. But then he sees Jordi, one of his math project partners, come speeding down the hall.

"Hey, Miles!" Jordi says, out of breath. "We've got a big problem." Jordi explains to Miles that a footbridge for the scale model of their nature trail they're building in math class has broken and that they need to go to the school's makerspace to 3D print another piece to replace it. Miles, the group's communicator, uses the iPad in his hand to update his group's online calendar, which tracks their tasks for project time and their whereabouts. He sends an update to their math teacher; nothing more is needed in that regard since they're already certified to use the 3D printer. Jordi, the group's manufacturer, texts their group's designer, Alicia, to confirm which file should be used for the printing. Once they have their assignments in order, Miles knows he can return to preparing his digital slides for the school board. But first, he has to help with morning meeting.

He checks the time and, sure enough, it's 7:40. He rings the cowbell, a little more confidently than the last time, noticing a smile from Ms. Phillips and a thumbs-up from Dare and Ted, older classmates whose turn it is to run the meeting. With the slow migration of eighty students and teachers toward the "Kiva," their team's meeting space, he realizes he's starting to get the hang of it.

MEETING THE NEEDS OF YOUNG ADOLESCENTS

The opening vignette is an amalgam of real students and personalized learning going on in several of the fifty schools we have worked with over the past decade to implement personalized learning in the middle grades. We created it to illustrate a number of critical aspects that form the structure and purpose for this book. First, we want to vividly convey what school life can look like for young adolescents when they are authentically engaged in learning that is personally meaningful, appropriately challenging, technology-rich and driven largely by them. This is personalized learning at its best. Second, we want to demystify the critical roles and vital functions teachers carry out in such an environment. Third, we want to debunk the myth that personalization means that students work alone in front of screens all day, demonstrating instead how learning can be both personal and social, both technology-rich and active. And fourth, we want to share how teachers we've worked with in dozens of schools have leveraged larger system innovations to bring personalized learning to life for their students.

Miles's morning reminds us just how much is possible during the middle school years. And how much those years in grades five through nine matter. Middle grades experiences have a great impact on the degree to which students close achievement gaps, graduate from high school, and are prepared for and pursue postsecondary education.[1] In many ways, Miles's experience represents much of what we hope for all middle schoolers. After all, early adolescence is a time when many students begin to experiment with their myriad identities. Miles's day is rich with opportunities to explore his identity, whether it's creating his self-portrait or declaring proudly in his advisory's video that he speaks three languages. And while many young adolescents want to assert their individuality, they also want to fit in, craving a sense of affiliation and belonging to a group. Like Miles as he boards the bus each morning, many middle schoolers may be anxious on a daily basis about whether they'll be included among their peers. Yet he arrives every day to his advisory, a time specifically structured to establish and reinforce belonging, and he serves as a valued mentor to a younger student grappling with her own exploration of identity and affiliation. Advisory period also helps strike a balance since Miles, like most young adolescents, wants and needs the support of caring adults—their reliable acknowledgment, guidance, and validation—even as he works toward greater independence. Importantly, he knows that wherever he is on his quest for identity, he is honored and integrated into the larger team community. Yet his advisory program and its video project, like the self-portrait, were the product of teacher work and planning. Ms. Phillips and her colleagues recognized that knowing their students better, and helping them know themselves and each other, is fundamental to engaging and lasting learning.

Young adolescents also want learning to be personally meaningful as they grapple with life's moral and ethical questions and seek a sense of purpose in the world. Miles's inquiry group is engaged in project-based, technology-rich, collaborative work that culminates in presenting a real proposal to an authentic audience: the school board. A real proposal to improve the school's campus by establishing a nature trail for students and the community to experience and learn from. The project connects him with a small group of peers engaged in a collective effort to make an impact on their world. His job of ushering his team through their transitions, like Sarah's management of the team's technology, lends real weight to becoming more responsible. And mentoring Maria on her PLP, watching her find her place on the team, and witnessing her struggles as a learner, reminds him every day how far he has come and how everyone deserves the support he's gotten. But his exploration of shared purpose, his respite from the constant jockeying for social status that can alienate even the most resilient of young adolescents from school, is not an accident. It was intentionally designed by his teachers to create more personally engaging learning opportunities.

Further, young adolescents want to be recognized for the effort they put into the work they care most about. For Miles, that includes his soccer, his artwork, and his work on the trail project. His school's system for personalized goals, proficiency-based assessment, and digital PLPs, gives him a way to readily translate the learning he values most into a language of achievement also valued by his school and community, while also leveraging the technology he loves. Just as he tags his self-portrait to visual art proficiencies, he can tag his summer soccer to teamwork skills, his Lego robotics to computer science, his budget projections to mathematical modeling, and his safety and ADA compliance to proficiencies in local and national governance. And in the course of figuring all that out, by experiencing how domains of human knowledge and skill are categorized and intersect, it's easy to imagine that Miles is on at least as sound a path to lifelong learning as he would be in any other setting. Miles's teachers are not the first to value young adolescent identity. Nor are they the first to see how project-based or service learning, even classroom jobs for students, can significantly increase student engagement and improve classroom culture. But as much as teachers and students know how vital these practices can be for young adolescents, the prevailing system of subject classes and traditional testing push these deeper, lasting experiences to the margins. Instead, Miles's teachers have embraced an assessment plan that allows them, along with their students, to catalog and evaluate authentic evidence derived from personally meaningful learning. Miles is not only deeply engaged in learning, he knows it matters, not just to him, but to his teachers and community as well.

We'd love to see such learning opportunities available for all young people, so we are heartened to see schools across the United States increasingly adopting these and other key aspects of effective middle grades practice. What's more, as our colleague and postdoctoral research associate Steven Netcoh observed, for the first time in our memory, these efforts are taking shape as part of a broader policy agenda to personalize learning as a way to meet the diverse needs and interests of students.[2] For example, "in order to make schools more personalized and improve student outcomes," thirty-three states currently require individualized learning plans for middle or high school students and another ten states have similar plans in place without a mandate.[3] In fact, only six states demonstrate no state-level activity or enabling policies promoting competency-based education, a key feature of most personalized learning environments.[4] The national trend toward personalized learning is not without its critics and contradictions, which we address directly in the pages ahead. In spite of the controversy, this book shows how educators, regardless of their school or policy settings, can channel the power of personalized learning into more effective and rewarding schooling experiences for young adolescents and themselves.

When schools are places to direct important projects, assume vital leadership roles, and safely and openly explore identity, young adolescents can discover the joy and excitement of competence and efficacy, traits that predict persistence and resilience as students confront inevitable challenges on their paths to adulthood and beyond. Middle schoolers deserve opportunities to identify issues of personal relevance; to learn about those issues in appropriately interdisciplinary ways; and to draw upon an array of experiential, technological, and human resources to promote that learning. They deserve to be supported along that learning journey by knowledgeable mentors who care about their growth and development, and merit authentic audiences to whom they can demonstrate their achievements.

WHO ARE WE AND WHAT'S OUR CONTEXT?
Personalized Learning in Vermont

Recently, Vermont educators and legislators recognized the need for students to assume greater authority for, and engagement in, their learning. While Vermont's consistently high secondary school graduation rate is enviable, students in poverty complete high school less often than their more affluent peers, and Vermont's percentage of students pursuing postsecondary education is well below the national average.[5] These challenges, among others, spurred the passage of Act 77 in 2013, known as the Flexible Pathways Bill, which called for a more personalized system of education. Act 77, the Education Quality Standards, and their accompanying policies, shifted schools away from the traditional Carnegie-unit, seat-time credits and toward personalized, interest-driven demonstrations of competency-based learning, or what Vermont refers to as Proficiency Based Graduation Requirements.[6] As a result, Vermont students may now work toward high school graduation through a wide variety of pathways, including community-based internships, paid or volunteer positions, summer experiences, college courses, and online courses. One critical component of the bill is the mandating of personalized learning plans for all Vermont students in grades seven through twelve as a means of creating these personalized pathways. PLPs, developed by students in collaboration with teachers, families, counselors, and relevant community members, are meant to inform and document students' individual pathways to graduation.[7]

The Tarrant Institute for Innovative Education

Designed by researchers and teacher educators at the University of Vermont, the Tarrant Institute for Innovative Education has partnered with more than fifty middle level schools and districts over the past decade. Made possible by a generous gift to UMV by the Richard E. and Deborah L. Tarrant Foundation, these institute-school partnerships vary greatly in their vision and process. Each establishes its own pathway to better teaching and learning. What they share is a set of bedrock principles for the institute's work. One, the initiatives need to be grounded in effective middle grades practices, as represented by the extensive literature on how best to serve the learning and developmental needs of young adolescents.[8] Two, plans need to embrace innovative technology integration to deepen and extend those practices. Three, initiatives need to reflect what we know about effective school change, like the need for coherence and collective efficacy.[9] Finally, and perhaps most fundamentally, the initiatives must incorporate effective professional development, what teachers need for their own growth in the midst of change they value.[10] Since the passage of Vermont's Act 77, we've helped our partners stay true to these principles as they leverage the PLP to design flexible pathways and craft proficiency- (or competency-) based assessment systems in the interests of young adolescents and their teachers.

The teacher and student work products featured in this book stem from these partner schools across Vermont. The schools represent a range of demographics that, like most schools, present both challenges and opportunities. For example, some serve a student population that includes more than 50 percent eligible for free or reduced-price lunch, with almost 30 percent English language learners and more than 30 percent receiving special education services. Some are located in refugee-resettlement communities that speak more than thirty languages. Other schools in relatively affluent suburbs serve predominantly White populations, with fewer students who are receiving special education services or learning English. Still other schools are located in rural communities, with 50 percent of students eligible for free or reduced-price lunch and 60 percent of students receiving special education services. The dozens of schools from which we draw examples also present considerable variety in terms of building configurations, including preK–6, preK–8, 5–8, 6–8, 7–8, and 7–12 schools. What all of these schools hold in common is the desire to improve the learning and lives of the young adolescents in their charge.

For more than a decade, we have conducted research on various aspects of the work. We've studied various elements of personalized learning environments, such as the influences of choice and goal-setting on the student experience, and the potential for students to inform teacher learning.[11] We have analyzed the teacher experience, including the dispositions, roles, and professional growth related to key aspects of personalization.[12] We've studied the use of teacher action research as a strategy for professional learning.[13] We've examined promising pedagogies to couple with personalized learning, including project-based learning, service learning, and genius hour, within and across content-specific settings.[14] And we have learned a great deal about the intersections between effective middle grades practices and technology integration, and the implementation of 1:1 (one student, one device) laptop, tablet, netbook, or Chromebook environments in more than two dozen schools.[15] Over the past decade, our partner educators and students have helped us understand a great deal about what works and what does not. This book is the result of both research and practice, and, importantly, represents the hard work of Vermont educators and students during a time of considerable transition.

MAKING THIS BOOK WORK FOR YOU

The purpose of this book is to help you create personalized learning environments for young adolescents by leveraging the PLP. Because of the strong alignment between personalization, middle schools, and the developmental needs of this age group, we believe the best of personalized learning is within reach of many teachers, schools, and districts, regardless of the context. We hope this book offers useful insights for those of you in states such as Maine, New Hampshire, Colorado, and Oregon that have already adopted student-centered approaches to competency-based education. At the same time, we offer strategies to increase classroom-level personalization that educators in states such as Massachusetts, Illinois, and Wyoming can enact despite the lack of supporting policies.[16] We believe that the type of personalized learning we aspire to is possible in districts with low per-pupil spending as well as in districts spending far more.

Whether you are a preservice teacher or an experienced educator, this book will expose the conceptual background and practical underpinnings of how PLPs can help engage students in meaningful learning. We describe what an effective PLP is and illustrate how educators can create them at the middle grades, where students and schools are particularly well poised to take advantage of them. By detailing how PLPs, flexible pathways, and proficiency-based assessment work in concert, we show why and how to help students set personalized learning goals, identify flexible ways to achieve those goals, and document their learning in authentic ways.[17] Throughout it all, we illustrate how you can leverage technology to engage students and expand their access to learning. We introduce you to examples from successful teachers' forays into personalization, drawn from real examples of student PLPs and the practical tools and resources teachers used to scaffold success. And you'll benefit from illustrations of hard-won lessons learned as teachers tried—and sometimes failed—to launch PLPs. We hope that, upon reading the book, you'll be well equipped to take important steps toward personalization in your classrooms and schools.

While we've tried to be mindful of our readers' varied circumstances, we know we can't anticipate everything. To make this book work for you, we offer here a few suggestions. We hope they help you get as much as possible out of the concepts, strategies, and examples.

How This Book Is Organized

The book is organized into nine chapters beyond this introduction. As with this opening chapter, most begin with a vignette that illustrates the chapter theme. Like the case of Miles, these vignettes are composites of real schools, teachers, and students with whom we work. We include these depictions of personalized classrooms for several reasons. First, teachers often ask us what personalization looks like. Second, despite the many rich, real-life examples we include in this book, no single example can possibly capture the full potential of a personalized learning environment. And third, perhaps most importantly, as you prepare to increase the level of personalization in your own classroom or school, you will need a truly ambitious vision of what's possible in order to honor the significance of steps along the way.

After each chapter's vignette, we offer ways for you to "build your rationale" by connecting this work to relevant theories and research related to young adolescents and learning. As you consider increasing the personalized—and purposeful—nature of your own classroom, team, or school, you'll undoubtedly need to communicate about (and perhaps advocate for) these changes with various stakeholders, including other educators, administrators, boards, families, and communities. It's helpful to develop a strong rationale before doing so. You can draw upon this literature to justify to yourself, as well as to your students, colleagues, administrators, and families, the considerable time, effort, and risk that it takes for any meaningful change. Each chapter also contains examples and visuals of numerous work products that come from real students, teachers, and schools. We hope these convey both the ambition and the practical realities of their efforts.

We also invite you to consider a schema we've come to rely upon as we've dealt with the many vagaries of transitioning to more personalized learning environments: rethinking the use of time, space and roles. For this, Miles's morning is instructive once again. The vignette took place entirely outside our traditional notion of time, cutting off just as the team assembled for its morning meeting, the official start of Miles's school day. He anticipated a fluid movement in and out of his math class and the makerspace, and his presentation to the school board at their evening meeting at the town library, further stretching our typical understanding of school day, but also how we define the spaces in which learning happens. And clearly, Miles stretches our typical vision of student roles in his inquiry group, mentoring Maria, and facilitating a smooth transition for his team's launch of the day. Of course, his teachers, the school board members who agreed to hear his group's proposal, the state wildlife biologist who introduced them to nature trails, and the town lawyer who consulted on safety and accessibility, are all contending with somewhat novel roles as educators. We think resolving the understandable disequilibrium that often accompanies a shift to personalized learning lies in rethinking traditional notions of the time, space, and roles of schooling.

Chapter 1 (Personalized Learning for Young Adolescents) introduces you to personalized learning as an educational approach that encompasses many practices. We acknowledge its varying definitions in the field, describe what we mean by the term for the purposes of this book, and distinguish that from what we, in fact, don't mean. We present the three pillars of personalized learning, emphasize their interdependence, and share five key roles that educators play in personalized learning environments. Chapter 2 (Personalized Learning Plans) presents the underlying rationale for personal learning plans, helping you distinguish what PLPs do and don't do well. In it, we identify common threats for you to watch out for as you head down this path. And we offer a set of questions you may find helpful to revisit throughout the book as you design PLPs for your own purposes. Chapter 3 (Laying the Groundwork for Personalized Learning) recognizes the need to carefully prepare the classroom or school culture prior to tackling PLPs. In it, we describe how to scaffold both the teacher and the student cultures for personalized learning. We emphasize common planning time, shared resources and a responsive platform, as well as sustainable routines for individual and collaborative behavior. And we discuss the importance of social-emotional learning and executive functioning in a personalized classroom.

Chapter 4 (Launching PLPs with the Learner Profile) launches you into using PLPs with students at the start of a school year. The central aim of this chapter is to discuss how to design learning opportunities that result in evidence to populate the Learner Profile of the PLP with an emphasis on individual and collective identity. In chapter 5 (Designing Flexible Learning Pathways for Young Adolescents), we move into creating action plans for learning and creating flexible pathways for that learning. We place particular emphasis on the role of empowering pedagogies, such as project-based and service learning, in the context of personalization, and we provide lots of examples of student and teacher work. In chapter 6 (Scaffolding for Equitable, Deeper Learning) we continue to explore flexible pathways, emphasizing the various ways teachers scaffold for successful learning. And we consider strategies such as passion projects and genius hour, blended and maker-centered learning, and playlists and micro-credentials.

Chapter 7 (PLPs and Proficiency-Based Assessment) rounds out the critical functions of the PLP with the integration of proficiency-based assessment, describing how students can document and reflect upon authentic evidence of personal growth in the midst of personalized learning. We explore the unique role PLPs can play in translating authentic evidence of learning into an accessible and universal language of academic progress. In chapter 8 (PLPs, Goal-Setting, and Student-Led Conferences), you'll come to understand the power of the student-led PLP conference as an anchor practice and explore strategies for enhancing family involvement in that process. You'll also see how students' personal and academic goals fit into the PLP while considering how to provide appropriate scaffolding without what professional development coordinator Life LeGeros and the Crossett Brook Middle School leadership team deemed "over-schoolifying" the process.

Finally, in chapter 9 (Sustaining Innovation in Your Classroom, Team, or School), we acknowledge the very real effort—emotional, intellectual, even physical—educators expend in pursuit of educational change. We discuss the roles of personal and collective efficacy, as well as the importance of milestones along the journey. And we offer strategies for maintaining momentum by drawing on the significance of seemingly modest progress and personal commitments.

In some respects, this book covers concepts, opportunities, dilemmas, examples, and much more that we would ordinarily introduce to our partner educators over the course of months or years. Along the way, we would help them make personal meaning of it all and craft implementation plans that reflect their priorities and circumstances. We would encourage them to commit to bold timelines with significant, often public, milestones to mark and celebrate progress. We would ensure that they had thoughtfully planned backward from these milestones using the best planning and implementation practices we can come up with. We do this because we learned from life without such a plan as we tried to make change in our own classrooms. We remember how our hopeful summer plans sometimes collided with day-to-day realities. How overlooked minutia could undermine our best intentions. And when moving too fast—or too slow—at times sparked blowback from colleagues, students, or families.

For sure, the change portrayed in this book is hard work. But teachers are nothing if not disciplined planners, at least when it comes to practices they're familiar with. A remarkable number of the specific practices we describe are not new. Many have been honed to a series of highly reliable action steps using readily adaptable materials. Some of those materials appear here; others are easily found online or in other resources we'll point you to. What's far harder to find elsewhere is how these practices apply and interrelate to serve the particular needs of personalized learning environments. That's what you'll learn in each chapter. We hope the wisdom gleaned from the ambitious work of others, combined with your own scaffolded planning, offers you a useful entry point into improving your practice—at the classroom or school level—and increasing the engagement of young adolescents.

A Word about Words

Finally, if you've been looking into personalized learning, you've likely come across the term *personal learning* as well. The latter term conveys a deeper degree of learner autonomy than the term *personalized learning*, which, for some, suggests a more institutionalized—or schoolified—approach.[18] Advocates of personal learning point to learner autonomy as the key distinction between the personal and the personalized. You'll find an associated debate regarding the terms *learner* and *student*, with the former implicitly suggesting that learning happens anytime, anywhere and the latter relegating learning to the school building and day. And there are certainly many terms for the education of young adolescents, including *middle school, middle grades,* and *middle level.* The latter two terms are often chosen to convey that students this age need, and in fact deserve, specialized pedagogy, regardless of the type of school building they're in.

Given our considerable emphasis in this book on student self-direction and anytime, anywhere learning, it's fair to say that we are aiming more for personal learning than for personalization. And we surely hope it can be embraced for all young adolescents, regardless of which grades are represented within their school buildings. Yet, throughout the book you'll see we use various terms to describe the kind of learning we hope all young adolescents can experience, such as *personal, personalized, engaging, meaningful,* and *powerful.* We similarly rely interchangeably on terms such as *middle grades* and *middle school.* One reason is that drawing a hard and fast rule to divide these complex approaches and perspectives risks oversimplification. Another, frankly, is that it's unnecessarily mundane to rely on the same terms throughout an entire book! Most importantly, however, we wish to speak to educators on all sides of these issues. We believe teachers can support deeply personal learning within a personalized learning environment; conversely, we recognize that the reality of schools at times demands personalization without more personal aims. This is perhaps particularly true within public education, where the majority of our work resides. Regardless of the terminology, we agree with classroom technology experts Bruce Dixon and Susan Einhorn, who observed:

> We need to shift our thinking from a goal that focuses on the delivery of something—a primary education—to a goal that is about empowering our young people to leverage their innate and natural curiosity to learn whatever and whenever they need to. The goal is about eliminating obstacles to the exercise of this right—whether the obstacle is the structure and scheduling of the school day, the narrow divisions of subject,

the arbitrary separation of learners by age, or others—rather than sup-plying or rearranging resources.[19]

Whether you use the terms personal or personalized, student or learner, middle school, middle level, or middle grades, we are hopeful that you will find the right approach for your context, one that helps young adolescents become efficacious, empowered, and confident learners.

ONE

PERSONALIZED LEARNING FOR YOUNG ADOLESCENTS

Defining Personalized Learning

Just what is personalized learning? In general, it's considered "a variety of academic approaches to learning and instruction where teachers and students work together to tailor education around individual learner readiness, strengths, needs, and interests."[1]

Given the breadth of that definition, it's not surprising that the term has been, as one education writer noted, "used to describe everything from supplemental software programs to whole-school redesigns. As a result, the term has become a blank slate on to which supporters and skeptics alike project their own hopes, fears, and beliefs."[2]

It's also not surprising that the broad and inconsistent use of the term hinders our understanding of its effects. In a study of twenty-three charter schools implementing personalized learning for a minimum of two years, for instance, students made significantly greater gains on standardized reading and mathematics tests than their counterparts in a matched comparison group.[3] The researchers caution, however, that they were unable to identify "which particular instructional approaches may account for the positive student learning outcomes identified in math and reading."[4] Students demonstrated similar achievement results in a study of sixty-two public district and charter schools; again, however, personalized learning practices differed across the participating schools, making it difficult to identify which strategies were most promising.[5] These examples, and their potentially positive outcomes, call upon us all to be specific about what we mean by personalization.

At their core, most definitions of personalized learning identify the common goal of addressing the needs, skills, interests, aspirations, and backgrounds of individual learners. Personalized learning is often viewed as an alternative to the more traditional "one-size-fits-all" approach, in which all students, sorted by age, move at the same pace through the same instruction, assignments, and assessments. Leading researchers and practitioners typically agree that some version of the following three elements is important in a personalized system: (1) addressing an individual's needs, skills, identities, and interests; (2) offering a variety of learning pathways, usually in preparation for college and careers; and (3) assessing learning based on students' competency or proficiency.[6]

These elements were evident in Miles's classroom in the book's opening vignette. Miles set personal goals based on his own needs and interests as he focused on improving his soccer, reading, and computer programming skills. He and his peers pursued various learning pathways, strengthened by the targeted use of technology, as they worked individually and in inquiry groups on topics of interest to them. And Miles's learning was assessed based on an authentic demonstration of skills, such as his preparation for and presentation at the school board meeting.

Of course, meeting the needs of individual learners is hardly a new concept in education. Most educators are already familiar with approaches that center on students' needs. Differentiation and individualization, for example, are both well-represented in most teacher education curricula. When first introduced to the idea of personalization, some teachers understandably wonder what distinguishes it from these other approaches. A key distinction between personalization and its counterparts of differentiation and individualization is the explicit focus on students' ownership of their learning.[7] In a differentiated classroom, teachers provide explicit instruction based upon the learning needs of groups of learners; in an individualized classroom, teachers instruct based on the learning needs of an individual learner; and in a personalized setting, learners participate in the design of their own learning in collaboration with the teacher.[8]

Overall, then, we consider personalized learning to be an increasingly "student-driven model in which students deeply engage authentic and rigorous challenges to demonstrate desired outcomes."[9] It fosters partnership between teachers and individual students in the design of learning that emerges from students' interests, questions and needs, toward an aim of self-directed learning. These learning opportunities respond to the wide array of students' identities and attributes (e.g., cultural, cognitive, social, emotional, moral, physical) and often prioritize real-world demonstrations of proficiency in twenty-first-century skills, such as critical thinking, problem solving, citizenship, quantitative reasoning, and oral and written communication.[10] And assessment strategies complement these learning opportunities, using portfolios, performance tasks, learning exhibitions, and other means of evaluating authentic evidence of proficiency.[11]

We are conscious that, for some educators, personalized learning may feel simply like the latest fad. Indeed, educational reform initiatives inevitably stem from distinct perspectives and priorities. Some initiatives emerge to address a society's economic priorities, political interests, or social needs. Others arise from concerns about pedagogical effectiveness, such as tackling issues of equity or accountability. And still others surface from a more humanistic appeal for schools to address students' needs, such as agency, voice, efficacy, or meaning. Yet, one reason we are optimistic about personalized learning as an educational change initiative—so optimistic in fact that we took the time to write a book—is that it's rare that one initiative arises from all three perspectives. Yet, personalized learning has done just this. And, in its best manifestation, personalized learning can engage and empower youth at a critical stage of their lives: when they are exploring what their role is, and will be, in the world around them.

CHAPTER OVERVIEW

In this chapter we explore how different educational reform initiatives are defining personalized learning, with a particular look at technology's role. We then consider the match between the needs of young adolescents, the design of contemporary middle schools, and the aims of personalized learning. We also introduce the three pillars of personalized learning: personalized learning plans, flexible pathways, and proficiency-based assessment, and emphasize their interdependence. Finally, we explore the importance of student self-direction in a personalized learning environment and share five key roles that educators play in these spaces.

TECHNOLOGY'S ROLE IN PERSONALIZED LEARNING

Over the past decade, various organizations, proponents, and educators have emphasized and promoted different aspects of personalized learning, based on their purposes and priorities. We have seen personalized learning encouraged at the national level through federal grants, such as Race to the Top funds; mandated at the state level through legislation, such as Vermont's Flexible Pathways Act and New Jersey's Personalized Student Learning Plans; and driven at school and district levels by philanthropic organizations, such as the Bill and Melinda Gates Foundation and the Chan-Zuckerberg Foundation.[12]

Perhaps not surprising, given the prominence of these foundations, many people associate personalization first and foremost with technology. Some initiatives do focus on leveraging adaptive technologies to customize curriculum and instruction in order to allow individual students to work at their own pace. The Gates Foundation underscores the affordances of technology, stating that, "While the concept of personalized learning has been around for some time, advances in technology and digital content have placed personalized learning within reach for an increasing number of schools."[13] This emphasis on technology-driven approaches has not been without controversy. Some equate technology with big data and adaptive learning systems, expressing concern that these systems are redefining teaching, learning, and educational policy in ways that shift educational decisions from public school educators to private corporations.[14] Others assert that, when defined as "methods that use some form of technology to give students greater control over the content and pace of what they learn," personalized learning conflicts with what is known about the workings of long-term memory.[15]

Most often, however, we find that critiques of the practice stem from a constrained understanding of both personalization and educational technology. In our view, as Miles's classroom illustrated, technology for learning isn't an all-day, every day, self-paced march through strictly online curriculum. Frankly, we can't imagine a poorer match with young adolescents' developmental needs! Further, research also demonstrates that the simple substitution of in-person learning with online learning does not increase student achievement.[16] On the other hand, avoiding or eliminating online opportunities does not increase learning either.[17] Instead, research increasingly shows that blended environments, an informed integration of in-person and online learning, outperform traditional classrooms.[18] Educational psychologist Saro Mohammed summarized the research this way, "[B]lended environments significantly outperformed traditional face-to-face learning environments. So access and connectivity appears to be a necessary step, but just *one* step, in the path to improving outcomes using technology. For those who are seeking to implement blended learning, the exciting message is then: It's not *what* you use, it's *how* you use it that matters."[19]

We agree that how one uses technology matters a great deal. Again thinking back to the opening vignette, Miles and his peers relied on many technologies for learning. At home, Miles texted to manage his inquiry group's preparation for the school board presentation. At school, they seamlessly managed their broken bridge crisis by texting an absent teammate and using a shared online calendar to revise the group's task list and update their teachers with their new plans and whereabouts for the morning. Miles and his classmates routinely created and composed with technology, leveraging the podcasting booth, Lego robotics, iPad, Chromebook, class blog, and 3D printer to meet their goals. And they vividly documented their learning in electronic personalized learning plans (PLPs) capable of capturing and sharing their evidence of growth in all its forms. In short, Miles's world was full of technology, used in and out of school, by students and teachers alike, and yet his school life was far richer than any algorithm can generate.

Many young adolescents are at ease with technology. American middle schoolers average between six and nine hours a day using social media and the internet; playing video, computer, and mobile games; reading; listening to music; and watching online videos, TV, and movies.[20] This affinity for technology is one reason why personalized learning is such a strong match in the middle grades. Young adolescents have shown us that learning in a technology-rich environment is engaging, fun, and collaborative. It affords them opportunities for creativity, enables efficient use of their time, and provides them with helpful organizational tools.[21] Throughout this book, you'll see how technology can empower students to redefine how, when, where, and from whom learning can occur.

THE PARTICULAR PROMISE OF PERSONALIZED LEARNING IN THE MIDDLE GRADES

Young adolescents' affinity for technology is but one of several reasons why personalized learning is especially well aligned with the nature and needs of young adolescents. Personalized learning environments like Miles's classroom also hold great promise in grades five through nine because they respond to young adolescents' developmental needs for independence, responsibility, and competence.[22] They offer opportunities for autonomy and participation in decision-making at just the time that students express an increased desire for these chances.[23] Personalized learning environments can also exploit key design features of contemporary middle schools, such as block scheduling, teams with common planning time, flexible grouping, and teacher advisories.[24]

Additional characteristics of effective middle schools align with personalized learning environments. In its position paper, *This We Believe: Keys to Educating Young Adolescents*, the Association for Middle Level Education (AMLE) describes an appropriate education for young adolescents in four key terms: (1) developmentally responsive, (2) challenging, (3) empowering, and (4) equitable.[25] Similarly, when comprehensively implemented, a personalized learning environment directly responds to the varied developmental needs and cultural identities of this age group. It challenges students within their personal zone of proximal development. It empowers them with greater ownership over personal and academic goals and the distinctive pathways to achieve them. And with this flexible and responsive framework, personalized learning targets inequities by attending to students who face additional learning barriers, including students of color, students living in poverty, students who have experienced trauma, English language learners, and students with disabilities (see figure 1.1).[26]

We believe there are many connections between personalized learning strategies and the Association for Middle Level Education's widely recognized expectations for a positive middle grades experience. These connections convey not only how a personalized learning environment may be more familiar than you initially might think, but they also underscore the fundamental practices long promoted by middle grades advocates.

PERSONALIZED LEARNING AS A SYSTEM

The best of personalized learning is realized through a fundamentally reshaped system to know students better, design engaging learning opportunities, and leverage assessment for student growth, achievement, and accountability in personalized learning environments. It's a system that draws educational stakeholders together by bringing to the forefront and honoring the interests that each holds most dear in their duty as student, teacher, administrator, mentor, family member, and voter. And while it's built upon long established

FIGURE 1.1 **Intersections between AMLE's essential attributes and personalized learning**

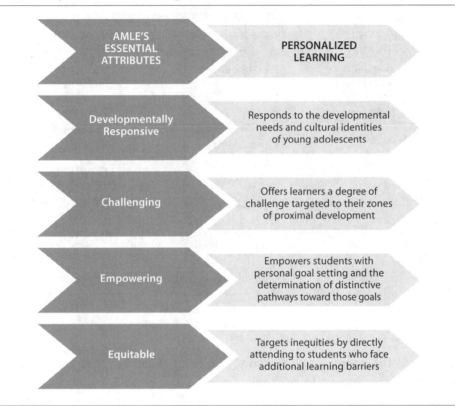

principles of good education, it has only recently become imaginable on a large scale, thanks in large part to some converging trends in educational technology. That may be a big reason it has never been suggested on a large scale before. It's this opportunity for scale that sets the movement apart from the many visionary classrooms, teams, and the occasional school who've demonstrated over many decades what personalized learning looks like. And while much of their work is well-represented in the visions and strategies now being discussed in central offices, state agencies, and other organizations, we see the current movement to personalize learning as the best chance yet to move beyond islands of innovation and make a learning environment such as is

FIGURE 1.2   **Three pillars of personalized learning**

The Three Pillars of Personalized Learning		
Personalized Learning Plans	**Flexible Pathways**	**Proficiency-Based Assessment**
Provide window into students' identities	Invite learning of personal and social significance	Honor authentic evidence
Position student as director	Promote powerful pedagogies	Remove seat time
Offer framework for goals and action	Welcome a variety of collaborators	Provide new language for learning
Create platform for engaging families	Value anywhere/ anytime learning	Emphasize transferable skills
		Track and report what matters
Knowing students well	**Creating authentic opportunities**	**Valuing students' learning**

MIDDLE GRADES COLLABORATIVE

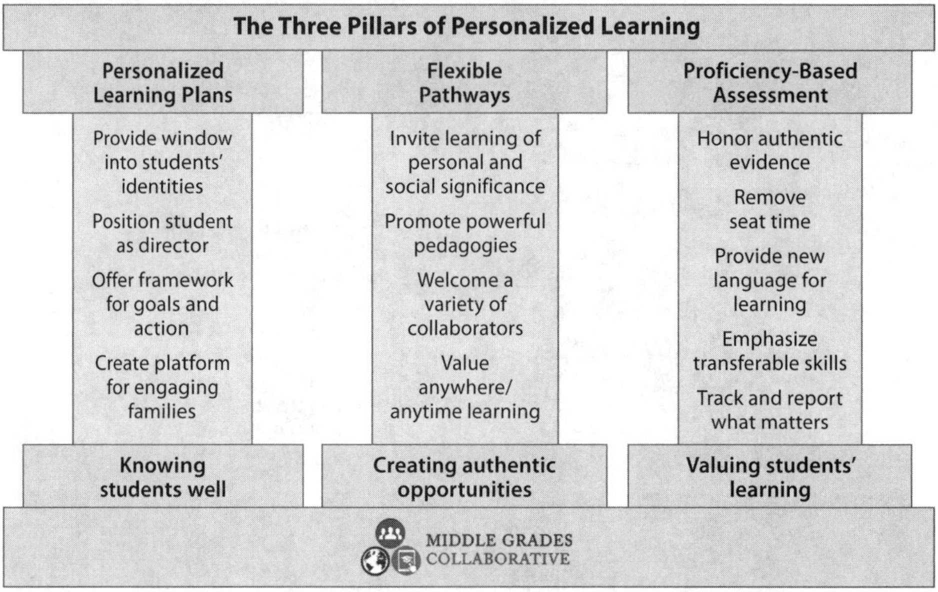

Source: Middle Grades Collaborative, www.middlegradescollaborative.org.

depicted in the opening vignette available to all students. That promise rests on a system that has three key parts, featured in figure 1.2, which we think of as the three pillars of personalized learning.[27] We introduce them here and dig deeper into each in chapters 4 through 7. They are personalized learning plans, flexible pathways to learning, and proficiency-based assessment.

Personalized Learning Plans

We saw how Miles, like his classmates, had a personalized learning plan that documented his academic and personal goals. The plan charted his pathways toward achieving those goals and cataloged evidence of his learning. It was accessible to teachers, his family, and selectively to his peers and mentors, but it was nonetheless his personal space, over which he felt real ownership. He expressed who he was from week to week, year to year, along with what he was learning and how he imagined his future. It was nearly always available online, from just about any kind of internet-connected device, on a netbook or Chromebook, a tablet or smartphone, at the town library or the community center. And you can imagine, well beyond the vignette, the many ways Miles might interact with his PLP. He could upload video and slides of his presentation to the school board and link to the project calendar he was maintaining for his project group. He could embed the spreadsheet he made to calculate the number and species of trees to be cleared for the proposed nature trail and add the interactive model showing the comparative impact on fauna of the nature trail from two competing land use proposals. To document his physical growth and development, Miles also might include videos of his soccer penalty kicks or cardio charts from the school's heart rate monitors in PE class. And if he helped with certain jobs at home, Miles might capture a quick audio reflection before bedtime. All of these examples of learning have a place in his PLP. Over the past decade, we have learned that the PLP can be a powerful lever for achieving this multifaceted vision.

In their review of research on equity and personalized learning, researchers Rashawn Ray, Lynne Sacks and Janet Twyman describe PLPs this way: "Typically co-created by teachers and students, personalized learning plans (PLPs) vary by school but generally incorporate individual student strengths and skills, skills gaps, and academic aspirations to chart students' progress toward both individual goals and classroom- or school-based learning targets."[28] The Great Schools Partnership, the lead coordinator of efforts by the New England Secondary Schools Consortium and the League of Innovative Schools to implement personalized learning in more than a hundred schools across New England, highlights in its definition the importance of student ownership, motivation, and out-of-school learning:

> A personal learning plan (or PLP) is developed by students—typically in collaboration with teachers, counselors, and parents—as a way to help them achieve short- and long-term learning goals. . . . Personal learning plans are generally based on the belief that students will be more motivated to learn, will achieve more in school, and will feel a stronger sense of ownership over their education if they decide what they want to learn, how they are going to learn it, and why they need to learn it to achieve their personal goals. . . . The general goal of a personal learning plan is to bring greater coherence, focus, and purpose to the decisions students make about their education. For this reason, plans may also

include learning experiences that occur outside of the school, such as internships, volunteer opportunities, and summer programs students want to pursue or books they would like to read. . . .[29]

Figure 1.3, a design guide for PLPs developed by the Great Schools Partnership and the Vermont Agency of Education, characterizes how six key design traits may be weakly or strongly represented in PLPs.

We also believe that within PLPs, students can finally document out-of-school learning in a format embedded in the system of schooling rather than pushed to the margins. They can collect and reflect upon authentic, often multimedia, evidence.[30] Further, PLPs serve key facets in a system of personalized learning. They prioritize student voice in the learning process, which according to psychological and pedagogical research, contributes to intrinsic motivation and engagement, the life blood of student-centered learning.[31] And PLPs emphasize lifelong learning by stretching a student's planning horizon, temporally and spatially, beyond their immediate classroom learning. By soliciting and amplifying students' own interests and aspirations, PLPs can drive teachers and families to imagine a schooling experience and a future that students find personally meaningful.[32]

Flexible Pathways

Personalized learning calls on us to reimagine the use of time and space, the where and when of learning that counts. Learning becomes more powerful when educators consider the school walls as permeable and the school day as malleable. Most would agree that youth have always acquired skills and knowledge in out-of-school contexts, such as when they care for younger siblings, assist a coach at the community center, work on the family farm, learn infant CPR to earn a babysitting certificate, join an after-school club, or volunteer at the animal shelter. Thanks to technology, options abound. A student may take an online coding class or use YouTube to learn American Sign Language or how to play guitar.

Thinking back to Miles, nearly every aspect of his life could be imagined as steps along his pathway of learning: work on the nature trail, mentoring Maria, painting his self-portrait, contributing to the advisory video, joining the robotics team, leading the summer soccer clinic, and coordinating his team's transitions. The idea of flexible pathways invites authentic, real-world learning

FIGURE 1.3   **Personal learning plan: design guide**

**Personal Learning Plans:
Design Guide**
May 2015

Traits of Personal Learning Plans	Weaker PLPs	Stronger PLPs
Are teachers, advisors, parents, and any other members of a student's personal learning team **actively involved** in the development and updating of the PLP?	A student creates the PLP alone, or with the help of one teacher. Parents are considered to be observers, rather than co-creators. The student completes the PLP, but content is adult-directed, rather than co-designed.	Students, advisors, family members, community mentors, and others who know the student well and support his/her learning help craft and/or revisit the plan. Parents report feeling more engaged and involved in their children's learning. Student has authentic voice and ownership of the process.
Is the PLP **easily accessible** to students, teachers, parents and other members of the personal learning team?	Students complete an annual PLP and rarely or sporadically revisit it. Parents see PLP at annual conference, after completion.	PLPs are easily accessible on-line to the learning team. There is a formal process in place to ensure that PLPs are revised and adjusted frequently, and formally revisited at least quarterly.
Is the PLP designed to help achieve **student and school goals via flexible pathways**?	Students and teachers report a lack of connection between the PLP and classroom learning experiences, ELOs or other pathways. Students use PLPs to set goals, identify strengths and weaknesses, and reflect on their learning within the structure of traditional classwork. PLP reflects student's individual goals and interests, although these are not connected to school goals or graduation requirements.	PLPs are an integral part of each learning experience, driving student ownership of their learning. The team considers various strategies to support academic, personal, and career goals including dual enrollment opportunities, service learning, internships, extra-curricular work and more. Teachers dedicate collaborative planning time to revise instruction and assessment based on individual PLPs and PLP trends amongst their students.
Is the PLP a vehicle for **meaningful reflection**?	Reflection only happens annually. Students engage in interest inventories, career or college exploration activities, etc . for post-secondary planning purposes.	Students use PLPs to explore and reflect on academic progress, personal goals, career exploration, and interests. In addition to goals, PLP includes plans and action steps as a road map toward achievement of these goals. Students, teachers, parents, and other members of the learning team reflect on growth and progress. Students use their PLPs to advocate for themselves as learners and to ensure that their time in school is used purposefully.
Is the PLP a thoughtful, inclusive **student profile**?	Information about the student on the PLP is mostly demographic in nature.	Information is included about student strengths, abilities, skills and values, in the academic sphere as well as relating to student's personal interests and learning styles. Teachers routinely look at student PLPs to tap into students' interests, skills, learning styles, and goals to teach more effectively.
Are all **critical elements** included, to assure compliance with Act 77?	Student identifying information is present, but dates of revision, team member involvement, or other details are missing. Sensitive or personal student data is searchable or unprotected.	Electronic format is embedded within or compatible with other, frequently used software. Plans are regularly saved or backed up in a secure manner. The format of the PLP makes it easy to see the history of the document. Advisory or guidance curricula provide clear PLP outcomes.

Source: Vermont Agency of Education and Great Schools Partnership,
https://www.greatschoolspartnership.org/wp-content/uploads/2016/11/PLPDesignGuide-v1.pdf.

that can cut across traditional subject areas, such as tapping mathematics to build a scale model of a nature trail, biology to prepare a species impact analysis, and language arts to distill it all into a persuasive speech to the school board. No two students have the same experience, even in whole-group, fully teacher-directed pedagogy. When students help chart a course, their experiences diverge from one another still further. Groups engage disciplinary knowledge for different purposes. Individual students stretch in their own particular ways. Within the same unit, a whole team of students may seek one set of learning outcomes while the unique paths of small work groups or individuals may align with various additional outcomes. Personalized learning uses flexible pathways to embrace the idiosyncrasies of students' interests, abilities, and learning experiences as the norm rather than the exception, as sources for purposeful design rather than threats to teachers' best laid plans. Flexible pathways are an essential response to any sincere implementation of PLPs. And it's pretty hard to imagine managing flexible pathways without all that PLPs reveal about students. Where else, after all, will teachers find all the personal information they need to support students along personally meaningful and flexible pathways? Where else will students describe in ever-changing detail who they are and who they want to become; identify and plan what and how they want to learn; chronicle and evaluate their progress; and communicate all this to those concerned about and able to support their education? Flexible pathways and PLPs rely upon each other. They are two pillars of personalized learning. The third is proficiency-based assessment.

Proficiency-Based Assessment

Many of us can appreciate that Miles's robotics team, soccer camp, and leadership roles are indeed learning opportunities which, perhaps, may have a more lasting impact on his life than some of what he learns as part of his standard school curriculum. Fewer of us, however, have seen these out-of-school or extracurricular experiences count toward achievement in the assessment and reporting systems of school. Even with flexible pathways to create opportunities and PLPs to coordinate and document his journey, we need to translate these experiences into a record of growth. How can we explain to families, the community, or education agencies that Miles's journey has yielded essential skills and understandings to graduate from high school, compete for a job, apply to college, or function as an informed citizen?

The answer lies in an approach to assessment which, like flexible pathways, is responsive to the idiosyncrasies of personalized learning. In the opening vignette, Miles tagged his uploaded self-portrait to an art proficiency. It was a routine yet methodical step to collect and reflect upon evidence of growth. He didn't tag his portrait as part of a checklist for completing an assignment. Rather, as he walked past his portrait in the hallway on his way to class, he realized that exploring examples of portraits, wondering how to represent himself as connected to—yet so different from—his classmates, and choosing the medium and colors, may have been what his art teacher calls an "artistic investigation," one of his sixth-grade visual arts proficiencies. Miles illustrates how a student, along with his teachers and other trusted adults, can build a body of evidence, regardless of the experiences that generated it, and sort it by content area proficiencies. In some PLP systems, he might regularly review progress by looking at a digital dashboard that summarizes the proficiencies he's pursuing, convey his status along established indicators of achieving them, and link immediately to any new evidence still needing evaluation. It's this evidence and the conversations it spurs, not syllabi and seat time, that clarify a student's personalized learning priorities for units, projects, or other experiences. With immediate access to his personalized plan, and schoolwide agreement on proficiency rubrics and scales, teachers can tailor their routine engagements and formative assessments to help a student make progress.

Just as important, however, a student can introduce evidence of proficiency that teachers played no role in, whether it was generated in or out of school, or captured in video, text, or nearly any other manner. With a robust PLP platform, and access to innovative technologies, students can catalog just about any kind of evidence. Proficiency-based assessment lends a universal language to districts and schools describing the critical knowledge and skills every student deserves to demonstrate before graduating from high school. And it's a language students can understand. Recall, for instance, that Miles chose not to tag his coat of arms to an art proficiency. He didn't look at other artists' work, gather the right tools for the medium, carefully plan and refine his work in a way he could describe as artistic investigation. He decided instead to tag the coat of arms, and his reflection on seeing everyone else's, as evidence toward an indicator of citizenship: to contribute to the enhancement of community life. PLPs and flexible pathways open the doors to seemingly infinite learning opportunities. Proficiency-based assessment helps us design and interpret these opportunities within a full-scale system of accountability.

The Interdependence of the Pillars

Let's come back to the idea that personalized learning comprises three components or pillars: personalized learning plans, flexible pathways to learning, and proficiency-based assessment. It strikes most educators as obvious that implementing one pillar at a time makes the most sense. For instance, instead of getting totally overwhelmed, how about launching PLPs in year one, proficiencies in year two, and flexible pathways only after those systems are in place? Even Vermont's legislation set PLPs for every middle and high school student as the first implementation deadline. This seemed reasonable to us. But many educators discovered that leading with PLPs often bombed! And upon reflection, it's not surprising. Why even have PLPs if you're not also offering the flexible pathways they're meant to inform? Why expect students to reflect on progress when there's not much to say other than, "I want to improve my grades." And why invest so much in PLPs and flexible pathways if the larger system rejects the legitimacy of the learning they produce? In table 1.1 we summarize some of the dangers of focusing too closely on only one pillar.

Having PLPs without personalized pathways and proficiency-based assessment to give them meaning simply doesn't make sense. It's just more work for teachers and students. And not particularly inspiring work either. A number of schools that led with PLPs failed so gloriously that students pretty much refused to play along. And when they tried again, they had to adopt entirely new designs and terminology just to get faculty, not to mention students, to give it another go. This way of starting small didn't work, but we've learned that another approach does: making student engagement your first priority.

We suggest you start with a manageable and highly engaging unit, project or personalized block of time. Consider seizing upon the most engaging time of year in your school, such as a favorite festival, community service project, or a tried and true unit you've been looking to reinvigorate. Some Vermont schools began with genius hours or passion projects, setting aside 90 minutes on five successive Fridays, during which the entire school paused its normal teaching schedule and students were given wide latitude to carry out personal projects. The key is to choose learning activities you're confident will yield student engagement, which often involves topics students care about and results in

TABLE 1.1 **The interdependence of the three pillars**

PILLARS OF PERSONALIZED LEARNING			RESULTS
Personalized Learning Plans	Flexible Pathways	Proficiency-Based Assessment	Engaging, authentic, and personalized learning
	Flexible Pathways	Proficiency-Based Assessment	Loss of engagement, authenticity and student voice
Personalized Learning Plans		Proficiency-Based Assessment	Loss of differentiation and ubiquitous opportunities
Personalized Learning Plans	Flexible Pathways		Loss of accountability, equity, and community support

products they share publicly. To discover what's engaging for students requires knowing them better, which even preliminary work with PLPs can help with. Knowing them better helps them discover personally engaging topics and projects. It's these experiences that generate authentic evidence worth collecting into a PLP. And it's this evidence that is best evaluated with proficiency-based assessment. Instead of focusing on one pillar at a time, do something manageable, fun and meaningful to students. Then simultaneously integrate initial pieces of each pillar you think can contribute most to the effort.

For instance, focus initial PLP development on honoring only the evidence students feel most strongly about. Experiment with a portion of the established schedule, calendar, or curriculum, one that you and your colleagues decide is worth risking with the iterative process of innovation. Introduce no more than one or two of only the most relevant and accessible proficiencies, such as those related to communication or problem solving. The point is not complete implementation of a personalized learning environment. Rather, you're designing an opportunity for everyone involved to begin to discover what personalized learning looks and feels like. Schools that have started off at a modest scale but with student engagement as their highest priority have triggered enough excitement among students, teachers, and families to sustain them through the hard work of broader implementation for years after.

Another important benefit of this approach is that, even in the course of taking some risks, everyone involved still spends most of their time on firm ground. Nobody has completely thrown out the systems and skills they've honed over the years: not the teachers, students, administrators, families, or school boards. In this way, personalization is not a direct attack on anyone but rather a well-considered exploration. Moreover, it reminds everyone that many aspects of the established system, and many established skills, remain important even in personalized learning environments. So-called traditional practices are still regarded as important options, and perhaps necessary, if they prove effective for particular students, circumstances or learning outcomes. And they frequently make sense as critical knowledge and skill builders for student success in complex and real-world projects.

Accountability and Personalized Learning

It's worth taking a brief detour now since one issue is rightfully near the forefront of any reader's mind. How is personalized learning reconciled with broader accountability systems? We have started to address this by sharing some of the underlying research: personalization makes sense given all we know about young adolescents and how they learn best. And promising findings are emerging that, when done well, personalized practices as envisioned in the three pillars can work at scale in much the same way they've been proven in any number of classrooms and schools for years. We will dig deeper into the supporting research as we look more closely at specific practices in the chapters ahead. But without some careful forethought, accountability pressures can undermine effective implementation of personalized learning. And much of that pressure comes from within us, in long-held habits of thinking about how best to make sure students are learning what we want them to learn. Let's start with how we think about standardized testing.

Contrary to some assumptions, even standardized tests have a vital role to play in personalized learning environments. We're not talking about the unhealthy, standardized testing culture too often bred in schools subjected to high-stakes accountability; we mean the well-designed, criterion-referenced, standardized tests that can reliably gauge some important knowledge and skills. They can be invaluable tools for raising red flags about students struggling with basic numeracy and literacy. Used appropriately and carefully, such tests can help identify systemic problems, particularly concerning equity. That's because they are both reliable and valid for measuring the limited range of skills and knowledge they address.

That said, standardized tests do not gauge student progress on many skills and dispositions vital to students' personal success and that of the communities they live in. Can students act with purpose and conviction in the world? Can they identify important problems, investigate them, propose solutions, and garner public support to take action? Can they collaborate, invent, and help others? Can they apply mathematics to real-world projects, conduct scientific inquiries, or write effectively for a variety of personal purposes and authentic audiences? These are just a few of the skills critical to communities, employers, and college admissions officers alike. They often distinguish youth who are resilient from those who are at risk, and they are what most people mean by a student well-prepared for adulthood. Even a brief glimpse into a single day in the life of students like Miles and his peers suggests that these skills can flourish in schools, and that over time, students can compile compelling evidence of achieving them. Yet these skills are notoriously difficult to measure. A portfolio of authentic evidence from personalized learning may convince any number of teachers that a particular student is proficient in one of these hard-to-measure skills. Yet no two teachers may ever be able to agree with much precision on why they are convinced. Moreover, no two students' portfolios will—or should—look alike. Even for the same skill, they will have different forms of evidence from different learning opportunities. Given these challenges, it's not surprising even many highly valued skills have gotten short shrift in schools focused primarily on "measuring" student achievement.

We have watched a number of schools and districts try to establish reliable assessments for personalized learning opportunities. It makes initial sense to create highly detailed rubrics and train teachers to use them with a high degree of inter-rater reliability, such that any trained teacher would rate the same piece of evidence the same way. But whatever benefit might arise from such considerable and expensive efforts is for naught if the rubrics don't work for students. Or as reliability wanes with teacher turnover or time since the last training. When teachers or students are faced with novel forms of evidence. Or, as seems inevitable, when a new set of standards is introduced. Similarly, it can be tempting to translate cells on a proficiency rubric into numbers, and even average these numbers across multiple experiences or a whole set of indicators. These are attempts to project expectations for highly reliable assessment onto a highly valid but inherently unreliable form of assessment. They divert scarce time and energy away from more important implementation priorities, like helping teachers and students use proficiency language for continuous, formative assessment. And they can undermine the very purpose of personalized learning by compromising the authentic engagement, personal meaning, and idiosyncratic experiences that are at the heart of the endeavor.

A system with both proficiency-based assessment and standardized testing, however, needn't attempt the impossible: expecting each to do what it will never do well. Personalized learning lets us focus on the learning experiences that matter most, while standardized testing can ensure we notice when students—or whole groups of students—are slipping dangerously behind in basic skills. Standardized tests aren't likely to go away and they will continue to improve. So focus on how they can serve you with what they do well and free up personalized assessment to fulfill its unique role: to help each student develop highly valued skills too often left behind in a system focused primarily on standardized assessments. That may be your best chance to address the critical shortcomings and undo at least some of the damage done to schools by the improper use of standardized testing. But that chance will be wasted if we try to standardize personalized learning.

RETHINKING ROLES

Assessment and accountability are just two of the concepts educators reconsider as they implement personalized learning strategies. Many describe a shift in their thinking about the roles of teachers and learners. When and where does learning happen? What kinds of learning "count"? Educator and author

Will Richardson rightly observed, "The ability to learn what we want, when we want, with whomever we want as long as we have access creates a huge push against a system of education steeped in time-and-place learning."[33] Making learning personal calls upon teachers to reimagine how they undertake their work and what new roles students will play.

Student Ownership and Self-Direction

One of the primary reasons we can now imagine new roles in this business of teaching and learning is the continued evolution of technology. Gone are the days when the amount of existing knowledge about a subject was relatively finite, the schoolmistress or master was the holder of that knowledge, and students had to come to the schoolhouse physically in order to learn. Technology opens doors to learning in previously unprecedented ways, as students now have at the press of a button nearly ubiquitous access to information and mentors from across the globe. In many instances, students can choose when and how they want to learn and they can do it from most anywhere.

For this reason, and others, we believe a model of personalized learning that fails to acknowledge the importance of student ownership and self-direction is incomplete. As we illustrated in the vignette, Miles's inquiry group felt a sense of responsibility to complete its project, not for a grade, but rather in order to successfully pitch the nature trail to the school board. Miles felt connected to his self-portrait in part because he chose the medium. And we can imagine that his self-worth was informed also by how well he supported Maria, his PLP mentee.

We agree with Rickabaugh's assertion that, "Unless students are given voice and choice in their learning, opportunities for personalized, real-time feedback as they progress, access to a personalized learning path, and opportunity to build toward real independence as a learner, they will not build key capacities to survive and thrive in the rapidly changing work and life world where they will spend most of their adult lives."[34] Others similarly emphasize the role of student ownership as a key feature of personalized learning, believing student self-direction to be a critical outcome of this approach.[35] The Nellie Mae Foundation, partnering with Jobs for the Future, includes "student-owned" as one of the four features of learning in its Student Centered Education Ecosystem.[36] The Great Schools Partnership identifies student voice, and "increasing the level of choice and personal responsibility students have in the instructional process" as an example of how schools and educators might personalize learning for students.[37] Research further underscores the importance of student ownership, because providing students with autonomy and choice in determining the path to meeting their learning goals can increase their feelings of academic engagement.[38]

The opening vignette conveyed this potential of ownership and self-direction as Miles and his peers assumed new roles in their learning environment. Self-directed learners must be planners of their learning, managers of their projects, and assessors of their progress. They must extend these roles into being effective collaborators in the more complex dynamics of working with groups and teams. Some roles involve whole-class leadership, such as Miles coordinating team transitions, Sarah managing the team's technology, and Dare and Ted leading morning meeting. Others are focused at the small-group level and are more task specific, leveraging real-world roles such as designer, manufacturer, and communicator for a complicated project like planning and advocating for a nature trail. Still others—as a mentor and PLP partner, for instance—seize upon natural intersections across the domains of social, emotional, and academic development. Students benefit as their partnership cultivates belonging, leadership, sustained support, and accountability to the norms and routines of the team and its PLP process. These roles provide important and personally rewarding growth opportunities to students. In addition to promoting their social and emotional development, it's in the course of occupying these roles that students deeply engage in critical thinking, collaboration, communication, and problem solving, all skills regarded as vital to their long-term success as learners, workers, and participants in democracy.

Adopting new roles is central to how young adolescents explore autonomy, identity, affiliation, and a meaningful place in the world. These roles are also essential in high-performing personalized learning environments. Personalized learning pioneers Barbara Bray and Kathleen McClaskey propose that, in a fully personalized learning environment, the learner:

- monitors and adjusts the learner profile as he or she learns with teacher as a partner in learning;
- is an expert learner with agency who applies innovative strategies and skills to redesign and achieve learning goals in the PLP;

- expands the learning environment in and outside of school to include the local and global community;
- self-directs how, when, and where he or she monitors, adjusts, and achieves learning goals in the PLP;
- designs challenging learning experiences based on interests, aspirations, passions, and talents;
- independently applies tools and strategies so he or she can explore deeper and challenging experiences that extend learning and thinking;
- learns at his or her own pace and demonstrates mastery with evidence of learning in a competency-based system;
- self-selects extended learning opportunities based on college, career, and personal and citizenship goals, as well as his or her interests, aspirations, passion, and purpose;
- designs assessment and showcases evidence of learning through exhibitions that involve parents, peers, teachers, and community.[39]

The shift in student role, with its emphasis on student self-direction and leadership, inevitably raises the question, what does the teacher do in a personalized learning environment? What is the teacher's role? As we explore in greater detail throughout this book, the hundreds of teachers we have worked with assume many different roles in their classrooms, teams and schools. Our research points to five roles that show particular promise in the personalized context: empowerer, scout, scaffolder, assessor, and community builder. To some degree, teachers have always played these roles, but personalization stretches them to devote considerable time and energy to refining, mastering, and executing them. After all, the students in personalized environments aren't simply able to take on their new roles. The opportunities are created purposefully by their teachers.

In figure 1.4, we illustrate the intersection between students' tasks in a personalized learning environment, as defined by Bray and McClaskey, and the roles teachers adopt in response to these tasks in order to facilitate learning, as identified in our research. We have identified four teacher roles (empowerer, scout, scaffolder, and assessor) that correspond with Bray and McClaskey's student tasks (the wedges that are connected to the term "student" in the graphic). The fifth teacher role, community builder, serves in a more global capacity as

FIGURE 1.4   **Teacher and student roles in personalized learning environments**

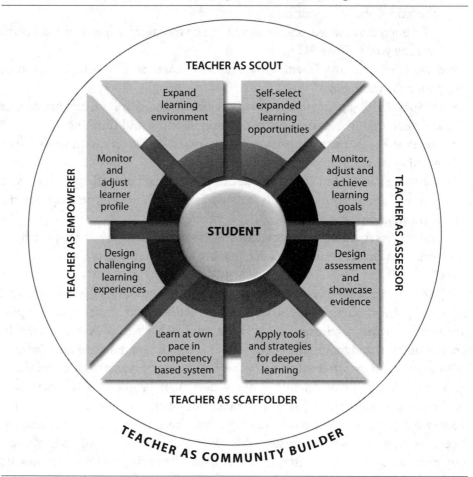

it cuts across various domains to create an effective personalized—yet also collaborative—learning environment.

Teacher as Empowerer

A classroom like Ms. Phillips's in the opening vignette, one that is intentionally student-run, does not happen by accident. The many structures and processes in place require planning, such as the multiage mentoring program to help manage the PLP process and the certification process for using the 3D printer or other expensive or complicated resources. And although many of the classroom roles—technology manager, transition coordinator, and morning meeting leader, for instance—can be developed in collaboration with students, each needs to be identified, clarified, and nurtured in order to be sustainable.

Much of the personalization in this kind of classroom is built upon a foundation of effective technology integration that may require teachers to strongly advocate for ambitious investment in technology as a key resource for empowering students. Teachers and students alike need to regularly leverage digital tools, such as a robust platform for housing the PLPs and online calendaring, that will help them manage the various aspects of goal-setting, project management, and self-directed learning. They benefit from straightforward communication tools like chatting and texting, and regularly access tablet, cameras, and digital slideshow software for documentation and presentation of their work. In their role as empowerers, teachers like Ms. Phillips seize upon opportunities large and small to give students more control over their learning in and out of school. They partner with students to monitor and adjust their learner profiles over time. And they help students develop the capacity to design and manage challenging learning experiences based on their passions and aspirations. Over time, as students assume greater responsibility to go along with their new roles, teachers identify new challenges that students face and adopt additional roles to address them.

Teacher as Scaffolder

For students to flourish in their self-directed environment, each new element needs to be carefully scaffolded. As scaffolders, teachers assist students in learning at their own pace in a competency- or proficiency-based system. They help students gain independence in exploring challenging experiences that extend their thinking. This kind of scaffolding was evident in the vignette, as Miles's art teacher trained him and his peers for life in the studio environment she created in her classroom. Before she could expect students to make informed choices and productive progress at the media stations, she trained students on how to plan their use of studio time, use the stations efficiently, seek appropriate help even if she wasn't immediately available, and clean up swiftly and responsibly.

Teachers we've worked with have arrived at similar conclusions after carefully scaffolding students' leadership roles or designing the certification programs for using complex technologies, such as 3D printing, video equipment, and power tools. Still, other teachers have learned to create explicit training materials for PLP mentors and their partners, eventually creating PLP handbooks containing all the necessary templates, guidelines, and timetables to prepare for a successful student-led PLP conference with parents. In essence, we've observed that students and teachers alike come to appreciate that self-direction can be challenging for young adolescents, just as it is for adults. But, importantly, educators can scaffold the understanding and mastery of it just as they previously scaffolded for more traditional, teacher-directed environments.

Teacher as Scout

Even well-scaffolded classrooms yield some unexpected surprises, however. As students launch their own less predictable learning adventures, teachers may find themselves acting like scouts, trying to stay one step ahead to increase students' likelihood of fruitful discovery and success. One art teacher we know revamped her studio stations several times after discovering how students actually use the resources and what they need along the way. For example, in response to repeated requests for help with a select number of rudimentary skills, she added short video tutorials to each station. She also researched her colleagues' curriculum and calendars to identify key opportunities to tap students' need and passion for artistic expression. Sometimes, scouting takes the form of anticipating useful forms of expression. One of our partner teachers pondered how to convince more students to use podcasting as a reflection and presentation tool. The podcasting booth became an immediate hit when students realized it was a safe space to speak private thoughts and produce much more professional recordings than out in their noisy classroom. And teachers must also serve as scouts in helping students recognize the feasibility of their goals. One educator recalled, with a chuckle, counseling a student that building a life-sized elephant out of soda cans might be a bit too ambitious for a one-week project. "How about a scale model?" she suggested.

As scouts, teachers also help students expand their learning environments. They assist them in learning how to self-select expanded learning opportunities that go beyond the school walls to include broader communities, near and far, and extend outside of school hours. As evidenced by Bray and McClaskey's list, these include opportunities to explore college, career, and personal and citizenship goals, as well as students' aspirations, interests, and passions.[40] And teachers help students develop the skills to showcase evidence of their learning in front of authentic and relevant audiences. With expertise in young adolescent development and pedagogy, along with the adult judgment honed by many more years of life experience, teachers are positioned to scout fruitful, productive, and safe journeys for their students even as they foster self-direction.

Teacher as Assessor

Teachers have always been assessors, but even experienced teachers find this role substantially transformed in a personalized learning environment. Teachers can now use students' PLPs to create project groups, as well as guide them in their choice of learning opportunities to meet proficiencies. A considerable part of the assessor role is helping students develop the skills to design and achieve their learning goals, self-assessing effectively along the way. As part of their project planning, students can create custom assessment plans based on their targeted proficiencies, including individualized rubrics to guide formative self-assessments and teacher feedback, and audience feedback forms for use at public presentations. No two assessment plans will look exactly alike, but they will all be grounded in the same proficiency language. And throughout the project, students can also collect evidence of their group's performance against group norms and collaboration proficiencies. It can take a few years for educators to fluently scaffold for students a personalized assessment system that works with their district accountability framework, but the integration of digital PLPs with proficiency tracking platforms, coupled with well-scaffolded PLP partnerships, can make a huge difference. Gone are the days of the standard gradebook, for sure!

Teacher as Community Builder

If you're an educator, you likely know that much of the engagement, authentic challenge, and support that students experience rests on a strong school and classroom culture. Behind the busy activity of Miles and his friends in the opening vignette was extensive and collaborative forethought on the part of his teachers. It is the educators, after all, who make sure their students have accessible hardware, a PLP platform responsive to the nature of their students' fast-paced lives, and leadership opportunities that stretch students in ways they can be proud of. But all the parts and pieces of a personalized system can serve, as well as result from, a strong culture.

The focus on building community within a classroom, team, or school is a critical, and too rarely explored, aspect of effective personalized learning environments. We saw Ms. Phillips connecting personally with Miles as he arrived to school after she consulted his PLP, where she was reminded of his love of soccer, his group advisory video—"I know three languages!"—the coat of arms activity, and the self-portrait. Teachers we work with appreciate how much students share about their out-of-school lives: their families, their hobbies, their hopes, and their concerns. But they also see how much students appreciate being acknowledged, and seeing their peers acknowledged, for being whole people, not just for who they are in school. These activities and others that follow forge relationships among peers and between teachers and students that sustain each person and the team as a whole throughout the year. Their sense of community is reinforced daily at morning meeting, when they come together to celebrate the team and organize each day. And it doesn't take long for teachers to realize that they can play community builder and assessor at the same time, seizing on these community-building activities for baseline assessments of writing, math, and technology skills. It's upon this solid foundation for a learning community, built with the developmental and pedagogical insights of collaborative teachers, that you can launch a personalized learning environment.

Each of these teacher roles—empowerer, scout, scaffolder, assessor, and community builder—is central to creating robust and healthy personalized learning environments. Contrary to myths emanating from those seeking to monetize student learning, personalization of the sort outlined in this book cannot be teacherless or teacher-proof. Rather, the essential roles of teachers in personalized learning environments are those farthest from the reach of automation. While an algorithm can determine which equations challenge each student, it is teachers who come to know students as personal learners. Whereas online tutorials can present a logically constructed progression of direct instruction, it is teachers, as human beings and developmental specialists, who can navigate the complex and continuous interplay of individual and social dynamics in a personalized learning environment. And while automated assessment has already broached the domain of creative writing tied to standard genres, for instance, teachers and their students are those in the position to evaluate the authentic evidence that emerges from personalized learning.

As Bray and McClaskey noted, "Personalizing learning is not something that someone does *to* a learner. It is about learners owning their learning and teachers guiding the process. When this happens, teacher and learner roles change and that impacts the school culture."[41] Indeed, while we believe much of the power of personalization resides in the shift of control from teacher to students over much of what, where, and how they learn and demonstrate knowledge and skills, we have learned that this does not render the teacher obsolete. On the contrary, in this era of anytime, anywhere access to information, helping students become self-directed learners is a key facet of an educator's work. And if you're wondering how on earth you can take on any more roles, keep in mind the sage advice our colleague and professional development coordinator Scott Thompson has honed to an indispensable mantra for busy teachers: *The people doing the learning should be doing the work!* (Consider tattooing it to the back of your hand.) He means the planning, the doing, and the evaluating. In running their own classroom for the good of all, students are also learning to run a community. And as he points out, there are a whole lot more of them than there are of us, so why can't they be their own best resource? He's right, of course. As educators, we can't take on an infinite set of roles. Instead, we suggest doing the necessary work to cede to students some of those roles and all the rich learning opportunities they entail.

LOOKING AHEAD: A MATTER OF PURPOSE

Conveying the engagement of students like Miles, and how they can benefit from the practical and real-world aspects of their learning, excites us. We hope it excites you too. But understanding the ingenious functions of PLPs, flexible pathways, and proficiency-based assessment doesn't make the prospect of personalized learning a whole lot less intimidating. Rest assured you can take it slow, with manageable steps at a time. It takes years to transition to a personalized learning environment, and we would all be wise to trust our own iterative process along the way. A rigid, formulaic approach to implementation won't be any more effective for personalization than it has been for other innovations. Indeed, no two of the more than thirty-five schools we currently work with are going about their transition to personalized environments in the same way. Local context, from the community level down to the uniqueness of every teacher-student relationship, is simply too important to the ultimate success or failure of any significant change.

Throughout the chapters to come, we offer a road map of sorts, including recommendations for stops along the way, optional scenic detours, and hazard signs to keep you safe. Fortunately, it's a journey on which you can set your own pace and choose your own adventures. We'll help you map at least the early stages of your trip as you work your way through the chapters. We've discovered a couple interesting caveats on the dozens of journeys with our partners. We share them with you in the chapters that follow because they are a bit counterintuitive. They've tripped up and slowed the progress of too many teachers already. We encourage you to follow the smoother course others now have charted.

Hopefully, this overview of personalized learning has sparked some ideas for your own ambitious vision of your classroom, team, or school. To move that vision forward, as well as to justify it to others, you'll want to consider quite explicitly *why* you want to make learning more personal. Chapter 2 (Personalized Learning Plans) will help you do just this. In it, we outline a number of reasons teachers identify for adopting PLPs, explore the various stakeholders they consider as they do so, and provide student and teacher examples to convey the nature of this work. Onward!

TWO

PERSONALIZED LEARNING PLANS

Purposes and Opportunities

The principal strides swiftly down the hall toward the middle school. She's feeling quite behind, facing a pile of unread email and a leadership team meeting this afternoon, but she needs to pass on a quick message to a teacher. She turns the corner toward Mr. Larmar's room and hears an excited, purposeful buzz pouring out of the room and into the hallway.

As she walks in, she sees students all over the room. Some are standing in small groups, conferring as they lean in over laptops. Some are spread out on the floor with a giant map and pieces of poster board. One pair has their heads almost touching, earbuds in, engrossed in viewing a video on a tablet, and taking notes. A few other kids are on bean bag chairs reading. She smiles to herself, thinking, "This is certainly light years from when I went to school. We sat in rows and listened to lectures. Compliance was the most important thing."

The principal scans the room for the teacher, not finding him. She's not alarmed, however. She knows he is here somewhere, orchestrating all of this student engagement. The room has the feel of young entrepreneurs in Silicon Valley, all working toward the next great innovation. Finally, her eyes settle on Mr. Larmar, seated at a low table with one student, who appears intensely engaged. The student speaks animatedly, showing him her computer screen. He listens intently, pauses in the silence between her words, then asks her a question. She stops, pulls her computer on her lap, and begins to work again. At this point Mr. Larmar notices the principal standing in the middle of the room—but no one else has. The students own the space, they own their learning, and they are deeply engaged in it, no matter who is present or not. Mr. Larmar walks over, and the principal conveys her message.

Cassandra didn't see the principal enter. She was too busy showing Mr. Larmar the latest entry in her personalized learning plan (PLP): the civics project she's been working on. The class has been learning about how local government operates, and she's documented her learning with a sketchnote she created. It connects the three branches of government to their local city governance and then to her personal interest in issues of animal welfare. In it, she illustrates her new understandings of the interrelationships among the three branches of federal government, her local government, and her work with abandoned and stray animals in her city. Once a month for as long as she can remember, she's been helping her mom, who works in a veterinarian's office, vaccinate, spay, or neuter stray animals. Cassandra has seen first-hand how the overpopulation of animals leads to their suffering and she wants to do something to stop it. When Mr. Larmar asked students to link their learning about governance structures and lawmaking to local issues, she jumped at the chance. Her classmate, Marcos, is also concerned about animals, and they teamed up to volunteer at the local animal shelter and draft legislation, which they will eventually present to local city council members. This both exhilarates and terrifies her. Right now, however, Cassandra is adding aspects of the project to her "highlight reel" in her PLP, the parts of her learning she is most proud of, in preparation for her student-led conference later in the day.

She shares the sketchnote, slideshow, and personal reflections with Mr. Larmar, and he does what he always does—asks her questions about her work instead of telling her what to do! It is both difficult and helpful, she thinks. He pushes her to think for herself and make adjustments based on his questions. This time, he asks her if she's looked carefully at the opposite perspective—someone who thinks that the city's finite resources should be spent on humans instead. Cassandra pulls her netbook onto her lap and gets back to thinking and writing about a counterargument.

Later that day, Cassandra's dad rushes in from a busy day at work. He just barely makes it for his scheduled student-led PLP conference and thinks to himself, "I just want to hear from the teacher! Why do I have to go through my kid? I really don't have time for this." He takes a deep breath, pushes through the door, and sees Cassandra with her netbook open, papers spread before her, and Mr. Larmar seated next to her.

During the conference, Cassandra lights up when explaining her civics project, talking so fast he can barely keep up. Her fingers move quickly on the computer, using her PLP to show her dad the statistics on abandoned animals in the city, taken from the data she collected from local politicians, veterinarians, local nonprofits, and the animal shelter. Her self-designed graph shows an increasing rate of growth in the population of these animals. When she links it to the city map, she shows him the particular increase in strays and abandoned animals that she and her partner Marcos identified in a five-block area. This is the area they plan to target with their legislation, she explains. She describes the bill's plan to raise awareness and resources in this neighborhood in their bill. Cassandra clicks to a slide showing a letter to residents, then to a poster she and her partner created on Canva, a graphic design website, and finally to the website she and Marcos started on this issue.

Cassandra confesses that, before this project, she was terrified of making phone calls to people she didn't know. She smiles as she tells her father that she had to do this several times for her research, and that she feels much more confident now. She also explains that she never really understood how maps and data intersect, but she finally sees not only how they connect but also how they can tell a story of what is happening in a community. Lastly, she tells him that she and Marcos have different communication styles and that they've had to learn to work through that in order to create the letter, website, and poster. Finally, she pushes the netbook back, breathless.

Her dad's mouth is agape. It's like he is seeing his daughter for the first time, he thinks. When did she become so capable? When did she learn how to see a problem, tackle it like this, using data, maps, writing and art? He is speechless. In fact, in this moment, all he can do is smile at his daughter and her teacher.

BUILDING YOUR RATIONALE: CULTIVATING A SENSE OF PURPOSE AND AGENCY

Cassandra is fortunate. Her volunteer work has already helped her develop a sense that she can make a difference in the world. She exuded enthusiasm in her PLP conference for being able to draw upon those outside passions for the purposes of school. Of course, not all students bring that level of purpose to the classroom, but the classroom can be a fertile place for helping students develop it. The vignette illustrates how teachers draw on many aspects of personalized learning to engage their students. Mr. Larmar invited students to connect their learning in a personally relevant manner, encouraging them to identify issues they cared about deeply. He opened the door to collaborative learning for students with similar interests. He helped them find authentic ways to apply their learning to make a difference in the world. And he leveraged the PLP as formative assessment, enabling him to provide thoughtful, just-in-time feedback. In turn, Mr. Larmar's principal recognized student engagement when she saw it and made space and time in the schedule for this type of learning. Cassandra's father suspended his disbelief in the usefulness of a student-led conference and, in return, was wowed by his daughter's new learning and her powerful sense of efficacy. And Cassandra herself bravely brought her best self to the project, working purposefully to accomplish something she believed matters in the world.

While purpose may be thought of as part of a personal search for meaning, it also has an important external component: "the desire to make a difference in the world, to contribute to matters larger than the self."[1] The role of purpose speaks to many facets of the best personalized learning: the power of a learner finding a sense of purpose in the world, the purposeful way a student learns to assume greater control over the learning, and indeed the clarity of purpose a teacher gains in shifting to a more personalized approach. The Association for Middle Level Education regards students and teachers "engaged in active, purposeful learning" as one of its sixteen characteristics of successful schools for young adolescents.[2]

It is not enough for learners to simply be allowed to move at their own paces. Nor is it sufficient for learners to have a degree of choice in their topics of study or the form of their final products. Rather, personalized learning—like that illustrated in the vignette—can manifest a heightened sense of purpose in the world. Early adolescence is a critical period for cultivating a sense of purpose. In this stage of life, students begin wanting to dedicate themselves to something beyond self-preservation or self-advancement.[3] And purposeful youth demonstrate a number of positive attributes, including prosocial behavior, moral commitment, achievement, and high self-esteem.[4] Unfortunately, despite the clear benefits of discovering a purpose, only 20 percent of teenagers report having one.[5] When youth lack purpose, finding little or nothing to which to dedicate themselves, they often struggle to acquire motivation later in life. Damon and colleagues explain, "Research has shown that the personal effects of purposelessness may include self-absorption, depression, addictions, and a variety of psychosomatic ailments, and the social effects may include deviant and destructive behavior, a lack of productivity, and an inability to sustain stable interpersonal relations."[6] The value of purpose continues well beyond early adolescence and throughout the life span, resulting in consolidated identities and deeper senses of meaning than those without a sense of purpose.[7]

Relatedly, one outcome of purpose is agency, or the "power to make our own decisions and choices, take meaningful action, and see the results in our own development and learning."[8] When students see the positive results of their purposeful work, their confidence in their ability to make a difference increases. Educators and authors Eric Toshalis and Michael J. Nakkula suggest that educators should consider "the contributions that motivation, engagement, and student voice make to the experience of human agency. If education is, at least in part, intended to help students effectively act upon their strongest interests and deepest desires, then we need a clearer understanding of how to cultivate that sense of agency."[9] As they are afforded more opportunities to develop agency in authentic contexts, students increase their competence, confidence, and creativity. Their skills improve, their belief in their capacity to learn is strengthened, and they come up with their own ideas for innovation.[10] In sum, students who develop a sense of purpose and agency fare far better than those who do not. And, as educators, we can create places of learning that foster a sense of purpose and agency for the sake of students' positive development, their engagement with learning, and their contributions to society.

CHAPTER OVERVIEW

Speaking of purpose, we know that people have a variety of purposes for reading this book. Perhaps you're reading it because you're looking for a way to make the learning in your classroom more personalized. Maybe you're considering implementing PLPs. Possibly you've been enacting personalized learning for a while but are seeking a structure or format that can help you take it to the next level. Or perhaps you're working within a system that has mandated personalized learning. You might be feeling some stress about how you'll possibly add one more thing to your plate.

In any case, we suggest that PLPs can offer you a clear and practical opportunity to advance your most ambitious vision of education. Whether you are pursuing personalized learning on your own, implementing it with the support of colleagues, or responding to external requirements, holding a deeper purpose for the PLP offers you the chance to align it with your own professional growth. Being clear about your own purposes can help you rein in what might seem like an overwhelming prospect and guide you along the complex path of design and implementation. In the sections that follow, we describe how various purposes for PLPs can serve teachers, students, parents, and invested others. We explore what PLPs can do well and what they don't do well. We also identify a number of common pitfalls or obstacles to realizing the full potential of PLPs, drawn directly from our work in schools. We explore these pitfalls and offer suggestions for how your purpose can clear your path to successful PLPs. The chapter concludes with an opportunity to declare the purpose that works for you, your first step to creating a plan for PLPs. Throughout, we include specific examples of personalization in practice, drawn from real schools, educators, and students in Vermont.

SERVING MULTIPLE STAKEHOLDERS

Why adopt PLPs? It's important when undertaking change in general, but particularly when implementing novel change like this, that we communicate compelling purposes every step of the way. One of PLPs' greatest advantages is that they can serve multiple stakeholders in ways that other tools do not. Unlike the familiar report card, for example, which primarily addresses a parent or guardian audience, the PLP can be leveraged for your benefit (and that of your colleagues) to inform personalized instruction, flexible pathways, and proficiency-based assessment. At the same time, as Cassandra's father experienced, it can help parents understand more deeply their child's progress and interests. The PLP also can provide a foundation for classmates to find common ground and build a sense of classroom community. And for invested others, such as community mentors, the PLP can be a platform for building relationships and exploring opportunities for collaboration. One might imagine, for example, the shelter director's joy at seeing Cassandra's new skills, knowledge, and commitment so vividly reflected in her PLP. By virtue of their inherent transparency and, in the case of digital versions, accessibility, PLPs can make students' learning and identities available to all of these stakeholders.

We know it can be challenging to develop a clear vision while facing the many moving parts of personalized learning. We suggest you take stock of the types of learning experiences that your students currently experience and then identify the critical gaps that PLPs can fill that would otherwise impede your progress toward personalization. Chances are, you're not starting from scratch. Few classrooms need *all* of what PLPs have to offer. We know that some teachers already do a remarkable job at eliciting and making smart use of students' identities. Others are very experienced at integrating real-world learning into their classrooms. Still others have been using standards-based portfolio assessment for years. This chapter is about helping you identify *your* purposes and which aspects of the PLP represent the greatest challenges and welcoming opportunities in *your* context. How can PLPs help you build toward personalized learning?

Begin by asking yourself this question: When during the school day or year are my students most engaged in learning? It might help to think about when students ask to work through lunch or stay after school, or when they arrange with partners to work on a project over the weekend. Identify what makes these moments different from others in your classroom or school. Next, consider any or all of the following questions:

- What life opportunities do I hope my students will engage in when they launch into adulthood eight to ten years from now? As citizens, wage earners, and family members?
- What kinds of learning would I like to see more of in my classroom or school?
- What kinds of learning do I wish were valued more by the rest of my school system?
- What kinds of evidence of learning and growth do these learning opportunities produce?
- How can I welcome this evidence into a system of student record-keeping?
- Who are the stakeholders in my educational community and what evidence or experiences do they need in order to support the learning I want for my students?

Answering these questions may help you deepen the purpose for your PLPs by focusing attention on learning opportunities that reflect twenty-first-century skills and other critical gaps in current school offerings. At the same time, the questions can help you narrow the purposes for your PLPs, thereby focusing your energy on what the PLPs need to accomplish and highlighting lower priorities that could otherwise burden your design and implementation.

IDENTIFYING YOUR PLP PURPOSES

What purposes do PLPs serve? When asked this question, the teachers we work with offer many different answers. At times, the PLP addresses their students' needs. At other times, the purposes are focused on more what PLPs can do for the teachers as facilitators of learning. Still other purposes relate to the needs of families, community members, or mentors. Table 2.1 summarizes some of the more common and productive reasons our teachers identify for embracing PLPs, based on each stakeholder type.

TABLE 2.1 **Sample PLP purposes by stakeholder type**

For students	For teachers	For families	For invested others
help students explore their identities in a safe and respectful place	learn more about students	provide a broader representation of what their children can do	discover common ground for collaboration with students
ensure students feel known as individuals	manage idiosyncratic learning pathways	help families stay connected to their young adolescent	cultivate a rich and common vision for learning within the community
provide students with a mechanism to know one another better	assess student growth more meaningfully	address parents'/ guardians' concerns or anxieties about their child's schooling and future	value the expertise within the community
allow students more control over their learning	collaborate with colleagues more effectively to address student needs	provide documentation for use during transitions from school to school	expand notions of where learning happens
For all stakeholders			
see early adolescent development through an appreciative lens			

For Students

Teachers most often articulate PLP purposes with student interests in mind. Here are five of the most common and productive purposes we encounter in our work with partner schools:

To help students explore their identities in a safe and respectful place.
One of the most important developmental tasks for young adolescents is to construct their unique sense of identity.[11] While, of course, identity development occurs across a lifetime, early adolescence is often when we first begin to think about how our identity may affect our lives. More challenging still, it comes at a time when we are often self-conscious about those identities.[12] Explored more fully later in this chapter, the PLP can provide a space for students to explore and document their developing selves. When invited to identify their attributes, values, skills, and aspirations, students ask themselves—and others—questions they may not have previously considered. And because identity is complex and changes over time, it's important that PLPs also be dynamic and revisited regularly.

To ensure that students feel known as individuals.
As they transition from childhood into early adolescence, middle schoolers are developing an increasing sense of individuality. Much of the contemporary middle school is constructed around this need. Teacher advisories, for example, are designed to ensure all students are well known by at least one adult in the school building.[13] Interdisciplinary teams are a means to break down the larger school unit into smaller, safer communities in which students can express their individuality.[14] When teachers leverage PLPs to help students discover and communicate their identities, interests, and imaginings of the future, they also send a clear signal to students that their school—and the system—cares about them as individuals. PLPs are a powerful mechanism for conveying to students that who they are matters to others.

To provide students with a mechanism to know one another better.
One of the conundrums of this developmental period is the young adolescent's dual need for individuality and acceptance. Middle schoolers often want to stand out as individuals while also being accepted by their classmates. Young adolescents crave connections with their peers. They seek a social environment where they feel like they belong and where they can create meaningful

relationships. We know these connections are important; students who have positive relationships with peers exhibit better mental health and more successful adaptation to their environment than those who do not.[15] With teacher guidance, the PLP can provide a platform for exploring and sharing common interests. We saw this illustrated in the vignette of Cassandra and Marcos, as they decided to partner on the shelter project after seeing each other's commitment to animals expressed in their PLPs. The PLP can convey students' unique attributes while revealing possible intersections with the interests and identities of their peers, offering rich fodder for shared exploration and deep, well-rounded relationships.

To allow students more control over their learning.
Another classic characteristic of students this age is the desire for greater independence. The chance to adopt new roles and assume increasing responsibility helps young adolescents develop a sense of personal efficacy.[16] Middle schoolers crave the opportunity to demonstrate what they're capable of; planning aspects of their learning offers them a powerful way to do so. This shift toward greater student ownership is a key component of personalized learning, providing learners with practice in making decisions, determining personally relevant goals, and identifying engaging pathways. Because of their inherent transparency and order, PLPs make it possible for teachers to hand over some control to students while still maintaining awareness of each student as an independent learner.

For Teachers

While the PLP can benefit students in the ways we just described, teachers also typically recognize its potential to inform their work as facilitators of learning. Recall from the last chapter that in addition to familiar roles, teachers of personalized learning serve as Empowerers, Scouts, Assessors, and Community Builders. The PLP helps teachers come to know students better, which in turn helps teachers discover ways to strengthen relationships, plan curricular content, inform instructional strategies, and heighten student engagement. They also use PLPs to manage the many different learning pathways in their classrooms and to collaborate with colleagues more effectively.

To learn more about students.
Although we explore this idea in greater detail in later chapters, we'll note here that the Learner Profile section of the PLP is devoted to the exploration of a

student's current and future identities. This section is populated by the types of who-am-I artifacts you may already create in your classroom at the start of the year or the getting-to-know-you tasks students on your team complete when you're working on team-building. Because the PLP provides an accessible and transparent format, as students include evidence of their interests and passions, you're in a position to discover new ways to guide a student's personal pursuits. You're also able to look across PLPs for collectively engaging topics as you plan curriculum for small or large groups. And because the PLP is an evolving document as students reflect upon and update their interests and identities, it continues to provide critical information to drive engagement throughout the year.

To manage idiosyncratic learning pathways.
As learning becomes more student-directed, it doesn't take long for teachers to realize the importance of keeping track of the many different learning trajectories in their classroom. Accounting for students' varied paces and pathways quickly becomes both important and challenging. Similarly, teachers recognize that the myriad topics or concepts under study require a reliable system of documentation. Because significant amounts of work and learning happen outside of the classroom, teachers can't possibly observe it all. Instead, the videos, images and testimonials accumulating in students' PLPs can provide ample evidence that projects are on the right track. PLPs, when thoughtfully integrated into the learning environment, can help you manage the many learning pathways your students are traveling.

To assess and communicate student growth more meaningfully.
Some teachers we work with are seeking more holistic ways to assess and communicate student growth. They know that more traditional assessments and reports don't capture what is often most important to students and their families. Grades on tests and quizzes, and even rubric scores on proficiencies, are already available. These teachers are eager to establish a continuous narrative about each student's learning experience that conveys more complex learning stories. Other teachers want to diversify how they go about fostering student reflection and assessment. The PLP provides an ongoing platform for students to reflect on authentic evidence of their learning, their goals, and their progress toward mastering various proficiencies. This type of formative assessment is helpful for teachers and students alike to gauge current mastery and plot future steps.

To collaborate more effectively with colleagues.
The potential for the PLP to communicate student growth can similarly focus conversation and collaboration with teaching colleagues. If you're a member of an interdisciplinary team, you likely know how rare and valuable common planning time can be. Using that time effectively includes conversing in targeted and meaningful ways about how to support students. Teaching teams can routinely review student portfolios for clues on how to streamline student workloads and to align teacher expectations with the deep learning students are engaged in. Too often, competing demands from different classes can undermine the depth of learning and spread students too thin. The PLP is designed to provide helpful and holistic insights into a student's experience, to enable teachers to identify themes across these experiences, and to provide focus to those collegial conversations.

For Families

As teachers consider their PLP purposes in light of families' needs, they quickly recognize the mutual benefits. Not only can PLPs bring families along on this journey of personalization, they also help families stay connected with their young adolescent and learn that much more about their child along the way. Here are some PLP purposes that teachers identify as serving the interests of families.

To provide a broader representation of what their child can do.
Unlike standardized tests, PLPs are intended to provide a more complete picture of a child. Through this multimodal representation of what a learner can do, families can see a wider variety of skills and interests than what is covered by state tests. Some students perform poorly on standardized tests in spite of otherwise grasping and enjoying tested subjects. Whereas others may not excel in the traditionally tested subjects, the PLP provides a space for celebrating their talents and abilities. The opportunities to see broader representations are often restricted to open houses, poetry slams, or science fairs, for example, because teachers can orchestrate them only so often. As the vignette of Cassandra depicted, her father had not seen his daughter in action at the shelter; it was through her PLP entries that he came to understand what she was engaged in day to day during the project. With PLPs, these important learning experiences become a regular part of the conversation that parents, students,

and teachers have about continuing progress. With the changing nature of society and the rapidly evolving economy, parents' and guardians' academic concerns are extending well beyond grades and test scores toward twenty-first-century skills. Does my child collaborate well? Is she a problem solver? Is he intimidated by large groups of people? Does she express herself well in front of others? PLPs can answer these questions directly, in stark contrast to standardized tests.

To help families stay connected to their young adolescent.
For some students, early adolescence is a time when they begin to shift their allegiances from their families and toward their peer groups. Parents understandably feel the growing distance. Whereas it was once cool to be the homeroom parent, it's not uncommon for parents to be banned by their middle grade child from volunteering or chaperoning school events. Further complicating matters, at just the time that students start to pull away from their parents, the school environment also becomes more fragmented. Often, the self-contained classroom gives way to the interdisciplinary team or traditional junior high model, leaving parents to wonder how to communicate with teachers in this new structure. PLPs, particularly when bolstered by student-led conferences, offer a common platform for conversations about how students are growing across their curriculum as well as how they are maturing and revealing moral and ethical parts of themselves. PLPs invite discussion about how students are finding their place in the world, identifying with their communities, and discovering their resilience as they bounce back from the social, personal, academic, and familial challenges that are part of their daily lives.

To address parents' and guardians' concerns or anxieties.
PLPs can provide a running record of learning that families can access, or be directed to, at any time. It's not uncommon for parents to express concern about the pace of learning or degree of challenge in the classroom, whether they have children with a history of high achievement, special education accommodations, or a pattern of disengagement. Whatever the concern, imagine being able to balance anxious parents' perspectives about their child with a rich and diverse record of learning that in many instances captures healthier dimensions of their child's development. PLPs give us a chance to replace that impulse to say to worried parents, "Trust us," with something more akin to, "Let's look at the evidence." And that evidence is often far more compelling

than a list of grades or scores. They also show more vividly than other reporting tools how their child's school experience is—or can be—customized for him or her.

To provide documentation for schooling transitions.
At times, parents or guardians need to facilitate a child's transition from one school to another. It can feel overwhelming as they wonder how a new teacher will come to know their child as well as the last one did, how they might convey the student's learning interests and preferences, or what areas of academic and personal growth are in greatest need. Because the PLP is designed to communicate this important information to various stakeholders, it is already well-positioned to do so during school transitions as well.

For Community Members

Teachers, students, and families may be the more obvious stakeholders in the educational venture, yet the community at large—both local and global—can benefit from the thoughtful use of PLPs. As flexible pathways legislation pushes to expand learning opportunities beyond school, and as teachers increasingly adopt community-based pedagogies like place-based or service learning, adults and peers outside the school walls can become key players in student learning. They also have a need to know a student they're collaborating with and are often in the best position to help a student gather and reflect upon the authentic evidence of their learning together. The following are key ways in which PLPs can serve the community's interest in student learning.

To discover common ground for collaboration.
It can be intimidating to consider the world beyond the school walls as a locus for learning for young adolescents. What roles will people and organizations play? How will you find fruitful areas for collaboration? How can you quickly establish meaningful relationships between student and community partner given the fast-paced learning lives of students and schools? An experienced and skilled collaborator first wants to know something about the people with whom they collaborate. A system that values students' opportunities to connect with people outside of school places the sharing of stories at the forefront of establishing partnerships. Vivid, multimedia PLPs tell a student's story in ways that are particularly accessible to potential collaborators, often regardless

of their own educational backgrounds. It's hard to imagine a better way to explore possible collaboration and find common interests and histories that can be the start of a productive relationship. PLPs succinctly capture students' identities and sense of self, present vivid examples of learning they value, identify sources of their passions and interests, and pose questions they are currently pondering. For example, we might imagine that PLPs helped Cassandra and Marcos convey to the shelter director that important learning will happen and convince her to accept them as volunteers in her very busy shelter. What's more, PLPs are presented in a student's voice, which makes them accessible to potential partner peers as well. With a digital, media-rich PLP, students can just as readily share their story with a collaborator across the room, across town, or across the globe.

To establish a common language and vision for learning within the community. As we look toward the future, lists abound with critical skills for college, career, and life success. Among the skills most in demand for 2020, the World Economic Forum identifies problem solving, critical thinking, creativity, coordinating with others, emotional intelligence, and decision-making.[17] *The Handbook of Research on Technology Tools for Real-World Skill Development* similarly identifies thinking skills, social skills, global skills, and digital skills as vital for future success.[18] PLPs, by capturing in vivid and accessible terms these skills in the learning lives of young adolescents, can galvanize a community's commitment to personalized learning. Through a child's voice, they can demystify student-directed learning, flexible pathways and proficiency-based assessment and empower community members to fulfill their role as collaborators in student growth. A farmer knows the importance of effective communication when seeking a loan from the bank. A mechanic running her own shop knows how important it is to think entrepreneurially in order to grow a business. The financial analyst, the custodian, the professor, the electrician, and community members from all walks of life regularly need to think critically, reach out to mentors, join associations, gather information, and learn new technologies. Often, they need to do many of these things at the same time! Just as Cassandra's father in the vignette, they readily recognize these skills and dispositions in a PLP. And they are invariably impressed to see them in the work of 10- to 14-year-olds because, regardless of background, they know these skills matter for life.

To value the input and expertise of the community.

Community members have a great deal to offer young people in personalized learning environments. Focusing the PLP on skills that are applicable across careers, identities, and generations welcomes everyone back into the schools that too many find alienating. PLPs focused on these universal priorities can lead students, teachers, and others to see the strengths in their community and invite many more people to share their expertise with students. We have seen students interested in creation stories interview a local imam, rabbi, and priest; those eager to learn to cook meet with the owners of a newly emerged Nepalese dumpling house and an African corner market; and those with a goal to learn a new language consult with a local resident at the senior center. In our more rural communities, students interested in technology connected with a local dairy farm, orchard, and machine shop to see how each employs twenty-first-century technologies; those with a passion for research surveyed the library and newspaper archives to explore local history; and one student with a passion for cars interned with a town mechanic, which led to a paid part-time job. It's these community members, after all—like Cassandra's mom and dad, the animal shelter director, the veterinarian and, of course, Mr. Larmar and the principal—who live the relevant and real-world lives young adolescents so desperately want to be a part of. They are the positive role models for students who can strengthen community bonds as a result.[19] The PLP is a ready platform for developing students' interests and goals, connecting these with expertise in the community, and documenting the results alongside and on par with the rest of their learning.

To expand notions of when and where learning happens.

Finally, the transition to personalized learning can challenge the expectations of all stakeholders, not least those most removed from the perplexing talk of school reform. PLPs can help us engage directly with members of communities near and far in redefining where and when learning happens. Students' PLPs can convey persuasively that learning outside of school counts and that community members are valued by the school system as mentors and knowledgeable resources in their own right. If personalization of this sort is to flourish, we'll need the community to understand what it looks like, why it's important, and the roles community members can play as accountability systems evolve, costs shift, and new job descriptions emerge. We've never had a more powerful public relations tool for school change than the PLP.

Across Stakeholders

To see early adolescent development through an appreciative lens.

Unfortunately, society can be full of disdain for the stage of early adolescence. You don't have to look far to find book and movie titles proclaiming middle school as the worst years of one's life. And most middle grades teachers are familiar with the responses they receive when divulging their profession to others. Regrettably, students are also aware of this negative perception by much of the world around them. By developing vibrant PLPs, revisiting them regularly, and sharing them across these stakeholder groups, we have a chance to acknowledge the rapid pace of change and growth experienced by every student. We can reframe development as continuous and positive rather than reinforcing the negative stereotypes so often hoisted upon this period in students' lives. Perhaps PLPs can help society get past its obsessions with students' use of social media and instead support and celebrate all the other ways they want to engage with the world. Viewing personal development through a positive lens can transform the stress that is common and potentially debilitating for young adolescents, bewildering for families, and alienating for many in the community. Instead, we can offer regular opportunities to reflect, honor, and reimagine these changes in ways that help foster resiliency.

EXAMPLES IN ACTION

Let's look at several examples of how teachers and leaders in Vermont schools use PLPs to serve their stakeholders. We will continue to use these real-life anecdotes throughout the rest of the book to help illustrate personalization in practice.

PERSONALIZATION IN PRACTICE Lamoille Union Middle School

Lori Lisai and Joseph Murphy, educators from Lamoille Union Middle School, developed an array of Geography of Self activities for students to explore their identities.[20] One of these tasks invites students to think about and share aspects of their lives in the form of an Autobiographical Map. The idea of being an explorer and cartographer of one's own life is compelling to many young adolescents. In table 2.2 we share how Lisai and Murphy help students represent their lives in this way.

Figure 2.1 is one example of maps students have created in response to this task. In Trinity's Island, you'll note that she includes relationships in her map key,

TABLE 2.2   **Autobiographical map instructions: Lamoille Union Middle School**

Autobiographical Map

We can learn about geography of a place by studying a map. A map is simply a representation of something real. Geography of Self asks you to be the cartographer, or mapmaker, only the land you seek to represent is yourself. What might a map of you look like?

Symbolism is an important tool we use to express how we feel about things, how we see things, and how we think about the life we live. For this portion of the project, you will use your own version of map symbols to create a visual representation of who you are.

READY . . .
Start by brainstorming a list of what is important to you. Include the following:

1. your full name
2. names of people who are important to you (family, friends, etc.)
3. life-changing events (things that have happened in your life that have shaped its course)
4. your favorites (pet, memory, vacation place, book, film, food, subject, music, part of the day, thing to think about, etc.)
5. any other details you deem important to who you are

SET . . .
Now, consider the different types of land features on a map. Our world is comprised of peninsulas, islands, archipelagos, mountains, rivers, streams, waterfalls, tundra, taiga, desert, plains, steppes, and plateaus to name just a few. Think about the meaning of each land feature, and how you might use that meaning to represent, or symbolize, something of importance to you. Have a look at some examples at this link here. Notice how the artist of "My Lifesland" chose certain land features to represent important people in her life; for example, she drew a volcano and called it "Dad."

Now, plan out a rough draft of an autobiographical map using the principles of map creation. Maps portray where things are located in relation to other things. Think about how to use this idea to represent who you are and what/who is important to you.

GO . . .
Using old school paper and colored pencils, create an autobiographical map. Include the following elements:

1. 5–7 different land features
2. 8–10 different symbols
3. a map legend
4. a unique compass rose

Source: Lori Lisai and Joseph Murphy, Lamoille Union Middle School.

including her mom and her dad's ex-wife. Trinity emphasizes animals by including her Archipelago of Pets, and cats, in particular, on Cat Beach. Her oasis (the kitchen) and the inclusion of a tiny suitcase next to a stone with "RIP" written on it provide fodder for questions that peers might pose as she shares her map with others.

FIGURE 2.1   **Autobiographical map of Trinity's Island, Lamoille Union Middle School**

Source: Trinity Masi, student, Lamoille Union Middle School.

PERSONALIZATION IN PRACTICE Cabot School

Sarah Adelman, a fifth- and sixth-grade teacher at Cabot School, wanted to provide a creative way for students to share their identities and learning preferences. She had several goals for this work: to learn about her students deeply, to create a platform for authentic, meaningful goal-setting, and to build community. Sarah invited her students to create Identi-trees, illustrating their interests as the branches; their important events, places, and people as the roots; and their goals as the leaves. Her students then uploaded these pieces of art into ThingLink, where they added digital links from the internet to documents, websites, photographs, or other links to express these concepts. Although we can't fully appreciate the linked version here, the image of Silas's Identi-tree in figure 2.2 demonstrates that he sees himself as quiet, confident, skillful, and mysterious. Among other things, he conveys his love of baseball and soccer, his goal to improve at skiing, and his desire to "find an undiscovered place." And he leaves us wondering what happened at the Orange County Fair! As his teacher, Sarah is presented with a number of entry points for building relationships and curriculum. Her project integrated art, technology, and expression. It grounded the PLP in self-expression and student identity while generating with remarkable efficiency critical insights and opportunities she can leverage for personalized learning.

PERSONALIZATION IN PRACTICE Burke Town School

At Burke Town School in West Burke, eighth-grade students launched a semester-long project to advance the United Nations' Sustainable Development Goals in their community.[21] As they began, they quickly realized that they needed to know their community better. Their teacher, Morgan Moore, asked the students to think of someone in the community who inspired them. Students then interviewed and photographed those community members and created block prints based on the photos. Next, with art teacher Carol Mason, they hosted a community art show at a local café, as shown in figure 2.3, calling it Humans of Burke, based on the Humans of New York website and portrait series.[22] Overall, the project emphasized getting to know and embrace one's community. Through their reflections, students shared that the experience gave them a sense of purpose and a new appreciation for the community as they helped its members feel known and important.

FIGURE 2.2　**Silas's Identi-tree, Cabot School**

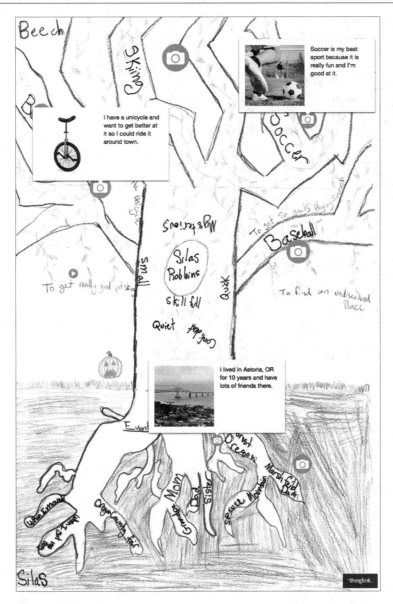

Source: Silas Robbins, student, Cabot School.

FIGURE 2.3   **The Humans of Burke art exhibition at local café, Burke Town School**

Source: Image from the cafelottivt Instagram account.

MATCHING PURPOSES WITH STAKEHOLDER NEEDS

We've explored some of what PLPs can do. Now let's consider for a moment what PLPs don't do. In this complex business of teaching and learning, your role often dictates the type of data needed to do your job well. Effective teachers need different information than district administrators. Similarly, school counselors require different data than principals. And families have their own information needs. Of course, this doesn't mean we aren't concerned about issues that reside outside of our roles. Teachers surely care about systems-level issues and district leaders similarly care about individual students, for instance. But it does mean that our responsibilities dictate the types of data we will find most useful in our daily work with youth. A quick review of the data needs of different players in education will help us isolate the unique contributions PLPs can make to the system as a whole. There's an inverse relationship between the utility of the PLP and the number of students one is responsible for. The farther your role is from the individual student, the less immediate the applicability of the data within the PLP. Let's explore this in greater detail, with a particular focus on the stakeholders we've not already considered previously in the chapter.

State or District Level Leaders

System leaders are accountable to the communities they serve. They routinely need to share information that communicates the system's effectiveness. Therefore, to do their job well, they need data that can answer broad questions. Is the district meeting basic standards in literacy and numeracy? Do glaring inequities across schools or sub-populations of students exist? Are there flaws in teacher preparation or system functions? Are our schools safe places? These systems-level, accountability-oriented examples are the concerns of system leaders, school boards, top administrators, and the political interests of state and federal legislators. Their policy responsibilities need to address system-level issues and concerns. District leaders' interests often are best served by quantitative data that can be analyzed to answer systems-level questions, such as the demographic analyses of standardized test scores. But often, systems-level data does not tell the whole story of learning and growth taking place in schools.

A PLP's focus on the individual generally renders them less helpful to administrators for many of their purposes. However, PLPs can still be powerful when state and district level leaders need to keep the conversation grounded in the work of students. At times, for example, leaders wish to showcase examples of learning opportunities that occur within their schools, when making a case in a legislative work group, at a coalition of school boards, or to a policy committee. In these cases, the PLP can remind us all of the human element at the core of our work, an element that statistics and policies can sometimes mask. But PLPs, along the lines we've previously described, are not intended to provide a reliable picture of the distribution of basic skills across the whole system, for instance.

Principals and Other Building-level Leaders

Principals and other building-level leaders require similar information that reveals how their school population as a whole is doing. They need to understand the level of student engagement, as it relates to behavior, achievement, and the functioning of the school community, much of which cannot be readily measured through standardized tools. Principals also need to balance that holistic picture of the school with more intimate knowledge of student growth and interests. The PLP becomes more relevant as school leaders consider school culture and student learning. They benefit from the ability of PLPs to tell stories and illustrate themes that convey students' lived experiences. To do their job well, principals can use PLPs to bolster their own relationships with students and reach the ones who struggle. Imagine how a readily accessible PLP could enrich disciplinary conversations.

School Counselors and Special Educators

The PLP assumes still greater importance as we consider the roles of the school counselor, special educator, and related school personnel. As professionals often juggling hundreds of students on their caseloads, counselors and special educators frequently use standardized test scores, diagnostic batteries, and other quantitative data to clarify needs, categorize students, and coordinate services. But as they work directly with students, particularly those needing extra attention, they also require quick and easy access to what really makes a particular student tick. Counselors and special educators can benefit greatly from the rich and complex stories PLPs capture about their authors. They can reveal how a student describes herself now, or in the past, how she's developing academically or socially, what she's interested in or what she feels good about. The PLP can be an invaluable conversation starter as these busy professionals search for all-important bridges from where a student is to where she needs to be.

In a comprehensive system, each of these stakeholders requires different types of data to respond to different questions. These questions vary based on one's role and responsibilities. While PLPs don't answer the same questions as standardized tests, neither do tests afford the benefits of PLPs. Quantitative measures alone are unlikely to help a principal create a healthy and cohesive community. Test scores don't help the teacher divine the subtleties of a student's identities, abilities, interests, or passions. They don't create opportunities for social integration, assuage a parents' angst over their child's welfare, or record the evolving story of a student's sense of self, social connections, and intellectual development. At their best, PLPs are accessible, revealing, and user friendly. PLPs focus on those things that most stakeholders regard as important, which is not the same as focusing on everything every audience might want to know. PLPs can tell a story that reaches beyond the initial interests of any particular audience by striking essential, resonant chords with each one.

AVOIDING POTENTIAL PITFALLS

We've discussed what PLPs can do well, and what they can't. And we've explored the utility of the PLP in light of various stakeholder needs. Now let's consider possible pitfalls or obstacles to realizing the higher potential of PLPs. As you move PLPs from theory to practice, responding to the needs and interests of key stakeholders, the higher purposes of PLPs can be threatened by traditional mindsets, logistical challenges, and competing concerns. For instance, students' need to "own" their learning, including their PLP, may clash with a teacher's need to bring order to student work or the larger system's demand for integrated accountability and record-keeping. We offer here some patterns we've observed that have confounded early attempts at PLPs. In many, you'll notice the inherent connection between form and function. Table 2.3 summarizes these common pitfalls and how to avoid them.

TABLE 2.3　**Avoiding common pitfalls**

Instead of . . .	Try . . .
Overlooking the unmet need	Identifying your purpose
Expecting reliability	Prizing validity
Demanding uniformity	Enabling personal expression
Toppling any of the three pillars	Embracing meaningful curriculum
Equating choice with personalization	Inviting students into the conversation
Leaving families behind	Including PLPs in your family engagement strategy

Overlooking the Unmet Need

As teachers and administrators consider PLPs, they should answer these questions: What is the critical function we want PLPs to serve? What is the unmet need? What gap will PLPs fill in our classroom, team, or school? Not identifying this gap leaves a system vulnerable to dictating form by aiming for misaligned functions. For example, does the student struggle with decoding? Word recognition? Vocabulary? Tests can tease those out. A fine-grained analysis of literacy or numeracy skills is precisely what standardized tests are good at providing. We don't need the PLP to serve those purposes. Similarly, in our experience, it's practically by default that most schools we've worked with initially build subject-specific sections into their PLP design. But simply transferring an existing system's compartmentalized approach to learning can overburden PLP work and distract from the inherently interdisciplinary demands of personalization. Instead, commit to organizing the PLP to capture how well students apply communication skills to multidisciplinary problem solving, social and team dynamics, and multiple audiences, for instance. Set aside the necessary time with colleagues to identify the critical purposes and essential functions for your PLP system. We suggest you revisit table 2.1. Consider which, if any, of these purposes line up with your own hopes for the future and expand upon those you deem important.

Expecting Reliability

As we suggested in the last chapter with regard to personalized learning generally, one of the biggest threats to PLPs in particular is expecting them to do what they don't do well. Teachers and leaders sometimes expect PLPs to help them reliably measure and track subject-specific learning. Consider whether other systems do this well enough already. Pushed too far toward assessment, PLPs can end up looking like little more than a collection of scored rubrics. Turn to other facets of your personalized environment to bear the burden of cataloging test scores and systematically tracking progress on a full battery of proficiencies. We will discuss later in the book how technology can help integrate the distinct facets of the three pillars without undermining the distinct purposes of each. Preserve the PLP itself for students telling their own story of growth using authentic evidence of knowledge and skills they've applied to real-world challenges.[23]

Demanding Uniformity

It's not surprising for stakeholders in the upper levels of the system to demand uniformity across PLPs. That makes intuitive sense from a systems perspective. In our experience, however, it places at risk students' sense of ownership of their PLPs. Rather than demanding uniformity, enable the creative personal expression that students value in their PLPs. In a low-tech system such as a three-ring binder, this may simply mean allowing students to decorate the cover and determine how they might organize the documentation of their learning. In moderate-tech systems, such as a Google Site, Google Presentation or PowerPoint, students can freely decorate certain pages or slides, reserving other sections for required content and more standard layouts. And in more high-tech systems, as you'll see in the next chapter, an increasing number of PLP tools are built on database technology. These tools allow students to upload, tag, or label just about anything they want while giving teachers and administrators access to sorting and reporting tools to make their own meaning of student work, individually or across a larger population. In our experience, pitting personal expression against systems requirements is unproductive; without both, systemwide PLPs may not be worth the effort at all. Most fundamentally, without a sense of ownership, students will not be able to apply the thought, heart, and energy to garner significant benefits from PLPs.

Toppling the Pillars

Another common obstacle to realizing the higher purposes for PLPs and personalized learning is crafting a system that relies so heavily on one of the three pillars that the others are weakened or even nonexistent. Recall table 1.1 that illustrates the interdependence of the pillars? We've observed that this most often occurs when schools become intensely focused on the measurement of proficiency. While proficiency-based assessment is an important component of personalized learning, some schools become so mired in developing fine-grained targets, scales, and tasks for subject area proficiencies that they risk losing sight of what it looks like for students to engage deeply in real-world problems of personal relevance. One Vermont high school teacher recently noted, "We figured out that we cannot move forward . . . thinking that proficiency and personalization are separate components of or pathways to learning. We cannot plan for each separately, divvying up time between them like cake to siblings. We need to shift our thinking to see these as inseparable parts of the same system, not only relying on each other for integrity and purpose, but demanding each other in order to have any chance of transformational learning."[24] Within an exclusive focus on learning scales and proficiencies lies the risk of reducing the creativity and student voice in the process. The focus on fine-grained targets and scales is based on the assumption that we need to create a reliable program of proficiency-based reporting to replace (or be on par with) existing measures, such as tests. This assumption that grading must be replaced with something that is highly reliable, even at the expense of validity, overlooks the fact that the traditional system of A–F grading is notoriously unreliable and problematic.[25]

Instead of asking how you can translate your curriculum into proficiencies, targets and scales, we suggest you first ask: What does it look like for students to demonstrate their capacity as actors in the world, as civic participants, as problem solvers in society? The answer promotes a grander vision of outcomes than we typically expect from the backward design process. Then ask, how can we get students there? The flexible pathways you will then construct with students, colleagues, families, and communities will make proficiency-based assessment all the more necessary and relevant.

Equating Choice with Personalization

Mistaking student choice for personalization is another issue that sometimes emerges in this work. Student choice is indeed an important aspect of a personalized learning environment. Yet while it is necessary, it is not sufficient.[26] On one middle school team we know, the teachers earnestly wanted to ensure that all students could find their passions in the curriculum. Each student selected a personally meaningful topic and the teachers worked hard to create a space in the schedule specific to this pursuit. Yet, while there was an abundance of student choice, ultimately students spent each block of personalized learning time in the classroom sitting in front of computers, researching their chosen topics. In short order, many students began to demonstrate considerable disengagement. Yet why should we be surprised when, despite topical choice, very little about students' school lives had changed? This case is a reminder that personalized learning is not about students working in isolation in front of screens all day. It is about students leveraging technology as a tool, alongside research, collaboration, feedback, making, doing, and sharing, all of which are social, dynamic, and responsive. Rather than relying solely on students' topical choice to personalize their learning experience, consider the range of ways choice can be broadened to include not only what they learn but how, when, and where as well. Better yet, invite students into the conversation about how to make learning more meaningful. We showcase several examples of how to do this later in the book.

Leaving Families Behind

Finally, many parents expect their child's education to look a lot like their own. When they encounter something unfamiliar, they may need help seeing its utility or place. For example, parents can respond to PLPs with disappointment or frustration if they expect to see the data they are most familiar with, generally in the form of grades, and then don't. This is an ongoing issue for educators with any shift in assessment practices, but it needn't be conflated with PLPs themselves. For most teachers, and in most settings, the program of more traditional education is continuing alongside these forays into personalization, and the more traditional data still are being generated. The gap is not in parents' capacity to know if students are submitting work on time or getting passing grades; progress reports and online assignment trackers can still be useful if that's what families need to feel on top of things. The question of what to do about parents' expectations for grades can and should be pursued separately from the PLP agenda. Instead of simply expecting families to understand and accept this new thing called a PLP, consider the role of PLPs within your broader family engagement strategy. From the unmet need perspective, you may wish to preserve the PLP as a vehicle for conveying the deeper, more relevant and personalized learning opportunities that students are pursuing. Parents will appreciate the PLP as a gateway to new conversations with their child about their learning and development. But be sure not to strip them of other tools they need to parent their child for success in school.

KEY QUESTIONS

A central aim of this chapter has been to convey that you're designing PLPs for a specific purpose. And, as you might imagine, that purpose should inform

TABLE 2.4 **Vermont's critical elements for personalized learning plans**

Vermont's Personalized Learning Plan Critical Elements
(1) Plan Information (including the name of student and school, dates of PLP meetings, and names of participants in the PLP planning meetings);
(2) Student Profile (such as a student's strengths, abilities and skills, relationships, core values, baseline assessments, and interest inventories);
(3) Student Goals (both secondary and post-secondary, accompanied by proposed pathways);
(4) Action Steps (along with timelines and evidence that will demonstrate progress);
(5) Achievement of Action Steps (including progress toward goals and common learning expectations, as well as assessments and evidence of student learning); and
(6) Reflection (on the part of the student, teacher, and family members).

Source: Based upon a condensed version of Vermont Agency of Education resources, which can be found at https://education.vermont.gov/sites/aoe/files/documents/edu-plp-critical-elements.pdf.

its contents. In our experience, the contents of PLPs vary widely from student to student, school to school, and district to district. Vermont's Personalized Learning Plan Critical Elements are featured in table 2.4.[27]

While these elements are useful, we know that the contents of a PLP are most powerful when driven by the PLP's intended purposes rather than by an externally mandated list. Accordingly, the Vermont Agency of Education suggests that schools are free to include additional elements that "align to their own specific school and community values."[28] Educators sometimes think that PLPs should encompass all learning or evidence. Yet when PLPs are mistaken for the only reporting vehicle, they become cluttered with things they don't need. It becomes just another place to catalog grades, test scores, and behavior data. While these items certainly can be kept in the PLP, they also can be distracting and conflate conversations.

When we decided to write a book about personalized learning, and about PLPs in particular, we invited educators to tell us what they'd want in such a book. Teachers asked great questions about the purpose of PLPs: Is it a vessel for documenting evidence to graduate? Should it provide evidence for report cards? Is it used as an application for college? Are PLPs just a vehicle for demonstrating the proficiencies? They also asked about the audience for PLPs: Do these plans get presented to someone in twelfth grade in person or just submitted electronically? Is someone grading/judging them to determine graduation? If so, who? They wondered about content: What is required and what is optional in a PLP? Will this vary by grade level? Do all classes contribute to the PLP? Could we have a handy checklist by grade level of what students and teachers should be focusing on? And they asked about roles and responsibilities: Who will take the lead for the school, district or supervisory union? Who takes the lead with each student and when? Who chooses the digital platform? Who sets it up for 700 students?

We quickly realized that the answer to many of the questions was the ever-annoying "it depends," because so much rides on your purpose for the PLP and your own school circumstances. Although we can't answer those questions as directly as some might like, we offer a set of guiding questions for your team, school or district. Although the list is far from comprehensive, we think it can help you maximize the potential and power of the personalized learning plan. As you read the book and consider PLPs for your local context, you'll likely find it helpful to visit, and revisit, the questions we pose in table 2.5 either on your own, with your team, or with your school's PLP design committee.

TABLE 2.5   **Guiding questions for designing PLPs**

Guiding Questions for You or Your PLP Design Team

Purpose:
What is my/our purpose(s) for the PLP?
Are there primary and secondary purposes?
If so, what are they?
Who are the main stakeholders?

Audience:
Based on these purposes, who are the audiences?

Content:
Based on the purpose and audience, what is required in a PLP?
What is optional?
What degree of choice will students have in determining content?
How important is consistency of content across settings?
Will the content vary by grade level, classrooms or teams?
Will all classes contribute to the PLP?

Form:
What form will the PLP take?
How important is consistency of format across settings?
Will the format vary by grade level, classrooms or teams?
What degree of choice will students have in determining form?

Roles and Responsibilities:
And based on all of this, who will take the lead for the team/school/SU?
Who will take the lead with each student?
What is our "start-up" plan?
What roles will students play?
Who chooses the platform?
Who sets it up?

LOOKING AHEAD

As we've conveyed in this chapter, regardless of how you arrived at the prospect of PLPs, be clear about why you are implementing them. Teachers are familiar with the challenge of turning mandates into opportunities, which can sometimes feel like turning lemons into lemonade. Whether working alone or as part of a larger group, achieving your greatest hopes for PLPs and personalization will hinge on knowing how those hopes relate to PLPs themselves. Knowing that PLPs cannot serve *all* purposes, ask yourself which gaps in your practice you're trying to fill. The contents of the PLP should follow. Of course, there are lots of ways to organize PLPs, but for simplicity's sake within this book, we'll talk first about developing the Learner Profile, featured in chapter 4 (Launching PLPs with the Learner Profile); next about flexible pathways through the learning journey, featured in chapter 5 (Designing Flexible Learning Pathways for Young Adolescents) and chapter 6 (Scaffolding for Equitable, Deeper Learning); and then about assessing the learning, in chapter 7 (PLPs and Proficiency-Based Assessment). In all four, you'll gain a better sense of what belongs in the kind of PLPs you're striving to create. But before we do any of that, let's take a look at the type of culture you'll want to create in your classroom and school to prepare for personalized learning in chapter 3 (Laying the Groundwork for Personalized Learning).

THREE

LAYING THE GROUNDWORK FOR PERSONALIZED LEARNING

Reaching into the chicken coop, Angela remembers what things were like before. Before she started her sustainability class. She hated school. She knew that it wasn't for her. School was just something to get through. With her mom in prison, no one was even asking her about it anyway. Nothing made any sense and she wasn't sure she would even finish school. It all seemed so pointless.

Angela pushes the sleeves of her sweatshirt up. She opens the nest box, and reaches in, pulling out a beautiful blue speckled egg. She remembers how her cousin, the one she was living with at the time, told her she might just like this class. Angela rolled her eyes and thought, "Yeah, right." But here she was.

Back on the first day of class, the teacher had asked if she had any different shoes. When Angela shook her head, the teacher had smiled and offered her her muck boots. She'd announced to the class, "This class is yours. We have to continue the legacy of how to make our school more sustainable, but how we do it is completely up to you." In the background, reggae music was playing. Angela looked around in disbelief, thinking, "Is this really a class? You mean, you're not going to tell us what to do?" The next thing Angela knew, she was learning how to hold a chicken and how to use a power tool to fix the chicken coop.

Angela feels different now, just a few months later. She feels powerful because she can choose what to work on. She knows her purpose: to make their school more sustainable. Over time, she's begun to see herself differently. She has even started paying attention in other classes, even though they still aren't as fun. And she's started thinking she just may want to graduate after all, because, well, then she would continue to have more choices. The most important part? She's started to care. She wants to do well because her sustainability teacher cares. And other students in the class care. It feels good.

Angela likes being able to document the story of her learning in her PLP, which is in the form of a personal website. She's taken lots of pictures: the chickens, her classmates, the chicken coop's newly insulated roof, and her class' microbusiness selling local greens to the community. Angela used digital media to design the label for the packaging, and she posted that to her PLP as well. She feels proud when she scrolls through the latest PLP posts and sees these images, her reflections, and the various likes and comments from her fellow students and teachers. It feels like evidence that she matters, that she was here, that what she does makes a difference. This is her story. The one she wants to tell.

Angela walks inside to the scale and weighs the egg. She enters the weight into the class's business spreadsheet, which she manages. She takes a quick look at the latest productivity charts for the coop, relieved to see things once again on the upswing after last month's dip. But she knows it's too soon to say if the new, softer lighting she suggested is making the difference. She'd learned about that on a small hatchery blog she's been following. She takes a quick screenshot of the charts, uploads it to her PLP, and tags it as evidence for quantitative thinking. A few months ago, she never imagined even saying "spreadsheet" or "quantitative" and here she is, the project's numbers wiz. The hardest part isn't the math involved, it's getting everyone to input their data each week!

Angela looks out the window to see what her group is doing. They are just finishing up their jobs: watering the tower garden, checking the greenhouse plants, feeding the chickens. The students are focused on these tasks, but not rushing. They are purposeful. Angela likes that everyone gets to sign up for a job they want on the board, and that everyone knows what to do. It took them a while to get the hang of the jobs, and to believe in the independence and trust that their teacher placed in them. But after a few weeks, they had it down. Once her group finishes, they will settle into a table and work on the presentation for the school board about their microbusinesses, grabbing their computers and meeting like business associates.

Angela hears voices at the door of the classroom and sees the three teachers on her team, meeting as they often do. She hears one ask, "Is it OK if I borrow some of your students to be a practice audience for my class's school board presentation? They really need some peer feedback. I'll send over the Google Doc they can use for this, OK? I'll drop it in the team folder, in the curriculum planning doc. And see you for our PLC later." There are some quick nods, and the teachers are up and moving again.

Angela looks back down at the egg in her hand. Its pattern is just so beautiful. She takes a picture of it and uploads it to her website so her classmates can see it. Especially Sandra, who she knows is doing a project about eggs, their different patterns, colors, and sizes. It's funny, she thinks, but in this class, and on her middle school team, everyone seems to help everyone out. It is amazing how things can change.

BUILDING YOUR RATIONALE: STAGE-ENVIRONMENT FIT

In many ways, Angela's story is a great example of a student benefiting from a strong match between her developmental needs and her academic experience. Educational psychologist Jacquelynne S. Eccles and her colleagues describe this match as "stage-environment fit," the degree to which the school environment meets the developmental needs of the learner.[1] For middle schoolers, Eccles notes that "a poor 'fit' between the early adolescent and the classroom environment increases the risk of disengagement and school problems, especially for those early adolescents who were having difficulty succeeding in school academically prior to their school transition."[2] Certainly Angela experienced a poor fit prior to encountering her sustainability class. She was already contemplating dropping out of school and she hadn't even entered high school.

Because many young adolescents see themselves as increasingly responsible and deserving of adult respect, a school's "emphasis on discipline and teacher control and its limited opportunities for student decision-making" can result in a poor match for the learner, according to Eccles.[3] Sharing power through decreasing teacher control and increasing student responsibility is an effective way to increase this fit. The vignette of Angela's sustainability class illustrates a number of features that support this aim, as her teacher creates regular opportunities for student self-direction and decision-making. Angela and her classmates choose what to work on each day. They hold classroom jobs with authentic, rather than token, responsibilities. They run a legitimate business selling their greens to community members, and the chickens depend on them to stay safe, warm, and alive. This sense of responsibility carries over into the realm of safety, as well, as students are trusted to use power tools and expensive equipment in their work. In these ways, and others, decreasing teacher control and increasing student decision-making lies at the heart of ensuring a strong fit for middle schoolers.

Strong relationships are another important part of stage-environment fit for young adolescents. Often, students are transitioning out of long-lasting relationships in elementary schools and into middle schools with many more students and teachers. In her seminal article on the developmental needs of young adolescents, Eccles observes:

> The structure of some schools reduces opportunities for adolescents to form close relationships with their teachers at precisely the point in the early adolescents' development when they have a great need for guidance and support from nonfamilial adults. . . . These structural factors can undermine the sense of community and trust between early adolescents and their teachers—leading in turn to a greater reliance by teachers on authoritarian control and increased alienation among the students.[4]

At its best, personalization creates deep connections between teachers, families, community members, and students. When students explore their identities and interests, and share these with trusted mentors, they have a chance to foster strong relationships. And when positive relationships are in turn coupled with greater responsibility and self-direction, schools are well-positioned to meet the developmental needs of this age group.

CHAPTER OVERVIEW

This chapter walks you through laying the groundwork for personalized learning, at both the teacher and student levels. Drawing on the experience of teachers we work with, you'll explore some fundamental pedagogical priorities that sustain personalized environments, including teaching self-direction and executive functioning skills, integrating social-emotional learning, leveraging student leadership, and creating a strong sense of community. You'll see how teachers pursue these priorities by strengthening collaboration with colleagues and adopting critical norms, routines and habits of work for teachers and students alike. For those of you on teaching teams, we discuss the importance of common planning time and efficient resource sharing. We also offer you some key criteria as you consider adopting a platform for the PLP. Throughout it all, you'll notice the many ways that a teacher's role as community builder comes into play.

Our goal for this chapter is to position you to make smart choices about how to start PLPs in your classroom. Perhaps most important, we hope you'll make these choices with a powerful end in mind: a smooth-running environment of engaged and self-directed learners. Granted, it's a lofty and long-term goal, but even in the early stages, teachers have told us it's the environment they want to strive for. It's the environment they want to live in every day.

THE FOUNDATIONS OF A PERSONALIZED LEARNING ENVIRONMENT

Teachers we work with describe their successes with personalized learning as largely the product of classroom culture and personalized learning strategies reinforcing one another. When things fall apart, it's usually because one or the other is missing. Without attending to classroom culture, attempts at personalized and self-directed learning almost invariably fail. At the same time, the initial stages of PLP development can build the kind of classroom culture that serves as an effective foundation upon which to lay personalized learning strategies.

Teacher as Community Builder

Whether you're new to the profession or a more veteran middle school teacher, it doesn't take long to recognize the importance of building relationships with and between young adolescents. Students themselves tell us that "the climate of the classroom is important. In fact, they perceive it as influencing their engagement, and their ability to learn."[5] In the middle grades, an effective learning culture is one in which students explore and develop their identities.[6] This identity exploration is coupled with a strong need for peer approval, one of many reasons young adolescents need learning environments in which they feel safe to spend time at their learning edge. Such classrooms foster "risk-taking and help-seeking."[7] They promote enthusiasm for challenging tasks that are accompanied by support, and they feature traditions and routines that build students' skills in seeking that support. They integrate social-emotional proficiencies, such as self-awareness, responsibility, and cooperation, into the curriculum.[8] Teachers and students discuss and assess growth together, considering the learners' strengths and needs. And these personalized settings ensure that each student is well known by at least one adult in the building, a cornerstone of adolescent resiliency.[9]

We know that the start of the year is a critical time to establish the norms and procedures that will embody this inclusive culture well beyond the first few weeks. Arriving at common agreements among teachers and students alike sets the stage for a more productive and smooth-running year.[10] This is no less the case in a personalized learning environment. Too often, however, our best efforts at community and culture-building are cut short by the pressures of mandated curriculum, time for test preparation, or simply a lack of know-how. The interdependence of classroom culture and personalized learning, and how both can meet the needs of young adolescents, justify doubling down on the time and energy invested in building this culture while implementing PLPs.

PLPs Reinforce Classroom Culture and Community

Launching PLPs dovetails perfectly with creating just this kind of positive learning culture. Determining the purpose for PLPs draws collaborating teachers into important conversations about beliefs, values, and pedagogy. Students can act as co-designers, informing the purpose, format, and contents of the PLP for their class or team. Pairing students as PLP partners initiates effective peer collaboration for the rest of the year while also lightening the logistical load ordinarily carried by teachers. Many teachers use PLPs to ensure that all students acquire essential technology skills while also providing chances to scaffold digital citizenship. At the same time, teachers harvest critical baseline artifacts for each student's writing skills, social and emotional development, and computing skills. Overall, a thoughtfully planned, deliberately scaffolded, and reasonably paced launch of PLPs can bring collaborating teachers closer together, help them know their students better, create a healthy learning community, and set everyone up for a far more productive and enjoyable year. Let's take a closer look at what this all means for PLPs and personalized learning.

DETERMINING PEDAGOGICAL PRIORITIES FOR PERSONALIZED LEARNING

If we hope to respond to what students believe is important and worth doing well, we need a fundamentally different culture than what many classrooms currently exhibit. The personalized classroom should reflect student directed-ness, effective group work, small-group self-monitoring, and minimal but tar-geted teacher intervention. Because much of this may contrast with existing practices, it's important first to establish some common agreements among teaching colleagues, particularly if you're looking to implement PLPs on a teamwide basis. First and foremost, if the PLP is to be a collaborative endeavor, the design of PLPs needs to be a product of common agreements among you and the colleagues who work with your students, as well as with students themselves. Before the year begins, you'll want to set some clear and common goals and expectations about what high-performing classrooms look like and what will be a manageable, multi-year effort to create those classrooms. As we discussed in chapter 2, you'll need to come to agreement about why you're implementing PLPs. What kinds of learning behaviors are you hoping to pro-mote in your classroom or on your team? What habits of mind or dispositions do you value? What kinds of essential information are you hoping to derive from PLPs that will help engage all of your students in deeper learning? Ambi-tious and shared aspirations will keep you going through some challenging stages of implementation and equip you to make some important decisions along the way about what's worth doing, retaining, or casting off.

Recall for a moment Bray and McClaskey's rich list of skills required by learners in personalized learning environments mentioned in chapter 1.[11] We've featured many of these skills in the opening vignettes thus far. For example, students self-monitored their behavior and observed how group mates could play essential and complementary roles in order to complete complex tasks. Miles and his classmates were in charge of transitions, morning meeting, and technology resources. And we saw similar self-direction in Cassandra's and Angela's classrooms. When you consider the breadth and depth of the many, often new, roles for learners, you can begin to appreciate how cultivating this kind of student may require a shared commitment to some new pedagogical priorities, perhaps at the expense of others. Now is the time to seek agree-ment on a number of foundational principles and practices in personalized learning. Owning these as your priorities—your non-negotiables—in building a foundation for personalized learning, especially in concert with colleagues, may be the biggest single step you can take toward successful implementation of personalized classrooms.

Self-Directed Learning

As you might imagine based on these new skills for students, effective personalized learning environments are built largely upon the skills and dispositions of successful student self-direction. Fifty years ago, psychotherapist Carl Rogers concluded, "If we are to have citizens who can live constructively in the kaleidoscopically changing world, we can only have them if we are willing for them to become self-starting, self-initiating learners."[12] A half century later, as the world continues to change "kaleidoscopically," we need to consider how school environments can lay the groundwork for self-directed learning. At its most general, self-directed learning is a process in which people, with or without assistance from others, identify their learning needs and interests, set goals aligned to those interests, locate resources (human and material) that they may require, and select and implement strategies to achieve and assess that learning.[13] Here we share a few building blocks for a sustainable and systematic approach to the kind of classroom culture that supports the best of student-directed learning, that which is focused on both the personal and common good. In particular, we discuss the importance of teaching executive function skills, attending to social-emotional learning, building community, leveraging student roles, co-designing with students, and establishing core proficiencies in relation to self-direction and personalized learning.

Teaching Executive Function Skills

The ambitious vision of self-directed learning, and the challenging roles it requires of students, are well served by teaching executive functions. Think for a moment about all that you juggle as an educator, grappling with multiple ideas simultaneously, making hundreds of decisions daily, and self-regulating your actions and thoughts as you work with youth, colleagues, and families. These abilities reflect the basic executive functions of cognitive flexibility, inhibitory control, and working memory.[14] Just as you call upon them routinely as teachers, so too do learners need to develop them. The new responsibilities and opportunities presented in middle school can challenge the executive functioning skills of even the most organized of young adolescents. Often, students need to get up, prepare themselves for the day, and perhaps remember an instrument, lunch, and homework for multiple subjects. They may need to charge their school laptop or tablet overnight, pack their after-school gear, and review their transportation to and from school. And this is all before the school day officially begins! It's easy to imagine how executive functions affect overall school success, but they also have considerable implications for later life success. Students with strong childhood executive functions demonstrate better physical health, higher socioeconomic status, and fewer drug-related problems and criminal convictions as adults.[15]

While surely executive functions (EFs) are critical in any educational environment, they are all the more important in self-directed, personalized learning environments, as it is this skill set that helps learners to set and achieve goals, prioritize tasks, filter distractions, and control impulses.[16] They are what enable students to plan, remember instructions, and manage multiple tasks successfully. While we aren't born with these skills, we are born with the potential to develop them. EFs are both measurable and malleable.[17] Fortunately, personalized learning environments provide students with lots of practice in developing EFs while engaged in work they care about. With the PLP as a guide, you can help students break down a project into manageable chunks and identify reasonable timelines and plans for each piece. In busy, student-directed classrooms, students need to self-monitor while they are working, including being aware of critical times for focused attention and the potential pitfalls of multitasking.[18] Prioritizing executive functioning skills in the opportunity-rich environment of personalized classrooms contributes to a strong foundation for self-directed learning, one that can last a lifetime.

Students benefit from the explicit teaching of EFs, like the approach taken by the educators at Williston Central School. In figure 3.1 you'll see a page from their 11-page *Student Guide to Executive Functioning,* which they use to support students in this complex work. These one-page, bulleted summaries offer strategies for improving time management, planning and prioritizing, organization, metacognition, task initiation, flexibility, sustained attention, response inhibition, goal-directed persistence, working memory, and emotional control. Teachers on this team acknowledge the challenges of being a student and offer helpful strategies. Their students assess themselves on these EF strategies via a Google Form survey and use this self-assessment to set goals. At the same time, by being overt about these challenges, they convey a sense of community, a feeling that everyone is in this together.

FIGURE 3.1   **Excerpt from the Student Guide to Executive Functioning, Williston Central School**

Planning & Prioritizing

Explanation:
The ability to design a plan to reach a goal or complete a task. It also involves being able to make decisions about what's important to focus on and what isn't.

Strategies to improve Planning & Prioritizing:

- Make a list (most important to least important)
- Use a planner
- Use sticky notes for reminders
- Set reminders on your phone
- Text/Email yourself reminders
- Put different assignments on sticky notes and take away when something is done
- Work with a peer to plan
- Minimize distractions
- Do the least pleasant task first
- Use a watch or phone to keep track of time
- Use helpful websites (For example, the homework page)

Source: Williston Central School.

Attending to Social-Emotional Learning

In addition to helping students hone their executive functioning, teachers find attending to social-emotional learning (SEL) to be an important way to scaffold the skills and dispositions for personalized learning. There are many clear connections between EFs and SEL; SEL is the process through which "children and adults acquire and effectively apply the knowledge, attitudes, and skills necessary to understand and manage emotions, set and achieve positive goals, feel and show empathy for others, establish and maintain positive relationships, and make responsible decisions."[19] Fortunately there's plenty of evidence to make the case for spending time on students' social-emotional learning, particularly that it enhances positive youth development. In a meta-analysis of more than eighty SEL interventions, researchers found that participants fared significantly better in social-emotional skills, attitudes, and other indicators of well-being than their counterparts who did not receive the interventions. Even more promising, these benefits accrued regardless of students' race, socioeconomic background, or school location.[20]

The Collaborative for Academic, Social, and Emotional Learning (CASEL) identifies five core competencies of SEL: self-awareness, self-management, social awareness, relationship skills, and responsible decision-making.[21] Like other competency frameworks, CASEL's framework for SEL advocates for intrapersonal, interpersonal, and cognitive competence in relation to each of these competencies. Table 3.1 summarizes the five CASEL competencies and breaks down the core aspects of each.[22]

It's easy to imagine how many of the tasks required for scaffolding effective personalized learning might also foster students' SEL competencies. For example, students creating and sharing projects based on their cultural backgrounds can heighten self-awareness and build a stronger sense of classroom community. Self-assessing their progress toward learning goals can help with self-management. A service learning project can heighten social awareness. Peer mentoring and collaborative group work require relationship skills. And finally, expecting learners to reflect upon the process of self-directed learning strengthens their responsible decision-making skills. In figure 3.2, you'll see how one student reflected on responsible decision-making, a key component of SEL, as part of a yearlong service learning project in Cabot, Vermont.

Building Community

Building a sense of community in a classroom or team is far from a new idea. Much of the middle grades concept is predicated on safe and supportive community. In fact, among the Association for Middle Level Education's characteristics of effective schools for young adolescents is a school environment that is "inviting, safe, inclusive, and supportive of all" with an adult advocate

TABLE 3.1 **CASEL competencies for social-emotional learning**

Competency	The Ability To . . .	Core Aspects
Self-Awareness	Accurately recognize one's own emotions, thoughts, and values and how they influence behavior. Accurately assess one's strengths and limitations, with a well-grounded sense of confidence, optimism, and a growth mindset.	Identifying emotions, Accurate self-perception, Recognizing strengths, Self-confidence, Self-efficacy
Self-Management	Successfully regulate one's emotions, thoughts, and behaviors in different situations — effectively managing stress, controlling impulses, and motivating oneself. Set and work toward personal and academic goals.	Impulse control, Stress management, Self-discipline, Self-motivation, Goal-setting, Organizational skills
Social Awareness	Take the perspective of and empathize with others, including those from diverse backgrounds and cultures. Understand social and ethical norms for behavior and to recognize family, school, and community resources and supports.	Perspective-taking, Empathy, Appreciating diversity, Respect for others
Relationship Skills	Establish and maintain healthy and rewarding relationships with diverse individuals and groups. Communicate clearly, listen well, cooperate with others, resist inappropriate social pressure, negotiate conflict constructively, and seek other help when needed.	Communication, Social engagement, Relationship building, Teamwork
Responsible Decision-Making	Make constructive choices about personal behavior and social interactions based on ethical standards, safety concerns, and social norms. The realistic evaluation of consequences of various actions, and a consideration of the well-being of oneself and others.	Identifying problems, Analyzing situations, Solving problems, Evaluating, Reflecting, Ethical responsibility

Source: Adapted from The Collaborative for Academic, Social, and Emotional Learning, What is SEL? CASEL, https://casel.org/what-is-sel/.

that guides "every student's academic and personal development."[23] As we discussed in chapter 2, a common key purpose and outcome of PLPs is strengthened relationships, both student-to-teacher and student-to-student.

Attending to the culture and climate of the learning community is foundational for students to take intellectual and personal risks in front of each other. One step toward establishing that climate is giving students meaningful opportunities to learn more about one another. Christie Nold, a sixth-grade teacher on the Verve Team at Frederick H. Tuttle Middle School in South Burlington, wanted to start off the school year, and PLPs, with a more intensive exploration of identity than she had before. She hoped to help her students establish

FIGURE 3.2   **Keith's student reflection, Cabot Leads program, Cabot School**

CABOT LEADS | SPOTLIGHT

Student: Keith
Job Title: Concessions Manager

Job Description
My job is to help run the concession stand at all the Cabot High School basketball and soccer games. The skills I need to be able to run the concession stand are handling money, making correct change, making popcorn, using my people skills, being there on time, talking skills, and keeping an inventory of snacks and supplies.

Reflection
My favorite part of the job is being behind the counter helping people get what they need. I also like making the right change. It's a good way to practice my math skills.

I think that this job has made me more responsible. One day our mentor didn't show up so my partner and I set up and ran the stand by ourselves. It felt cool that we were able to do that without an adult.

Mentors
Mike Crocker + Rebecca Nally + Lynn Leho

Source: Keith Greaves, student, Cabot School.

a collective identity, one that honors diversity, respects others, collaborates effectively, and learns together. At the same time, she wanted to attend to students' needs as individuals.

Inspired by the Humans of New York website, Nold began the year by introducing her students to these powerful portraits and interviews of New York City residents. She then invited her students to create a Humans of Verve collection to culminate their study of photojournalism, storytelling, and identity. Through a series of lessons exploring the Humans of New York website, StoryCorps resources, and video production using WeVideo, students posted photos and captions of each student on the Verve team outside their classrooms. A QR code on each posting linked to each student's interview video. Through this work, learners expressed their individual identities, explored a collective identity, and started to gel as a team. Throughout the unit, Nold placed a high value on promoting diversity and inclusion.

Leveraging Student Responsibility in the Classroom, Team and School

Student leadership is a sure route to social-emotional learning, executive functioning and a smoother-running classroom. Most of us do many things in our classrooms that students could do. Recall chapter 1's opening vignette for a moment and imagine how smoothly your learning environment could run if you had Miles and his classmates assuming responsibility for classroom transitions, technology management, PLP mentoring, and morning meeting. Authentic responsibility for one's community powerfully reinforces team citizenship and fosters a respectful and student-directed classroom. Grounded in meaningful purpose, authentic challenge, responsibility for others, and student choice, it also mirrors the goals and prerequisites of personalized learning.

Authentic responsibility applies to everyday group work as well. The term *personalized* is not at all synonymous with *alone*. While teachers in personalized learning environments focus on the individual learner's strengths, interests, and aspirations, we also know that effective learning for middle schoolers is often collaborative. Young adolescents crave social connections, and their life in school is no exception. Collaborative learning taps this need and rounds out their sometimes-tenuous sense of belonging in the rest of their social lives. To scaffold collaborative work, we encourage teachers to look at Complex Instruction as an example of established roles for students engaged in problem-based learning (see figure 3.2).[24] Students rotate through roles such as facilitator, resource monitor, recorder/reporter, and questioner throughout the school year. A commitment to more equitable outcomes from group work drives thoughtful training on explicit roles, opportunities to practice and rotate through roles over time, and ongoing reflection that acknowledges students' growing competence in group performance.[25] This is one of many systematic approaches to effective group work. In this chapter's vignette, Angela defined and developed her role as quantitative data manager specifically to meet the needs of the chicken coop project. Other roles may be particularly apt for makerspaces or engineering projects. Once a system of roles has been adopted,

TABLE 3.2 Group work roles in Complex Instruction (excerpted and adapted)

<table>
<tr><td colspan="2" align="center">PROGRAM FOR COMPLEX INSTRUCTION
Skillbuilder: Role Playing Roles
Resource Card: Guidelines for Group Roles
https://complexinstruction.stanford.edu/videos/making-groupwork-work
https://ed.stanford.edu/sites/default/files/manual/skillbuilders_complexinstruction.zip</td></tr>
<tr><td valign="top">

FACILITATOR:
- makes sure everyone understands the instructions
- sees that everyone has a chance to contribute
- makes sure all group members participate
- helps people ask for and receive help when needed
- checks to make sure that the group is on task
- sees that the roles are being performed
- ensures the group discusses everything thoroughly
- calls the teacher if necessary

FACILITATOR SAYS/ASKS:
- Who is willing to take on the extra role of _____?
- Who will read the directions?
- Does everyone understand?
- Does anyone have a question?
- Who can show us how to do it?
- Does anyone know the answer?
- What do you think _____?

</td><td valign="top">

HARMONIZER:
- makes sure communication lines are open
- makes sure there are no put-downs
- encourages positive responses
- recognizes effort and contributions by individuals
- makes the group aware of individual contributions
- helps the group come to agreement
- helps the group form consensus

HARMONIZER SAYS/ASKS:
- What do you think _____?
- What is your opinion _____?
- _____ has a good idea.
- _____ made a good suggestion when he/she said _____.
- You did a good job on the _____.
- What part don't you agree with _____?
- How can we change this so everyone can accept it?
- What would you like to do?

</td></tr>
<tr><td valign="top">

REPORTER:
- makes sure the group product is completed
- sees that the product represents the group's best effort
- organizes the group's report for the class
- summarizes the activity to introduce the report to the class
- reports to the teacher and class on how the group worked together
- makes sure that all parts of the project are correctly labeled and handed in

REPORTER SAYS/ASKS:
- What do we need to do to complete this assignment?
- What is our final product supposed to be?
- What do we want to show in our report?
- What is the BIG IDEA for this activity?
- How can we show the BIG IDEA in our report?
- How do we want to put all of this together?

</td><td valign="top">

RECORDER:
- makes sure that everyone has notes or diagrams from the discussion/research
- makes sure everyone completes the individual report
- is responsible for seeing that the activity cards and information is returned properly
- helps the group identify different parts of the task
- lets the teacher know when the group is ready

RECORDER SAYS/ASKS:
- Does anyone need help with the notes or diagrams?
- Does everyone have the notes and diagrams they need?
- Does anyone need help with the individual report?
- Does everyone have the individual report?
- What are the different parts of this assignment?
- Shall I tell the teacher we're ready?

</td></tr>
<tr><td valign="top">

MATERIALS MANAGER:
- makes sure that all supplies and materials needed are available
- makes sure that materials are used properly
- supervises clean up and the return of all materials
- sees that the group's is clean and orderly

MATERIALS MANAGER SAYS/ASKS:
- What materials do we need?
- Do we need anything else?
- What can we use to _____?
- Are you through with _____?
- Will you help _____?

</td><td valign="top">

RESOURCE:
- looks up additional information for the group
- shares all additional information with everyone
- helps the group assign time limits to the task
- keeps the group aware of how much time is left
- encourages all members to make good use of the time

RESOURCE SAYS/ASKS:
- How much time do we need to do each part of the task?
- What other sources of information could we use to help us?
- We have _____ minutes left.

</td></tr>
</table>

Source: Adapted from Elizabeth G. Cohen, Rachel A. Lotan, Beth A. Scarloss, and Adele R. Arellano, "Complex Instruction: Equity in Cooperative Learning Classrooms," *Theory Into Practice* 38, no. 2 (1999): 80–86, https://doi.org/10.1080/00405849909543836.

students can assess the group's performance against the role descriptors, or against a more general framework for effective collaboration. The Buck Institute offers free rubrics for both individual and team performance in collaborative group work, excerpted in figures 3.3 and 3.4.[26]

Adopting an intentional and reflective approach to collaborative group work pays off immediately when students actually begin working with their PLPs. Many teachers we work with establish PLP partners to help students get each other up and running with a new platform and to hold each other accountable with checklists detailing required elements at any point. In these partnerships, pairs of students take responsibility for ensuring that baseline expectations for PLP development are met all along the way. Transitioning to a more personalized learning environment challenges the logistical abilities even of master teachers. And the prospect of juggling the profiles, goals, evidence, and reflections of a PLP while also creating space in your practice for more student-directed learning can be daunting indeed. But students can manage many of the day-to-day logistics of PLPs. PLP partners can make recommendations for entries, provide each other feedback on entries, and generally help to sustain a dialogue about learning. PLP partners are also helpful when students join a classroom or team midway through the school year. The new entrant benefits immediately from a relationship with a peer and receives much-needed support in understanding PLPs and the learning environment they've just entered. As with group roles more generally, PLP partnerships require clear descriptions of roles and responsibilities and adequate time set aside for thorough training. We discuss PLP partners more thoroughly in chapter 7 in the context of preparing for a student-led PLP conference. Figure 3.5 depicts an abbreviated version of a checklist used to prepare trimester PLP requirements used by students on the Swift House team at Williston Central School.

A number of Vermont schools have embraced even more expansive designs for student leadership. The Rumney Memorial School's Sixth Grade Leadership Institute is one such example. Using a service learning model, sixth graders analyzed their own interests and passions and identified what needs or challenges exist at the school. The students then learned to write cover letters and resumes and use these to apply for leadership positions at the school, including school photographer, sports reporter, chef's assistant, and member of the school's public relations team. Responding to the nature of young adolescents, many of the positions got re-titled in more engaging ways, such as Reading Hero,

FIGURE 3.3   **Buck Institute collaboration rubric for individual performance in group work**

COLLABORATION RUBRIC for PBL
(for grades 6-12; CCSS ELA aligned)

Individual Performance	Below Standard	Approaching Standard	At Standard	Above Standard ✔
Takes Responsibility for Oneself	▪ is not prepared, informed, and ready to work with the team ▪ does not use technology tools as agreed upon by the team to communicate and manage project tasks ▪ does not do project tasks ▪ does not complete tasks on time ▪ does not use feedback from others to improve work	▪ is usually prepared, informed, and ready to work with the team ▪ uses technology tools as agreed upon by the team to communicate and manage project tasks , but not consistently ▪ does some project tasks, but needs to be reminded ▪ completes most tasks on time ▪ sometimes uses feedback from others to improve work	▪ is prepared and ready to work; is well informed on the project topic and cites evidence to probe and reflect on ideas with the team (CC 6-12, SL.1a) ▪ consistently uses technology tools as agreed upon by the team to communicate and manage project tasks ▪ does tasks without having to be reminded ▪ completes tasks on time ▪ uses feedback from others to improve work	
Helps the Team	▪ does not help the team solve problems; may cause problems ▪ does not ask probing questions, express ideas, or elaborate in response to questions in discussions ▪ does not give useful feedback to others ▪ does not offer to help others if they need it	▪ cooperates with the team but may not actively help it solve problems ▪ sometimes expresses ideas clearly, asks probing questions, and elaborates in response to questions in discussions ▪ gives feedback to others, but it may not always be useful ▪ sometimes offers to help others if they need it	▪ helps the team solve problems and manage conflicts ▪ makes discussions effective by clearly expressing ideas, asking probing questions, making sure everyone is heard, responding thoughtfully to new information and perspectives (CC 6-12, SL.1c) ▪ gives useful feedback (specific, feasible, supportive) to others so they can improve their work ▪ offers to help others do their work if needed	
Respects Others	▪ is impolite or unkind to teammates (may interrupt, ignore ideas, hurt feelings) ▪ does not acknowledge or respect other perspectives	▪ is usually polite and kind to teammates ▪ usually acknowledges and respects other perspectives and disagrees diplomatically	▪ is polite and kind to teammates ▪ acknowledges and respects other perspectives; disagrees diplomatically	

For more FreeBIEs visit bie.org   ©2013 Buck Institute for Education

Source: Buck Institute for Education.

FIGURE 3.4 **Buck Institute collaboration rubric for team performance in group work**

Individual Performance	Below Standard	Approaching Standard	At Standard	Above Standard ✔
Makes and Follows Agreements	▪ does not discuss how the team will work together ▪ does not follow rules for collegial discussions, decision-making and conflict resolution ▪ does not discuss how well agreements are being followed ▪ allows breakdowns in team work to happen; needs teacher to intervene	▪ discusses how the team will work together, but not in detail; may just "go through the motions" when creating an agreement ▪ usually follows rules for collegial discussions, decision-making, and conflict resolution ▪ discusses how well agreements are being followed, but not in depth; may ignore subtle issues ▪ notices when norms are not being followed but asks the teacher for help to resolve issues	▪ makes detailed agreements about how the team will work together, including the use of technology tools ▪ follows rules for collegial discussions (CC 6-12, SL.1b), decision-making, and conflict resolution ▪ honestly and accurately discusses how well agreements are being followed ▪ takes appropriate action when norms are not being followed; attempts to resolve issues without asking the teacher for help	
Organizes Work	▪ does project work without creating a task list ▪ does not set a schedule and track progress toward goals and deadlines ▪ does not assign roles or share leadership; one person may do too much, or all members may do random tasks ▪ wastes time and does not run meetings well; materials, drafts , notes are not organized (may be misplaced or inaccessible)	▪ creates a task list that divides project work among the team, but it may not be in detail or followed closely ▪ sets a schedule for doing tasks but does not follow it closely ▪ assigns roles but does not follow them, or selects only one "leader" who makes most decisions ▪ usually uses time and runs meetings well, but may occasionally waste time; keeps materials, drafts, notes, but not always organized	▪ creates a detailed task list that divides project work reasonably among the team (CC 6-12, SL.1b) ▪ sets a schedule and tracks progress toward goals and deadlines (CC 6-12, SL.1b) ▪ assigns roles if and as needed, based on team members' strengths (CC 6-12, SL.1b) ▪ uses time and runs meetings efficiently; keeps materials, drafts, notes organized	
Works as a Whole Team	▪ does not recognize or use special talents of team members ▪ does project tasks separately and does not put them together; it is a collection of individual work	▪ makes some attempt to use special talents of team members ▪ does most project tasks separately and puts them together at the end	▪ recognizes and uses special talents of each team member ▪ develops ideas and creates products with involvement of all team members; tasks done separately are brought to the team for critique and revision	

Collaboration Rubic / Grades 6–12 / Page 2 For more FreeBIEs visit bie.org ©2013 Buck Institute for Education

Source: Buck Institute for Education.

FIGURE 3.5   **Sample checklist for trimester PLP preparations,
Williston Central School Swift House**

Swift House Trimester 2 Portfolio Requirements - March 2017
EMBEDDED/ADDED TO GOALS SECTIONS (DUE Friday, Mar. 10th)
____ Goal 1: Clear and Effective Communication
      ____ Paragraph Reflection - Why is this goal important to you? How are you doing on this goal?
Describe your successes and challenges. What are your next steps for making progress on this
goal? Are there adults or other resources that you need to help you make progress?
      ____ Evidence 1- with explanation- how does this evidence relate to Goal 1?
      ____ Evidence 2- with explanation- how does this evidence relate to Goal 1?
      ____ Evidence 3- with explanation- how does this evidence relate to Goal 1?
      ____ Evidence 4- with explanation- how does this evidence relate to Goal 1?
____ Goal 2: Creative and Practical Problem Solving
____ Goal 3: Informed and Integrative Thinking
____ Goal 4: Citizenship
____ Goal 5: Self-Direction

**COMPLETE & EMBEDDED IN TRIMESTER 2 REPORTS SECTION (DUE FRI.
MAR. 17th)**
____ Literature
      ____ Lit Group Self Evaluation from December (highlight one):

      Bud, Not Buddy   A Long Walk to Water   My Side of the Mountain
      The Giver   Island of the Blue Dolphins The Sea of Monsters
      Redwall   The Great Gilly Hopkins   The Lion, the Witch, and the Wardrobe

      ____ Lit Group Self Evaluation from January (highlight one):

      Guts   Wednesday Wars   Something Wicked This Way Comes
      Holes   Once Upon a Marigold   Diary of a Wimpy Kid
      Indigo   Murder on the Orient Express Tuesdays With Morrie

      ____ Lit Group Self Evaluation from Student Led Lit Groups (highlight one):

      Hunger Games   Silverwing   Artemis Fowl   Scribbler of Dreams
      Sarah, Plain & Tall Maze Runner   Trueflix Nonfiction
      Flipped   The Crossover   Mysterious Benedict Society

____ Writing
      ____ Final Draft of Narrative Writing & Self Evaluation
      ____ Independent Project Final Draft & Self Evaluation
____ Life Studies
      ____ Social Studies Self Evaluation (Mr. Hunt or Ms. Donnelly)
      ____ Science Class Self Evaluation (Ms. Skapof or Ms. Laberge)
____ Math
      ____ Class Self Evaluation

Source: Swift House, Williston Central School.

Media Ninja, Trail Builder, and Global Education Advocate. Each student was appointed a mentor, with whom they met regularly to reflect, receive feedback, and troubleshoot potential issues. The experience culminated in a community exhibition in which students share their learning with family and friends.[27]

Inspired by the Rumney Leadership Institute, Cabot School launched its Cabot Leads program, which offered students in grades 5–8 a menu of leadership opportunities throughout the school and into the local community so that every student can find a role they find personally interesting and meaningful. Figure 3.6 lists their mix of school-based and community-based positions. Opportunities for leadership and responsibility are rich fodder for compelling evidence and thoughtful reflection in a PLP. They cultivate students' executive functioning skills and social-emotional learning.

FIGURE 3.6   **Excerpt from the job descriptions for the Cabot Leads program, Cabot School**

Cabot Leads—Draft Jobs

Jobs

Position	#	Mentor	Description/Notes	Confirmed With Mentor
Library Advisory Committee	2	Nene Riley	Do you love books? Join the LAC to survey students and develop a wish list for book purchases for the library. Includes a field trip to Bear Pond Books in Montpelier in the fall and book club lunch meetings, along with other library work.	
Vermont Rural Partnership Representatives	4	Nene Riley	Participate in VRP's fall meeting in November; plan and write a proposal for a $2000 MS mini-grant project that supports the Cabot Community. Manage the project. Present the grant work at the VRP conference in May 2018. Involves 2 off campus days.	
Primary Recess Assistant	2	Donna Ferrario, Rachel Popoli, Carolyn Deasy	Do you enjoy working with little kids? Do you want to spend more time outside? The Recess Assistant will organize games and activities for primary-aged students that encourage them to be happy, healthy, and energized.	

Source: Cabot School.

Inviting Students as Co-Designers

Students can also play a leadership role in co-designing the PLP process itself. We've learned through experience that is it important to partner with students at all levels of planning, sharing, and creating PLPs. The whole concept of PLPs hinges on students feeling that they are in fact in charge of their own learning and this includes telling their learning story. Planning and implementing PLPs can be a powerful opportunity to invite students into designing the systems they'll be expected to use in a personalized environment. We have seen what happens when teachers bring an "Oh, something else we have to do!" mindset to this work. It translates directly into student apathy and negativity about PLPs. It is crucial that teachers and students view this as a creative tool for the storytelling of learning.

One way to frame the PLP as a positive experience is to involve students early and directly in the design work. A PLP leadership council can provide great insight, valuable marketing of the concept, and feedback for teachers. We have seen students lead efforts to redesign PLPs, and the result has been much more student buy-in and creativity. For example, over the past few years, the PLP (re)Design Project, coordinated by our colleague, professional development coordinator Susan Hennessey, has brought together students from schools all over Vermont to refine and reimagine approaches to PLPs.[28] The work began with a day of facilitated, cross-school exploration of each school's experience with PLPs. The following summer, the group reassembled for a full-day design-thinking workshop. They continued the redesign work into following the school year, sharing their prototypes, challenges, and successes.

Participating teachers were struck by how helpful it was to include students in this way. One stated, "The PLP (re)Design was a real eye-opener in seeing how students would prefer to create their own projects. It reminded me that, when given the right opportunities, students will jump right into a project and take the responsibility for their own learning and achievement." Another educator offered, "It reminded me that student voice needs to factor in much more than it currently does in our plan. We need to revisit what are our non-negotiables. Can we let students choose the platform? Their goals? Ways of reflecting?"

Students also found the PLP (re)Design Project helpful. In particular, it became a way to express their preferences for certain ways of learning. For instance, when asked, students often point to project-based learning as encapsulating personalization. Students from Shelburne Community School who participated in the PLP (re)Design process consolidated their feedback into this elevator pitch: "Our PLPs should have hands-on projects with more school time to work on them. We should have choice of a platform and an authentic audience (PLP fair, etc.) to share our learning." Similarly, Crossett Brook Middle School's student leadership team recommended which PLP platforms should be available to learners, what the different components of a PLP could look like, and how students' goals and projects should relate to one another.[29]

Of course, inviting students into the design and refinement of their learning opportunities needn't be restricted to PLP design. This type of student consultation can be an effective method for yielding a practical agenda about a range of school-change initiatives.[30] Research into student consultation reveals various benefits to students, including in self-esteem.[31] Students say they appreciate "being listened to and knowing that what you say is taken seriously," "feeling that you belong and that you can make a difference to how things are done," and "feeling that by talking about things and taking part in things you understand more and have more control over your learning"[32]

There are many ways students can powerfully lead in their personalized learning communities. Older students on multi-age teams can design orientation programs for incoming, younger students. Students can rewrite proficiencies, rubrics, and scales in their own words. And they can drive curriculum when teachers solicit students' questions, concerns, interests, and ideas for learning resources, activities, and ways of demonstrating proficiency in authentic, real-world ways. We explore these ideas in greater detail in the chapters to come.

Establishing Core Proficiencies

In chapter 2, we discussed the importance of identifying with your colleagues a shared purpose for PLPs. Similarly, considering how a PLP will connect to any number of standards or proficiencies helps to justify to yourself, and to others, taking the time for this work. While teachers often feel the weight of too many standards, those that align with the kind of personalized learning environment you're attempting to establish in your classroom can help students practice and acquire the skills needed for self-direction. Depending upon your context, you'll want to identify the proficiencies, standards, or expectations that align well with your PLP purposes. You likely have particular standards or proficiencies for which your grade level, team, or department is responsible. Perhaps you've identified specific proficiencies you'll be targeting this year. Maybe there is even a schoolwide focus on certain ones. Collaborating with colleagues can remind you all what you're aiming for, underscore the purposes you've identified for PLPs, and strategically divvy up the goals you have for your shared group of students. How do you already distribute the work of accounting for standards across colleagues? On interdisciplinary teams, it's typical for the content-oriented standards to be divided up accordingly. But what about the skills that reach across content areas?

If you're first looking to justify and guide an emphasis on self-direction, you may be able to draw upon graduation standards, depending on your setting. The Great Schools Partnership defines these transferable skills as "essential life skills that students should practice across content areas and will need in any form of postgraduate training, study, or career," and they include Communication, Problem Solving, Informed Thinking, Self-Direction, and Collaboration.[33] Most states have adopted some version of transferable skills, although they may use different terms. For example, Vermont's five transferable skills consist of (1) Clear and Effective Communication; (2) Creative and Practical Problem Solving; (3) Informed and Integrative Thinking; (4) Responsible and Involved Citizenship; and (5) Self-Direction.[34]

As you establish priorities for student outcomes from personalized learning, it makes sense to identify which proficiencies to focus on, at least for the first part of the school year, within the PLP. Tables 3.3 and 3.4 illustrate the types of skills that cut across content areas that can also unite your sense of purpose, provide continuity for students, and help shape the aspirations for teachers and students alike.

As the scope of PLP work begins to sink in, it might feel overwhelming. It's worth noting that students are not the only potential partners in this work. You have your colleagues throughout your school as well. Thoughtful school systems will imagine how students' skills and dispositions will play out in developmentally appropriate chunks throughout their career in school. For instance, Bennington-Rutland Supervisory Union's K–8 PLP Continuum (figure 3.7) mapped how, from grades K–8, students can develop the skills and dispositions to take full advantage of a robust and student-centered PLP process.[35]

You can readily imagine how any of the performance indicators of Self-Direction or Responsible and Involved Citizenship listed in tables 3.3 and 3.4

TABLE 3.3   **Vermont transferable skill: Responsible and Involved Citizenship**

Responsible and Involved Citizenship	
Performance Indicator	**Learning Target**
Participate in and contribute to the enhancement of community life.	I can build a proposal, which includes community connections, for an improvement in the community.
Take responsibility for personal decisions and actions.	I can take ownership for the outcome of my decisions or actions by explaining how my choices affect myself and others.
Demonstrate ethical behavior and the moral courage to sustain it.	I can employ empathy when considering others in a variety of contexts; I can take positive action to resolve conflicts, promote equity and/or solve community problems.
Respect diversity and differing points of view.	I can engage in open discussion and respond thoughtfully to differing points of view; I can explain how my words, actions, attitudes and behaviors may be interpreted by others including majority and minority groups and other cultures.

Source: Based upon a condensed version of Vermont Agency of Education resources, which can be found at https://education.vermont.gov/documents/proficiency-based-education-transferable-skills-scoring-criteria-responsible-involved-citizenship.

TABLE 3.4   **Vermont transferable skill: Self-Direction**

Self-Direction	
Performance Indicator	**Learning Target**
Identify, manage, and assess new opportunities related to learning goals.	I can evaluate and pursue opportunities that pertain to my learning goals and plans by monitoring my progress and adjusting my approach as needed.
Integrate knowledge from a variety of sources to set goals and make informed decisions.	I can utilize information from diverse sources to make decisions, establish goals, and devise plans with identified needs, resources and action steps.
Apply knowledge in familiar and new contexts.	I can apply a concept to a new or familiar context or setting.
Demonstrate initiative and responsibility for learning.	I can monitor and make decisions around my learning goals, identify my strengths and needs, and employ strategies that allow me to achieve my goals; I can self-start and manage my time by organizing and prioritizing to complete a task.

Source: Based upon a condensed version of Vermont Agency of Education resources, which can be found at https://education.vermont.gov/documents/proficiency-based-education-transferable-skills-scoring-criteria-self-direction.

FIGURE 3.7   **Excerpt from PLP K–8 Continuum, Bennington Rutland Supervisory Union**

BRSU PLP Continuum K–8

	K	1	2	3	4	5	6–8
Form Use	Drives teacher actions (not direct student tool).	Drives teacher actions (not direct student tool). — **students have simplified form.**	Drives teacher actions — students have simplified form. Steps not written but students can verbalize.	Simplified form. Includes all goal areas minus written steps, but students can verbalize steps. Students identify data sources.	Simplified form. Includes all goal areas. Students **are beginning to write steps with teacher guidance.** Students identify data sources.	Simplified form. Includes all goal areas. Students are **writing steps with teacher guidance.** Students identify data sources.	Revised PLP form.
Student Use	Exposed to components of PLPs via modeling and classroom activities.	Student PLP is in teacher-designed format — includes all components.	Student PLP is in teacher-designed format — includes all components.	Students may begin to reflect on goals and post evidence digitally.	Students may begin to reflect on goals and post evidence digitally.	Students reflect on goals, identify new goals, and post evidence digitally.	Students reflect on goals, identify new goals, and post evidence digitally.
Community & Disposition Goals	Whole class developed.	Whole class developed.	Whole class developed.	Whole class developed.	Whole class or individually developed.	Whole class or individually developed.	Whole class or individually developed.
Hopes & Dreams	Student developed.	Student developed.	Student developed.	Student developed — beginning to connect to goal areas.	Student developed — beginning to connect to goal areas.	Student developed — beginning to connect to goal areas.	Student developed and connections to goal areas exist if applicable.
Conferencing	Students share something they've accomplished and something they're working on. Can speak to their next steps.	Students share work samples and components of PLP in teacher-designed format.	Students share work samples and components of PLP in teacher-designed format.	Work samples, aligned to PLP, drive conference discussion.	Work samples, aligned to PLP, drive conference discussion.	Work samples, aligned to PLP, drive conference discussion.	Work samples, aligned to PLP, drive conference discussion.
Keeping Alive	Teachers use explicit goal language and goals are posted in classroom. Frequent modeling of goal setting.	Students reflect frequently, and collect work samples to demonstrate goal attainment. Goal setting process is ongoing.	Students reflect frequently, and collect work samples to demonstrate goal attainment. Goal setting process is ongoing.	Students reflect frequently, and collect work samples to demonstrate goal attainment. Goal setting process is ongoing.	Students reflect frequently, and collect work samples to demonstrate goal attainment. Goal setting process is ongoing.	Students reflect frequently, use e-portfolio to collect evidence of goal attainment. Goal setting process is ongoing.	Students reflect frequently, use e-portfolio to collect evidence of goal attainment. Goal setting process is ongoing.

Source: Bennington Rutland Supervisory Union.

could be woven into meaningful and robust learning for young adolescents.[36] Many of our partner schools have students self-assess, sometimes weekly, on their progress on these and other transferable skills, such as Habits of Work or Scholarly Habits. Integrating these skills into learning tasks can also help you catalog and validate the extensive investment in SEL, executive function, community, and leadership essential to personalized environments. Doing so means that these investments are not merely groundwork for the curriculum, they are the curriculum. If you haven't already, now would be a good time for you, and your colleagues, to reflect on your local, state, or national standards. Look specifically for opportunities to serve the developmental and identity needs of young adolescents, build a strong foundation for a personalized environment, and embrace critical proficiencies for lifelong learning. These powerful intersections are plentiful in personalized learning and will help focus your work for the first few months of the school year.

PREPARING THE INFRASTRUCTURE FOR PERSONALIZED LEARNING

With a shared purpose for PLPs and personalization, and new commitments to the pedagogical priorities inherent in personalized learning, it's time to turn to some of the mechanics needed for a personalized environment to function smoothly. In many cases, systems and routines you and your immediate colleagues have come to rely on are poorly suited, often counterproductive, to the changes you're trying to make. If we accept that none of us can make the most of this work alone, how will you collaborate? How much time will you devote and when? How can you each feel comfortable making the necessary sacrifices to commit to meeting times? What other norms and routines need to be established to make the most of that time?

If you already work closely together, you may know the answers to these questions. But if not, we suggest that you consider as useful starting points your approaches to common planning time, shared proficiencies, shared resources and calendars, and a robust PLP platform. Finally, you and your colleagues will want to translate all of what you've learned so far into streamlined norms and routines with students that are consistently reinforced so they keep your personalized environment on track and running smoothly.

Common Planning Time

Common planning time (CPT) is a period during the school day in which teachers on an interdisciplinary, partner, or grade-level team meet together to share instructional strategies, plan curriculum, design assessments, organize team events, discuss student issues, and communicate with parents.[37] In this chapter's opening vignette, Angela witnesses her teachers' ready teamwork as they manage the day-to-day and moment-to-moment work of sharing resources and grouping students based on needs. As you move forward with designing and implementing PLPs, effective collaboration becomes all the more important. Common planning time can be both promising and problematic. Research suggests that, in order to realize the maximum benefits to students, teams should have CPT for *at least* 30 minutes per session, at least four times a week.[38] However, CPT is often scarce, and even teams with daily CPT frequently report that they make poor use of their time.[39] Effective teams adopt practices that encourage efficiency and monitor how their time is used.

A strong start for making the most of CPT is to establish agreed-upon norms that teams can refer back to when they find their meeting is drifting off track. In figure 3.8, we see how a team at Leland and Gray Union Middle School in Townshend keeps its norms front and center at the top of the CPT agenda. Norms can be incredibly helpful in holding team members accountable for staying focused on student learning and for creating safe spaces for thoughtful, open dialogue and decision-making. We also see how the teachers use clear roles during the meeting time. Developing norms and roles will help your team function more smoothly and efficiently, as will having a commitment to maintaining a clear agenda and meeting minutes. Effective teams also use shared, readily available agendas and minutes to sustain the iterative cycles that classroom change requires.

The most effective teams we work with regularly dedicate a portion of their time to assess the quality of their collaboration. This need not happen at every meeting, but regular and consistent check-ins among team members gives everyone an opportunity to clear the air, raise possible issues, tune the team and, ideally, celebrate jobs well done. We challenge teams to rate themselves from time to time on the degree to which the team is living up to its agreed-upon norms. Table 3.5 provides a sample rating questionnaire that teachers often find helpful for generating focused discussion about their collaborative

FIGURE 3.8   **Common planning time minutes, Leland and Gray Middle School**

September 12, 2017 1:20-2:20

Norms:
- Follow a goal-oriented agenda that includes timeframes and deadlines when appropriate
- Start each meeting with a personal check-in
- Stay engaged in group agenda and group work
- Keep the whole team in mind
- Give and receive constructive, honest, and open feedback
- Present the opportunity for all voices to be heard
- Acknowledge and respect others' opinions

Successes:
- Consistency & Routine
- Trust & Relationships
- Collaboration with colleagues
- Keeping Expectations & Goals in Mind
- Co-teaching & sharing expertise
- Work that is purposeful & relevant
- Communication
- Students feeling secure about their identity
- Students supporting each other & us
- Us supporting each other
- Us supporting the students
- Students & adults having ownership & pride in accomplished work

Present: Pat, Mandy, Ashley, Jeanie, Elizabeth, Jason, Johanna

Facilitator: Johanna
Notetaker: Elizabeth
Timekeeper: Ashley
Norm Checker: Jason

Agenda Items
1. **Grading systems**
   a. How to incorporate habits of work
   b. Breakdown of grades
2. **Homework communication system**
   a. Some teachers use powerschool but not everybody
   b. Standing agenda item on Thursday so we will be able to share big projects and tests
   c. We will continue using powerschool to list assignments
3. **Chromebooks for classwork** (Exploratories)/D.Citizenship for band & chorus and next?
   a. All but 10 students have turned in their chromebook forms that was sent home by it
   b. Everyone would like to start using them tomorrow
   c. There are 5 students that were given their chromebooks, they need to bring this back
   d. Must all be returned at the end of the day but they can get it in the morning when they come into school or in passing times
   e. Going to worry about it going home when the time comes: could do the video assignment when it does go home
4. **Celebrations!**
   a. The kids really are enjoying what they are doing
   b. We are doing a great job of building community
   c. Let's do a town hall.
      i. Do Discovery
      ii. Begin the Town Hall at 1st period
      iii. We need to keep thinking about the other ideas
         1. Design challenge? Outside Activities?

Source: Leland and Gray Middle School.

TABLE 3.5   **Sample common planning time questionnaire**

Please use a scale of 1 (lowest)–4 (highest) to rate our team on our Common Planning Time norms.		
Norms	**How well do I ... ?**	**How well does our team ... ?**
Prioritize the meetings		
Start on time		
Populate agenda ahead of time		
Keep agenda moving forward efficiently		
Volunteer for/use clearly identified roles		
Avoid off-task behavior and conversation		
Keep thorough minutes		
Assign tasks equitably		
End on time		

practices and their CPT in particular. In addition to rating the team as a unit, we encourage individuals to self-assess their own performance in meetings as well. Adapt such a tool based on the norms your team sets. Even one monthly, ten-minute check in can go a long way toward improving the culture of your teacher team.

We also encourage teams to spend 80 percent of the meeting time on the kind of curriculum and creative program development required in personalized learning environments, with the other 20 percent set aside for specific student issues. Our experience suggests that if a team is spending more than the equivalent of one meeting per week on student issues, it should be looking for systems innovations—designing more engaging learning, for instance— rather than picking away at problems one student at a time.

Time to plan together, whether it's available during the school day or not, is critical for the implementation of teamwide PLPs and it can be leveraged with the help of some well-known strategies. But a valid argument can be made that poorly used CPT would be better used as additional contact time between teachers and students. Alternatives such as Professional Learning Communities follow much the same logic in cultivating effective collegial collaboration, and while they can complement CPT, and are certainly better than nothing in its absence, they rarely entail the daily intensity of CPT. Committing to the effective use of CPT maximizes your chances of reaping its proven benefits to student learning and may convince skeptical colleagues, administrators, and school board members to invest in daily CPT. And in our experience, effective CPT vastly improves a team's ability to design and implement PLPs and personalized learning.

Flexible Scheduling

Just as CPT alters how teachers use their time, we should reconsider how we organize time for students. Unfortunately, in too many schools, the established schedule reigns supreme. It dictates the teaching and learning practices rather than the reverse. To be fair, we understand that tension. School buses arrive and leave at specific times. The cafeteria, gymnasium, science lab, or other facilities often need to serve multiple groups of students. And sharing teachers across teams or grade levels can cause a ripple effect on other schedules.

At the same time, a school's schedule truly is where the rubber hits the road. A quick analysis of the schedule can reveal an educational community's values. What does your schedule say about your priorities? One key way to maintain your commitment to personalizing learning is to ensure the greatest degree of flexible scheduling possible. Defined as the creative use of school time that attempts to respond to the learning needs of students, flexible scheduling provides alternatives to the traditional fixed-period arrangement present in most schools.[40] Often characterized by longer blocks of time, it enables teachers to make choices according to learning needs and have more control over the learning environment.[41]

Whether you teach on a team or in a self-contained setting, committing to innovative and varied uses of time to serve the needs of students can deliver significant payoffs. Educators know that not all learning tasks require the same amount of time. For example, most of us are accustomed to discarding the regular 45-minute, seven-period schedule on days dedicated to field trips or school festivals. What if you made a commitment to make similar adjustments in the interest of day-to-day learning when you observe a mismatch between learning objectives and the schedule? A thorough conversation with colleagues about the pros and cons of flexible scheduling can help address possible concerns, clarify appropriate purposes for making schedule adjustments, and free you up to think more boldly about engaging and personalized learning opportunities.

Notice in figure 3.9 the dedicated flexible blocks built into the regular weekly schedule for the Alpha Team at Shelburne Community School. And see in table 3.6 how the Verve Team at Tuttle Middle School planned its schedule according to time needed at various stages of their passion projects.

Shared Resources and Calendars

Collaborating with colleagues to orchestrate CPT, shared expectations, and flexible scheduling, you'll soon realize that traditional file drawers and spiral-bound day planners no longer suffice. Fortunately, today's technologies are leading us to ubiquitous computing: online resources and collaborative opportunities that are available anywhere, anytime, and on increasingly mobile devices. High-performing teaching teams seize upon technologies that make the hard work of teaming more efficient and sustainable.[42] Beyond shared norms, agendas and minutes, how will you, as collaborating adults, establish a fluid, collaborative, digital environment that will help you maximize the personalized learning environment you're working so hard to create? Effective teacher teams establish online spaces in which they can collaborate, organize, and archive their shared resources. In the opening vignette, Angela's teachers referred to their team folder and their curriculum planning doc. In a personalized learning environment, sharing resources like these becomes critical, as students regularly carve out individual inquiries and small-group pursuits. Because this may represent a considerable shift in practice for many teachers, it's all the more important to improve communication and access to shared information.

Perhaps you already have file-sharing norms at your school or on your team. Whether you're cramming late at night with a teammate, home with a sick child, or covering for a teammate yanked from the classroom by a student emergency, teammates or other colleagues should know where key materials are stored and be able to access them anytime, anywhere. As an individual teacher, you'll want to ask yourself, what resources and files are critical to your learning environment? As a team, then, consider which of these are needed by teammates in order to collaborate effectively and serve students. The answers to these questions should help you design a useful online sharing structure for your teaching team. Figure 3.10 shows a straightforward file structure from the Leland and Gray Union Middle School team.

A well-orchestrated calendar is similarly important for middle grades colleagues to share as they collaborate in this work. A shared online calendar can

FIGURE 3.9   **Weekly schedule from the student handbook, Shelburne Community School, Alpha Team**

Alpha Weekly Schedule

Date:					
Period	**Monday**	**Tuesday**	**Wednesday**	**Thursday**	**Friday**
8:05-8:15	Prime Group	Prime Group	Prime Group	Prime Group	Prime Group
1 8:15-8:55	6th Lang 7th PE 8th	FLEXIBLE	6th Lang. 7th PE 8th	FLEXIBLE	6th Lang. 7th Music 8th
2 8:55-9:35	FLEXIBLE		FLEXIBLE		FLEXIBLE
3 9:35-10:35		9:55 8th PE			
4 10:35-11:15		6th Lang 7th Music 8th	6th Art 7th Art 8th Music		
5 11:15-11:55		6th Music 7th Lang 8th Lang	6th Art 7th Art 8th PE	6th Music 7th Lang 8th Lang	
Lunch/ Recess 11:55-12:25	Lunch/ Recess	Lunch/Recess	Lunch/Recess	Lunch/Recess	Lunch/Recess
6 12:25-1:25	☐ FLEX	☐ FLEX	☐ FLEX	☐ FLEX	☐ FLEX
7 1:25-2:05	6th PE 7th Lang 8th Lang	FLEXIBLE	6th 7th Lang 8th Lang	8th Art/Citi	6th PE 7th Lang 8th Lang
8 2:05-2:50	6th Skills 7th Skills 8th Skills		FLEX	8th Art/Citi	FLEX

Source: Alpha Team, Shelburne Community School.

TABLE 3.6 **Flexible schedule for passion projects: Tuttle Middle School, Verve Team**

Week of January 21st:	Project Proposal
Week of January 29th:	Project Proposal Review
Week of February 5th:	Block of Work Time (90 minutes)
Week of February 13th:	Block of Work Time (2 hours)
Week of February 19th:	Block of Work Time (90 minutes)
Week of March 8th:	Block of Work Time & Start Presentation Prep (2 hours) & Additional Block of Presentation Prep (90 minutes)
Week of March 12th:	Projects & Presentations Due!
Total Work Time:	8.5 hours (in school)

FIGURE 3.10 **Team folder structure, Leland and Gray Middle School**

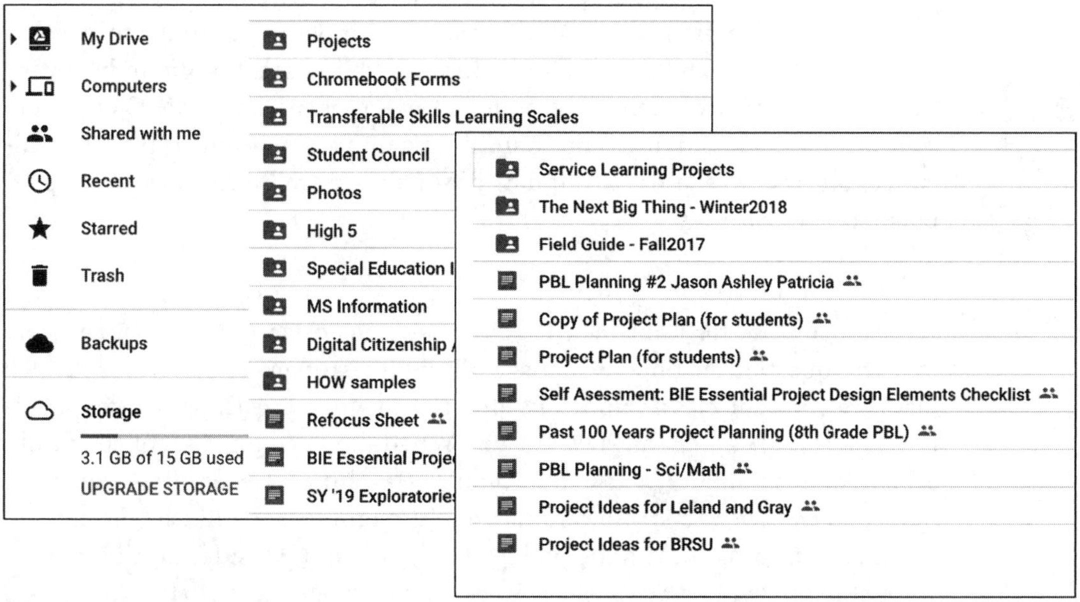

Source: Leland and Gray Middle School.

help convey what's planned as well as underscore what's been agreed upon. For example, Proctor Junior/Senior High School's leadership team planned PLP activities and content, and then delivered the plans to their teaching colleagues via Google Classroom. And, in figure 3.11, you see the first two months of the yearlong calendar of digital citizenship activities used by teachers at Leland and Gray Union Middle School. The common calendar, which was based upon resources from Common Sense Media, divvies up responsibilities and keeps everyone on track with the sequence of lessons aligned with the start-of-the-year demands of managing 1:1 Chromebooks and developing a respectful and welcoming learning environment.[43] Given the considerable reliance on technology in personalized settings in general, and with the PLP in particular, norms pertaining to digital citizenship are an important part of the curriculum.

As this work evolves, many teams come to realize that there is little to distinguish the expectations we have of ourselves for in-person behaviors and those we demonstrate virtually. Teachers at Peoples Academy Middle Level incorporated technology into creating digital name tags, for instance, and compiled a classroom set of short and easy video introductions by each student using TouchCast.[44] Completing a comprehensive list of activities such as those suggested by Common Sense Media provides ample opportunity to develop norms for general *and* digital citizenship, which is essential groundwork for their 1:1 iPad environment, just as it is for a personalized one. Collectively committing to the activities and coordinating implementation with shared calendars are keys to success and indicative of a team well-positioned to take on personalized learning.

A Common Platform

As your purpose for implementing PLPs becomes clearer, you will inevitably face the question of how to manage all of this student work. The right PLP platform for your classroom is the one that aligns with the purpose, priorities, and audiences for the PLPs. As with scheduling and teacher collaboration, a PLP platform should reflect the kinds of teaching and learning you value most and what your steps toward personalization may look like in the coming months. It also requires anticipating the future and considering the kind of work students will be doing years from now. Perhaps most challenging of all, selecting a PLP platform challenges us to think through issues of collaboration with our colleagues. This isn't as simple as changing grading platforms; PLPs

FIGURE 3.11   **Excerpt from digital citizenship lesson calendar, Leland and Gray Middle School**

Leland and Gray Calendar: Digital Citizenship Lessons
Source: Common Sense Media
https://www.commonsensemedia.org/educators/scope-and-sequence#grades-6-8
WEEKS WHERE LESSONS COVERED IN TA DURING SSR, READING AND ENGLISH
CLASSES WILL COVER SSR

Dates	Unit	Title	Description
8/28 – 9/1		**Care and Feeding** • Charging • Classroom use • On task use • School account • Travel • Shutting down • Workflow **Digital Life 101** • Self-image & Identity	Students are introduced to the 24/7, social nature of digital media and technologies, and gain basic vocabulary and knowledge for discussing the media landscape.
9/4 – 9/8 No school 9/4 Labor Day	1	Scams & Schemes • Privacy & Security	Students learn strategies for guarding against identity theft and scams that try to access their private information online.
9/11 – 9/15	1	Cyberbullying: Be Upstanding • Cyberbullying • Relationships & Communication	Students learn about the difference between being a passive bystander versus a brave upstander in cyberbullying situations.
9/18 – 9/22	1		
9/25 – 9/29	1	A Creator's Rights • Creative Credit & Copyright • Information Literacy	Students are introduced to copyright, fair use, and the rights they have as creators.
10/5 – 10/9	1	Strategic Searching • Information Literacy	Students learn that to conduct effective and efficient online searches, they must use a variety of searching strategies.
10/9	1	Unit 1 Assessment	
10/12 – 10/23 4 day week 10/15 = half day 10/16 = parent/teacher conferences 10/19 & 10/20 early release days	2	My Media • Self-image & identity	Students review their media habits and the array of media they use on a weekly basis, and reflect on the role of digital media in their lives.

Source: Leland and Gray Middle School.

invite teachers and students into the deepest day-to-day aspects of culture and pedagogy.

Because PLPs represent the whole child as a learner, it makes little sense for each teacher in a system to have her own platform. This is perhaps more obvious for teachers on interdisciplinary teams, but it is also true for those of us in self-contained classrooms, especially as we consider that our array of collaborators will only expand as the learning environment becomes more personalized. Inevitably, students ask to include evidence of their learning from many areas of their lives. Collaborating with the allied arts team (e.g., arts, music, world languages, physical education, technology), for example, provides students with opportunities to make interdisciplinary connections, and the allied arts are often the areas where young adolescents' interests and passions reside. Inviting these specialists to share in identifying the purpose of the PLP, the best platform for that purpose, and how students and teachers might interact with it, will facilitate students' later ability to gather evidence and reflection from those classes. In order to select a platform wisely, as with just about every subsequent step toward personalization you'll take, surrounding yourself with a high-performing and collaborative group of colleagues will make all the difference in the progress you make and your enjoyment of the journey.

Remember Miles's classroom in the book's opening vignette? It illustrated just a few ways in which technology can make personalized learning possible. Indeed, it is difficult to imagine a systemwide implementation of personalized learning without the opportunities technology affords. Recall that technology offers several advantages over bulky binders and hanging file folders often used to house student work. Whereas student work has rarely been cataloged by these older methods for anything more than a single school year, today's inexpensive data storage makes it possible to store samples of students' work across the entire school career. These days, digital videos and photography, animations, podcasting, and myriad other options substantially expand the ways in which students are documenting and expressing their learning. Electronic storage can be integrated into larger data management systems for a school or district and can conveniently travel with students from grade to grade and school to school. Online storage provides convenient access to student PLPs for additional, authorized audiences, particularly families and mentors, regardless of where they are located. All of these advantages together substantially increase the day-to-day viability and longer-term sustainability of PLPs to make significant contributions to student learning.

Of course, not every classroom has adequate access to technology to justify an online PLP platform. And in many respects, a binder of thoughtfully organized paper can garner many of the benefits of a PLP. Schools that have made extensive use of portfolios over the decades have demonstrated as much, particularly at the classroom level. With growing pressure on school systems to manage student data electronically, however, a paper-only approach may not achieve the systems-level benefits of PLPs. If you are in a relatively low-tech environment, it's worth considering how to leverage the technology you and your students do have access to. If your school has a shared laptop or netbook cart or computer lab, for instance, it can be signed out for a class of students to update their PLPs. Alternatively, a computer or technology class may be repurposed to assist students in developing their PLPs. Business plans, resumes, and other assignments in typical practical computing classes are rich fodder for PLP work. And the extensive use of smartphones by many students and families is an often-overlooked resource for managing PLPs, particularly for capturing video and audio evidence of, and reflections upon, learning. As you read through the following section on digital PLP platforms, consider the implications for whatever technology environment you operate in. Translate the critical factors we discuss into your plans for an analog or blended design for your PLPs. And reconsider what's possible after completing the chapter. Much of what's discussed may help you reassess the technology lives available to you and your students.

Certainly, not all technologies are created equal. Among the dozens of schools that we've worked with, and across the more than twenty years of working on school technology integration, we've learned important lessons about how to get the most out of a PLP platform. Foremost, it's important to decide what the PLP need *not* provide. This, of course, ties back to your purpose for implementing PLPs in the first place. There is always a temptation to find software that can do everything for a school, including housing student demographic and support services data, compiling test scores and grades, and related reporting capabilities. This temptation is no different when shopping for a PLP platform. Almost inevitably, we have learned that costly compromises are the chief result of seeking a single platform that does everything. For instance, one district we know prioritized a platform's ability to track proficiencies and failed to adequately consider user-friendliness. Rather than pilot the system with a willing group of teachers and students, the entire district's faculty was introduced to the system in the middle of the school year, distracting them from already ambitious experiments with personalization. The district dropped the platform altogether the following summer after it proved unworkable for teachers. Critical time, money, and professional development effort—and plenty of scarce political capital—can be wasted after stakeholders discover that, in exchange for doing everything, the new platform does nothing well.

Instead, we encourage seeking interoperability, or the ability of multiple platforms to speak to each other. We suggest you create a patchwork of different systems, one that satisfies the special needs of classroom-level stakeholders without undermining a larger systemic need to access and selectively report from across the entire dataset. For instance, seeking a system that students and families find welcoming for the purposes of their PLP conversations needn't conflict with federal reporting requirements related to special education services or subsidized meals. Fortunately, there is a growing list of PLP platforms available. And many purveyors of these systems have embraced collaborative interoperability as their best approach to satisfying the complex needs of schools in the process of personalizing education.

Most important, it is critical that teachers have a voice in the selection of a system and have a chance to pilot its features before final financial decisions are made. And our experience has demonstrated again and again that teachers and students quickly become adept at adopting platforms that respond to their needs, even if it means switching from time to time. It's when the time and energy spent on adopting a new platform feels for naught—when the tail wags the dog, so to speak—that resentment and frustration quickly escalate, and justifiably so.

One particularly significant challenge is balancing students' need to "own" their PLPs as a reflection of themselves with the system's need for a streamlined approach to accountability in student achievement and, just as important, equitable access to personalized learning opportunities. Meeting the first objective would seem to suggest student choice regarding platforms for their PLP, as students have frequently called for in our partner schools. The second objective appears to require a diametrically opposed approach: a single, standard platform that can automatically synthesize data from across a large set of

PLPs. We should first remind you of chapter 2's discussion of PLP purposes and stakeholders. The power of the PLP does not lie in offering lots of reliable data across large groups, either aggregated or disaggregated. It's not the best tool to meet the system's need for accountability in student achievement.

That said, educators still may find it useful to extract certain types of data across students, classes or teams. Students themselves appreciate being able to quickly search through and sort the considerable body of evidence they're able to collect in PLPs. And they want to express themselves regardless of the platform. If the platform allows for self-expression while also allowing educators to obtain the information they want, then both objectives are met. This is the sort of challenge databases are good at addressing. A growing number of platforms make it possible for students to upload and catalog just about anything, some of which may be valued only by the student, other items may be valued only by educators, and still others may be valued by both. The platform treats all the data the same, until it's tagged or labeled for particular purposes, such as "My best friend" or "Writing Proficiency 3.1." This tagging function helps students track their developing identities and their development toward specific proficiencies. It also allows teachers to filter and sort the data they need across their students' PLPs. We don't want to arbitrarily carve off the student's need for self-expression when self is in fact such a critical driver of personalized learning for young adolescents. Database technology can address this challenge if we incorporate both student and teacher objectives into the selection process.

With these basic principles in mind, you will want to identify clear selection criteria as you advocate for systems that attend the needs of the various stakeholders in your school community. We suggest you start by considering flexibility, efficiency, sustainability, expression, and reflection. In table 3.7 we offer questions to pose as you consider various platforms, regardless of your policy context, while remembering your ultimate purposes for the PLP. Judge the utility of platforms against your own criteria as well as those we offer here.

Set aside ample time to explore platforms, as you'll quickly learn that a number of emerging technologies have been created to help teachers and students in personalized learning environments in general, and for the creation of PLPs in particular. Be sure to test the platforms and their various templates to ensure they are functional and user friendly. Consider how well they align with the kind of learning environment you and your colleagues aspire to create. We don't endorse any particular platform to our partners but below we

TABLE 3.7 **Criteria for digital PLP platforms**

Criteria	Questions to Ask
Expression	Does it foster student expression? Can students personalize the design? Does it easily incorporate multimedia? Can students readily incorporate or link to external evidence?
Planning and Goal-Setting	Does it enable linking plans, goals, and proficiencies? Does it integrate student project planning and management?
Reflection	Does it support student reflection? Does it promote dialogue, such as commenting features, between the student and other audiences?
Flexibility	Is it flexible? Can students modify the PLP to respond to different audiences? Can students manage with whom their PLP can be shared both within and beyond their school? Can community mentors or family members weigh in on goals or evidence?
Efficiency	Is it quick and easy to use? Does it meet the daily needs of users? Is it available for students, teachers, and families to interact with at any time?
Sustainability	Can the student use it across years and schools? Does it integrate sufficiently with other data systems? Is it driven by a database, allowing tagging and filtering of evidence by proficiencies, for instance?

outline some of the tools they use regularly. By the time this book goes to press, there will inevitably be more options available, and the ones we include here will have been further refined.

Protean

Protean is a portfolio system for personalized learning built to be student-centric and designed to travel with students as they transition across buildings, schools, districts, and beyond.[45] It enables students to set goals; document evidence of their learning; align that evidence to goals, proficiencies and learning targets; and reflect on and share that learning. Teachers can view and assess learning in multiple ways. And it enables others (e.g., peers, family, community mentors) to provide input as well. Its tagging feature connects evidence of proficiency to both the standard and the assessment. With a strong emphasis on anytime, anywhere learning, a mobile app, a Chrome extension, and Google Drive integration, the platform empowers students to upload evidence from any aspect of their lives—in and out of the school building and day. A reporting functionality helps teachers and students summarize progress on proficiencies and personalized goals and customize reports for PLP conferences or other purposes and audiences.

Figure 3.12 shows a profile page excerpt from Grace, a student at Williston Central School, in her Protean-based PLP. In it, you'll notice the links in the header navigation to social and collaborative opportunities to "follow" other students. Grace can use the profile section as an "about me" space to highlight achievements, passions, current goals, and transferable proficiencies. She catalogs "learnings," including associated multimedia evidence and reflections, in a timeline (figure 3.13), and tags these items to goals and proficiencies for later sorting and filtering by students, teachers, expanded learning providers, and families (figure 3.14).

Google Sites

Google Sites has caught on as a quick and widely accessible way for students and teachers to create websites. Many schools have Google domains and use

FIGURE 3.12   **Excerpt from Grace's PLP profile using Protean, Williston Central School**

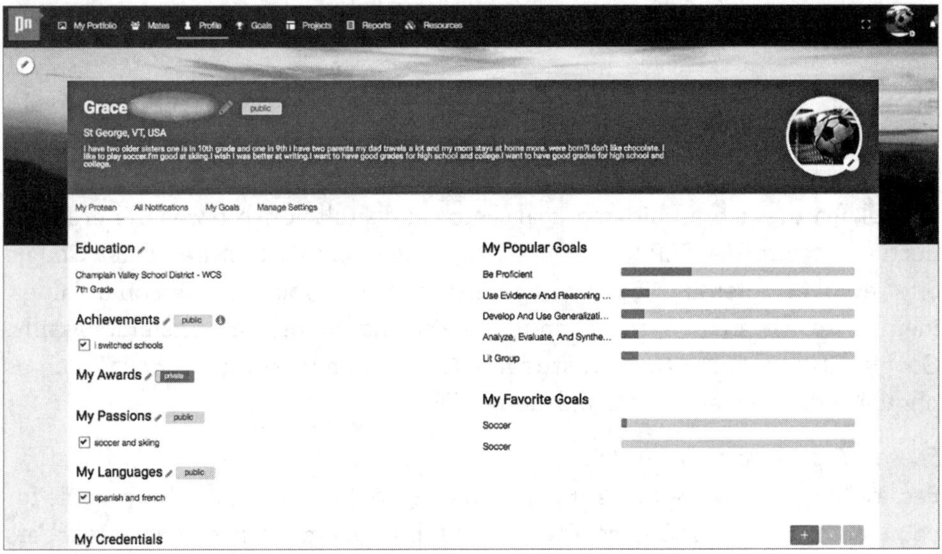

Source: Grace, student, Williston Central School.

FIGURE 3.13   **Excerpt from Grace's PLP timeline using Protean, Williston Central School**

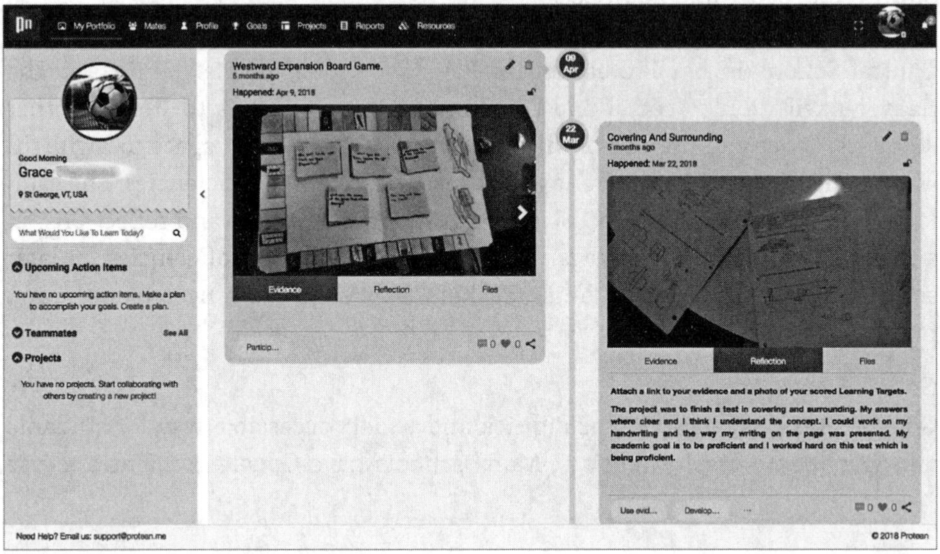

Source: Grace, student, Williston Central School.

Google Sites and its basic website functionality to help students create PLPs. In many cases, teams or schools provide templates or otherwise establish minimum required components for their PLPs. Nora, who attends Williston Central School, features a brief biographical sketch and a relationship web in her Introduction Page to her PLP (see figure 3.15). The overall structure of her Google Site reveals elements prioritized by her school, the focus on personal values, identity, self-awareness, goals and reflection, and lifelong or transferable skills. Google Sites makes it easy for students to embed authentic evidence, such as photos, videos, screenshots, and Google Docs.

Seesaw Digital Portfolio System
Seesaw[46] is an evidence gathering and sharing tool that is especially suitable for younger students. The Seesaw Digital Portfolio System offers students, teachers and families a wide range of functionality. Students can collect and annotate

FIGURE 3.14   **Excerpt sorting evidence by the Informed and Integrative Thinking proficiency from Grace's PLP using Protean**

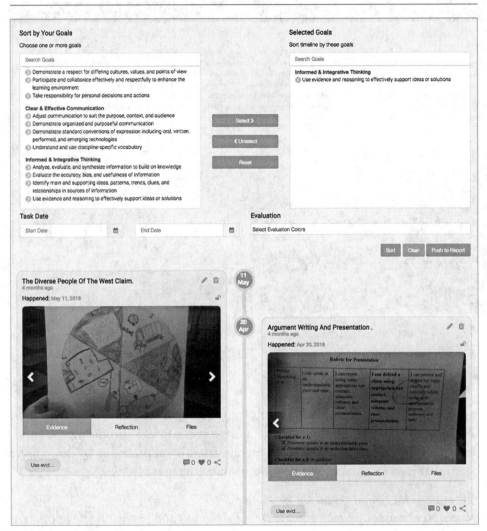

Source: Grace, student, Williston Central School.

FIGURE 3.15   **Nora's introduction page in her PLP in Google Sites, Williston Central School**

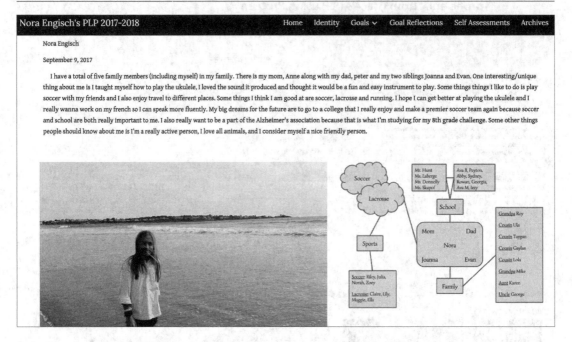

Source: Nora Engisch, student, Williston Central School.

multimedia, links, notes and drawings into journaling and portfolio features. The teacher dashboard summarizes class progress toward proficiencies. Families can receive notifications. And mobile-friendly apps and a QR code login feature enhances access for everyone, even younger students.

Other tools for building and showcasing PLPs

Many other emerging technologies can be put to good use in the development of PLPs, either as the primary platform or simply as a means to document evidence. These tools continue to improve over time, with easier interfaces, more options, and more outlets for student creativity. Some students in our partner classrooms have turned to website building sites such as Weebly and Wix to create visually appealing PLPs.[47] Students enjoy having a choice in how to represent themselves and their learning, and enabling this choice invites creativity and honors the technology skills many students bring to school. Slides and screencasting feature ways for students to guide their audience through their learning. For example, using Google Sites and VoiceThread to record a screencast, students can create a tour of their PLPs.[48] Students record themselves reflecting on their work and upload the recording to their site. These virtual tours enable students to share their work with families or community members even when they can't, or choose not to be, physically present. And with VoiceThread, for instance, families and community members can append a response to the presentation via text, voice, or video, establishing a dialogue that can continue over time. We will showcase the use of these, and other helpful technologies, in later chapters.

Building the PLP Machine

While it may seem logical to begin this PLP journey by training students on the nuts and bolts of accessing and populating their PLPs, the teachers we work with have found the opposite to be true. The platform is only one facet of a larger machine that makes PLPs work. PLPs have been most successful when teachers first encourage students to dive into meaningful work, such as exploring their identities through various reflective and visual activities, engaging in project learning work that has personal relevance and meaning, or venturing out to explore their community. Once students are deeply engaged in work they care about, teachers then begin to design scaffolds for (and hopefully with!) students to gather evidence of their learning.

As you'll see in the next chapter, students particularly enjoy opportunities to develop the portion of the PLP that describes who they are and who they want to become. This work also aligns well with creating a safe and healthy classroom community. Use engaging work like this as the context for introducing students to gathering evidence of their learning preferences, dispositions, and identities. With targeted, just-in-time scaffolding, they'll quickly learn where it goes, who has access to it, and how they can keep it updated. Some teachers couple scaffolding of these skills with sharing their own PLP, along with their own evidence and reflections about who they are, how they learn, and what they're passionate about. These teachers have seized upon what could be dreaded, step-by-step lessons in using a new platform, and turned it into the start of a school year grounded in knowing each other better and reshaping the relationships between teachers and their students.

It's easy to overlook how sophisticated your classroom likely already is. The seeming fluidity and invisibility of your current classroom mechanics is a product of that sophistication, built on top of the years of training in traditional schooling your students have already received. So yes, developing a smooth-running PLP machine for a personalized environment is understandably daunting. But the chapters ahead will help map it all out step by step. And in them, we'll also suggest essential first steps, after which the rest of your journey to personalized learning can unfold over time. Table 3.8 provides one strategy to break down the complexity of a PLP machine. Note that for each PLP task, we can ask critical logistical questions: What will be done? When will it happen? Where will it take place? Who will be involved? How will it be accomplished? For each question, we suggest some practical issues and opportunities to consider. Asking these questions will help you anticipate the decisions, logistical preparations, and scaffolding needed for effective PLPs. Moreover, these are the kinds of questions you can easily pose to students in order to collaboratively develop a PLP machine that works for them. In table 3.9 you'll see an example of how these questions might guide you in the implementation of an early-stage PLP roll out.

TABLE 3.8 **Anticipating the logistics of PLP implementation**

Task ➤	What ➤	When ➤	Where ➤	With Whom ➤	How ➤
	Task purpose statements Rubrics Exemplars	Expectations for frequency Schedules	Environment Resources Scheduling Accessibility Supervision	Norms and safety Preparation and training Access, privacy and security	Technical instructions Training time Mentoring and partnering Norms and routines
Express Self					
Set Goals					
Plan					
Document					
Reflect					
Share					

TABLE 3.9   **Sample logistics of early stage PLP implementation**

Support Student Learning	Plan	Implement
Express Self	Develop activity introducing student to portfolio concept; video example; speaking with experienced students	Teach students the overall portfolio process
Set Goals	Create rubrics and form(s) for goal-setting (written, templates, checklists)	Post resources with links to all materials students need to support their goal-setting
Document	Create rubrics, exemplars, and multi-modal strategies for evidence gathering and tagging (via blogging?) Design lessons/activities to teach evidence gathering	Post resources with materials and screencasts to support evidence gathering
Reflect	Design lessons/activities to teach reflection Create rubrics and form(s) for self-reflection (written, templates, checklists)	Teach students to evaluate and reflect on work to understand who they are as learners Post resources with links to all materials students need to support their reflection

Establishing Team Norms and Routines

We could have referred to the importance of norms and routines for students much earlier in this chapter, but we chose to hold off until the end. Not because they're least important but rather just the opposite. They are so important, in fact, that they should reflect all of what's come before. They should characterize your pedagogical priorities for self-direction, EF, SEL, student leadership, and a robust learning community. They should promote more engaging learning opportunities, regardless of when and where they occur, and facilitate a PLP process that students own and value.

Most teachers are used to establishing classroom rules, norms, and routines. As you consider the dynamic and student-directed character of a personalized learning environment, what norms and routines will help your students be successful? How will you scaffold passing off to students control over key decisions? Just as we attended to norms and routines for teachers in personalized classrooms, so too should we attend to these when the students arrive to start the year. Of course, norms and routines can be introduced at any time of year, and they must be reinforced throughout the year to yield much benefit. But launching the year with norms and routines makes the most sense. The teachers we work with invite students into the process. They hold class or teamwide meetings for students to brainstorm what such spaces should look like, feel like, and sound like. And they find that students in their classrooms, like so many young adolescents, are quick to identify the importance of belonging and affiliation, of respect and dignity, of risk-taking and growth. Partnering with students like this makes sense given the end game of student direction but also as a practical way to deal with the novelty personalized learning. After all, this is no longer about rules for classroom management and compliance; it's about norms and routines that result in a learning environment that's effective for students. That's something you'll need students' help to figure out.

It may help to build on norms and routines you already have underway in your school or classroom. Widespread models like Responsive Classroom, Developmental Design, and Positive Behavioral Interventions and Supports overlap significantly with a personalized vision of healthy and productive classrooms. And many of the strategies, norms, and routines may come in handy in personalized learning. But as any legacy system currently in place, they should be examined thoughtfully and tweaked as necessary—or tossed out—to align your system as a whole with your purposes for personalization. Of course, traditional norms of preparedness still have their place; norms in a personalized, student-directed learning environment are multifaceted. In contrast to many traditional norms for classroom behavior, teachers at Leland and Gray Union Middle School adopted the following habits of work to emphasize civic responsibility, collaboration, and participation:

- **I always take the initiative** and am responsible for my own learning and contributions.
- **I have strong communication** skills and take on **leadership roles** within my group.
- **I encourage others** to be involved in what we are learning.
- **I take a leadership role** in discussions and work with my team to complete our goals.
- I seek out and complete **additional** opportunities to further my group's goal and improve the school.

Finally, as you negotiate this culture shift in your classroom and strive to increase student self-direction and personalization, students may be resistant at first. It makes sense: self-directed learning *is* more work! When first asked to assume more ownership of their learning, students may push back. Don't worry. If this happens, rest assured, you're on the right track. Keep going!

LOOKING AHEAD: BUILDING UPON THE FOUNDATION

In earlier chapters, we made the case that PLPs can be a powerful gateway to personalized learning. This chapter laid the foundation for realizing that vision. Personalized learning is a marked departure from traditional teaching. The learning culture in which it takes place—and the culture in which PLPs make sense to students—must change to match it. Teachers we work with quickly realize the importance of collaborating closely with colleagues. Their students appreciate when each classroom they walk into shares common norms and routines for behavior and workflow. These teachers enjoy opening a student's PLP and seeing into a child's learning life rather than a sterile maze of menus and matrices. And they especially welcome working in partnership with students as those students take on greater responsibility for classroom life.

These rewards are the product of great effort. It requires rethinking how time is organized and used by teachers and students; how the space for learning may stretch out into community; how the culture of that space has to work for self-directed students; and how the shift in important roles from teacher to student needs constant attention on the path to personalized learning environments. And each new goal, strategy, platform, and set of norms and routines calls upon a teacher as scaffolder to ensure these innovations pay off for students, teachers, and other stakeholders.

Establishing the teaching culture was only the first step toward creating a transformed student culture. Fortunately, creating that culture is the product of well-known strategies, any number of which you may have used in the past. Creating a personalized learning environment merely invites teachers to take their past work on classroom culture one step further—or perhaps three or four. Whereas a student-centered culture made life more pleasant in traditional classrooms, personalized learning relies almost entirely on an empowering culture. That's why the skills for self-directedness and collaborative group work are foundational to launching PLPs. That's why now is the time to embolden your student citizenship and leadership programs. And, oh yeah, it'll make your life—and your students' lives—in a personalized learning environment a whole lot more pleasant!

In the next chapter, we illustrate how educators build on this solid foundation, discussing the role of the Learner Profile and providing examples of teacher and student work. We describe ways to share students' evidence of growth with various audiences, emphasizing the particular power of the student-led conference. And, lest you feel a bit overwhelmed, we show how other educators have simplified the initial PLP implementation process, sharing resources that you can adapt for your use in your own classroom or school.

FOUR

LAUNCHING PLPS WITH THE LEARNER PROFILE

Jamal sits waiting for his mom to arrive. He can't believe it but he's sweating. "This shouldn't be a big deal," he tells himself, "It's just my mom. Why does this feel so different?" He doesn't like being the center of attention. At the moment, he feels like crawling under a rock.

Jamal stares at his identity wheel. He created it with his advisor, Ms. Perez. She encouraged him to dig deep into his identities, and explained that they are fluid, shifting, especially in adolescence. But he's not sure he has ever said some of this stuff to his mom. It feels vulnerable and scary to him, but also necessary and important. "Breathe," he thinks, "Just breathe."

Mr. Jenkins, his math teacher, sits next to him, going through his papers. Jamal's mom rushes in from the hospital, still in scrubs, and sits down with a smile. Jamal takes a breath and opens his computer. Up pops his identity wheel. On it, Jamal has listed his visible, or public, identities: age, gender, racial identity. It also shows his more hidden identities, ones he is still learning more about himself. He looks at the screen, and not his mom, because it's easier. Like Ms. Perez said, it's OK if he looks at her intermittently, after he gets his bearings.

Jamal points to the computer and describes to his mom that he feels like an introvert in an extroverted world. Sometimes just going to school, with all that outward emotion and interaction, just exhausts him. And when he comes home at night, after *practice or after-school clubs, he is so tired he can barely answer her questions at dinner about how his day was. He can barely talk, because he has done so much outward living and he needs quiet time to recharge. When he's in his room, listening to music, reading comics or playing a video game, he is taking some down time to try to regain his balance and energy. Ms. Perez helped him see this from a personality trait survey and activity they did in advisory, and he included the results in the identity wheel in front of him. "I don't mean to be rude, Mom, really, at dinner or on the way home." He finally takes a moment for his eyes to flit to his mom's. "I just need to balance out the day. I do want to share with you, but maybe just not right away?"*

He goes on to explain that sometimes he needs some quiet think time in class before talking or acting. He is learning to advocate for that and finding ways to show the teacher what he knows without having to talk in front of the whole class all the time. His math teacher nods, because the two of them have worked out a system using email and Google Classroom to check in on math assignments.

While reading for his literacy class, he posts questions for his teacher on a shared Google Doc, because it's easier than trying to raise his hand and voice his questions in class. His teacher, Mr. Daniels, gives him credit for participating in this way. Mr. Daniels is also helping him share his thoughts in small groups as a stepping stone toward more public speaking.

His mom sits, listening intently. She sees for the first time her son as a reflective, engaged learner, exploring who he is and how this affects his learning experiences in school. She'd thought he was just moving into being a noncommunicative teenager, and this had saddened her. Now, though, she sees him with new eyes.

Jamal moves on in his PLP to share his highlights page with his mom. There are photos from the Philadelphia History Museum that his middle school team visited recently. His teacher jumps in and describes how the team coordinated this visit with an integrated unit on adversity. On this trip, students were invited to explore topics and exhibits that sparked their own interests, that they could select to research back in school. They were to collect artifacts, reflections, and ideas on the trip, and document these on their PLP, which they would then use as a springboard for inquiry and exploration.

Jamal flips through the pictures and stops on a photo of Octavius V. Catto. He pauses, and asks his mom, "Do you know who this is?" His mom tells him that the name looks familiar, but that she isn't sure. Jamal flips over to his Google presentation. There, he begins showing pictures and sharing his writing about Octavius, and his work for public education, voting rights, and citizenship in Philadelphia in 1870.

Jamal's voice grows a little louder as he shares artifacts from the Taking a Stand for Equality exhibit at the museum, and how Octavius was a teacher, athlete, and civil rights leader. Jamal takes a breath before explaining to his mom that this man is a hero of his, that he only learned about him from the trip to the museum, and that he was shot at the age of 32 for his views and leadership. On the last slide, Jamal reads a fictional letter from Octavius to Jamal about current civil rights struggles, charging Jamal to persevere and continue his work. Jamal finally looks up from his presentation.

"Jamal shared this letter and presentation this morning during advisory," Ms. Perez explained to his mother, "and the students were stunned." She turned to Jamal. "I don't think they had ever heard you string that many words together in a row! The letter felt like it really was from Octavius. How did you feel when the students asked questions and applauded?"

At that, Jamal only smiled.

Ms. Perez continued, "The museum is creating professional development for teachers using this exhibit, and I think we should have Jamal share his work with them as an example, and maybe more students can be inspired by Octavius Catto, and your work, Jamal."

Jamal's mom saw in her son a leader that she always knew was there but hadn't been expressed yet. Today, she saw him clearly, and it gave her comfort and hope. She, too, could only smile, nod and say, "Thank you."

BUILDING YOUR RATIONALE: IDENTITY DEVELOPMENT

Like Jamal, middle schoolers are grappling with forming personal and social identity as they explore different ideologies, affiliations and behaviors. In fact, identity formation is widely considered a key task of psychological development during these years. The process of positive identity development is predicated on forming a healthy self-awareness, high self-esteem, and strong self-efficacy.[1]

As young adolescents face the questions, "Who am I?" and "Who do I want to be?" their growing cognitive development brings about increasing self-awareness and, with it, the ability to imagine abstract and multiple possibilities for the future. Young people this age often view themselves in relation to the tasks and skills they perform well and become increasingly eager to experiment with various roles and experiences.[2] At times, this experimentation can result in friction or strife with those around them. One reason that family conflict is greater during early adolescence than in later adolescence is because parents and teens understand each other better when the adolescents have a clearer identity.[3] Middle schoolers' search for identity and self-discovery also may amplify their feelings of vulnerability among their peers.[4] Overall, while the development of identity is a lifelong process, research is clear that those who achieve a well-developed identity and positive self-esteem in adolescence experience a more satisfying adulthood than those who do not.[5]

For these reasons, among others, it's important for students to have safe spaces for this experimentation. The challenges of students' ongoing identity development call on us as educators to create supportive opportunities for exploration, particularly in diverse groups. By offering a range of identity-related activities, Jamal's teachers in the opening vignette did just this. Jamal learned about his nature as an introvert, what he needed during the day to recharge and regroup, and how to communicate those needs to his teachers and family. Generating thoughtfully constructed entries for the Learner Profile section of a PLP, like those Jamal created, can help students develop a sense of personal and collective identity. At the same time, these entries can serve as baseline artifacts for assessment. As professor and middle grades advocate Chris Stevenson put it, "Meeting these personal human needs must be a primary goal of middle level schooling."[6]

Personalized learning can work hand in hand with young adolescents' identity formation. It presents students with authentically engaging opportunities to discover more about themselves and their relationships to the world around them. At the root of this engagement is the value students ascribe to the work they're doing.[7] It's through a purposeful dialogue about who they are, what they care about, and who they want to become, that students can string together personalized learning opportunities into a path of deep growth and learning. This is what the Learner Profile section of the PLP is really about. And that's why our teachers use the Learner Profile to launch not just PLPs but also their learning communities.

With a focus on Learner Profiles, getting students up and running with their PLPs in the first months of school can help build a highly effective learning community, one marked by mutual respect and a commitment to making a positive difference in the world. The key is to embrace the Learner Profile as a representation of self and social discovery. It's students' opportunity to trace who they are as individuals and who they are in reference to the world around them. Teachers can design activities to learn more about their students' out-of-school lives and quickly gain insight into their academic abilities and needs. Personal essays, art projects, podcasts, and video shorts are effective, readily accessible, vehicles for self-expression. And each produces compelling artifacts for a Learner Profile and assessable baseline products for writing and communication.

Thoughtfully crafted community-building activities can inform students' grasp of their social identities and provide fodder for their Learner Profiles while also setting the stage for complex, collaborative, and personalized learning opportunities throughout the year ahead. All of this work can be done to kick off the school year with activities that are fun, highly engaging, developmentally appropriate for young adolescents, and nonetheless challenging, such as hikes, urban outings, ropes courses, game days, and scavenger hunts. These activities can encourage students to express their identities and establish the social connections that can make the classroom a powerful place for social-emotional learning. Assignments that prompt reflection upon these experiences generate still more assessable artifacts for Learner Profiles and baseline determinations. And this intentional and multifaceted approach to community-building drives collective construction of norms for collaboration and general behavior.

In short, Learner Profiles can address the following requirements for effective student learning in the middle grades:

- Young adolescents need opportunities to grapple with their personal and social identities for healthy development.
- Safe, caring, respectful, and productive learning communities are the product of collaborative efforts to know one another and construct social and behavioral norms.
- Truly personalized learning requires that educators know students well, personally, socially, and academically.

CHAPTER OVERVIEW

In chapter 2, we identified four main ways that PLPs serve teachers: to learn more about students; to manage idiosyncratic learning pathways; to assess and communicate student growth more meaningfully; and to collaborate more effectively with colleagues. In the chapter ahead, we describe how the Learner Profile is the linchpin for knowing students well. We lay out the justification for the Learner Profile and walk you through how to populate PLPs with these first important entries. You'll see how developing Learner Profiles can invite powerful culture-building activities that are well suited to launching the school year. Next, we emphasize the importance of students sharing their Learner Profiles with authentic audiences, including families and the community. We wrap up this chapter by illustrating how you can manage this initial rollout of PLPs over the course of the year, drawing upon helpful frameworks developed by our partner schools.

WHAT IS A LEARNER PROFILE?

The Learner Profile is regarded as an important component of an effective PLP by a broad range of organizations. The Institute for Personalized Learning describes Learner Profiles as "co-created by educators and learners and comprised of rich, current information regarding each learner."[8] The institute identifies four dimensions of a Learner Profile: demographic data that represent the student's current circumstances and learning history; a snapshot of the student's academic status drawn from a variety of data points; the student's learning-related skill set, such as tools, habits, strategies that support independent learning; and potential learning drivers, including the learner's aspirations, potential motivational hooks, and career plans.[9] The organization Next Generation Learning Challenges suggests that a Learner Profile may capture "student strengths and gap areas, motivation and goals, learning styles, and other personal data related to their learning experience and needs. . . ."[10] Bray and McClaskey similarly contend that a Learner Profile should invite students to consider their strengths, interests, and challenges in relation to how they access information, engage with content, and express what they know, linking it to the Universal Design for Learning principles of engagement, representation, action and expression.[11] And Vermont's Agency of Education recommends that, within Learner Profiles, students identify their strengths and challenges; complete inventories such as a Myers-Briggs Inventory, career assessments, and interest surveys; and respond to questions like the following:

- Who am I? *What defines me as a person and member of my community?*
- How do I learn? *How do I learn best to meet my academic goals?*
- What are my skills and interests? *What do I like to do and what do I do well?*
- What is my future path? *What do I want to do with my life after high school?*[12]

Regardless of your particular framework, at its core the Learner Profile should convey the multifaceted nature of your students' identities: the personal, academic, and social; the existing, exploratory, and aspirational. The Learner Profile helps teachers, families, and the learners themselves to understand the learner better. In the opening vignette, Jamal relied upon the tasks he completed during advisory time, including a personality trait survey and an identity wheel, to share information about himself. As a result, his mother came away with an enriched understanding of her son's nature and needs.

Like many aspects of the PLP, integrating the Learner Profile into your first weeks of school serves multiple purposes. Both the act of creating entries for the Learner Profile and sharing the results with different audiences can yield important outcomes. Learners take stock of who they are as they confront the challenges of a new school year while buttressing their resilience with increasing self-awareness and deeper connections with others. As the teacher, you come to understand the learners personally, socially, and academically. And as students carry out the activities for the Learner Profile, you have ready-made opportunities to illustrate norms, routines and expectations for your classroom, such as workflow, collaborative editing, and digital citizenship. You can leverage the evidence generated for the Learner Profile to conduct important formative assessments of essential skills. As students share their Learner Profiles, families gain new insights, as did Jamal's mother, about their emerging adolescents at a time when many children are seeking greater independence.

DESIGNING LEARNER PROFILE TASKS

Because a primary task of early adolescence is identity development, generating evidence for the Learner Profile is a particularly good match for students in the middle grades. So much of effective pedagogy for this age group rests upon a teacher's willingness and ability to tap into students' identities to foster learning. We can encourage students to create prose, poetry, or podcasts about their identities; allow them to design avatars for games that explore their idealized selves; or base curriculum on the compelling questions they ask about their rapidly changing selves and their emerging sense of their futures. These are just several of the hundreds of ways our teachers invite students into the central purpose of the Learner Profile: to learn and share about themselves.

Generating the Learner Profile is about understanding the individual and collective identities of the children you live with every school day. In turn, this understanding can drive smarter decisions about where to take your learning community. It's your chance to connect with each student, up front and with deliberate speed, in ways most of us only realize with a few. It's a vehicle to *make* those things happen rather than letting them happen. In that sense, how we go about Learner Profiles is an issue of equity, calling on us to connect with each student as soon as possible.

Learner Profiles are best started at the beginning of the school year, so it's important to begin designing them well before that. We know there is a great deal riding on those first weeks of school. You need to get to know your students, establish a learning community that will thrive throughout the year, introduce norms and routines of the shared learning space, and conduct early formative assessments on various skills. Few of us have given ourselves permission—or been encouraged—to spend the first eight weeks of school the way we would if we took seriously young adolescents' need for a respectful, rather than compliant, environment. Students want a respectful classroom because they know it's the best chance for them to be who they want to be. They seek a meaningful purpose for being there and appreciate the collective power of others being on that journey with them. During the first few weeks of school, this means dedicating time to considered reflection about personal identity as a launching-off point for establishing a collective identity, one that is grounded in shared purpose, respectful negotiation, trust, and honesty. Rather than being "just one more thing," constructing the Learner Profile can help you accomplish all of these tasks.

Many teachers already have a number of activities to launch the school year, so it's worth considering what already works well in your classroom or team to help students explore who they are. Perhaps you ask students to compose a podcast or memoir to tell their peers more about their backgrounds and where they come from. Maybe students complete interest inventories or learning preference surveys so you have a better sense of what engages each student. Perhaps your team participates in an annual ropes course or field trip that would prove good fodder for reflecting on one's leadership skills.

When thinking about Learner Profile tasks, consider for a moment your blind spots as a teacher. Think about the student you don't quite understand and try to identify what's missing. Is it because you share so little history? Are unconscious biases getting in the way? Is the family challenging to connect with? Or perhaps you simply learn differently or have radically different interests, background with schooling, or dispositions? Establish a sample of students that present the greatest challenge to you. Reflect on the cultural outliers, the ones that may feel at risk because their life experiences, racial identities, or backgrounds seem vastly different from those of their peers and teachers. The behavioral outliers, the ones who you just can't seem to reach and are at risk of a downward discipline spiral. The cognitive outliers, either the students who have developmental disabilities or the ones to whom you wish you could offer more advanced opportunities. Perhaps the students you know have strong academic abilities but appear aloof or disinterested in class. Maybe those students who are at significant risk and come to school hungry or have an incarcerated parent. In any of these cases, knowing the students better will help you respond to their needs better. Keep these students in mind as you review our sample activities in the next section. Then pose these questions:

Does the activity . . .

- respond to your stated purpose(s) for doing PLPs? (Are students composing, creating, or depicting something that will help you meet one or more of your purposes?)
- result in student-created artifacts that will help you understand your students better? (Are they reflecting on aspects of their cultural identities or increasing their understanding of their own development?)
- help build the culture you need for personalization and self-direction, as discussed in chapter 3. (Are they connecting socially around the assignments? Are students engaged in work that introduces them to the team's norms and routines, such as effective group work, smooth workflow and equitable access to technology?)
- engage students? (Do students find personal meaning in what they're doing? Do they persist in spite of challenges? Are they coming in to work on it during lunchtime? Are they telling their families about it?)

- align with the common proficiencies or standards you and your colleagues value for PLP work? (Are there authentic products that complement other assessments of students' abilities, such as diagnostic or standardized test scores?)

LEARNER PROFILE EXAMPLES

With those five questions in mind, consider how students might explore and express their identities in your classroom or school. While it's likely you already have a number of ways you build community and knowledge of your students, here are a few highly engaging ways some teachers have generated entries for Learner Profiles.

Autobiography

Autobiography is a common and relatively accessible way for students to introduce themselves to their PLP audiences. It also teaches students a genre—the brief biographical sketch—with broad appeal for academic and professional purposes. Don Taylor, a teacher at Main Street Middle School in Montpelier, provides his seventh and eighth graders with the guidelines in table 4.1 to get them started on their PLP Biographies.

Educators on the Swift House team of Williston Central School also use the brief biographical sketch as a component of their Learner Profiles. Nora, an eighth grader on that Williston-based team, offered the following to introduce readers to her learning journey:

> I have a total of five family members (including myself) in my family. There is my mom, Anne along with my dad, Peter and my two siblings Joanna and Evan. One interesting/unique thing about me is I taught myself how to play the ukulele, I loved the sound it produced and thought it would be a fun and easy instrument to play. Some things I like to do is play soccer with my friends and I also enjoy travel to different places. Some things I think I am good at are soccer, lacrosse and running. I hope I can get better at playing the ukulele and I really wanna work on my french so I can speak more fluently. My big dreams for the future are to go to a college that I really enjoy and make a premier soccer team again because soccer and school are both really important to me. I also really

TABLE 4.1   **Writing your PLP biography, Montpelier Main Street Middle School, Team Summit**

Writing Your PLP Biography

Directions: As part of your Personal Learning Plan, you will be responsible for a short biography (of yourself) that introduces you, your page, and your goals/mission. This biography should be accompanied by an appropriate picture and should illustrate the important characteristics, achievements, goals, and activities that make you an individual. Please note that your biography should be written in the third person. Additionally, it should be between 100–200 words in length for your personalized learning plan. In the future, you may be asked to create versions of different lengths. Use any brainstorming, teacher advisory activities, or any additional resources to develop background ideas for the biography.

Bio Pre-Writing and Writing Process

Step 1: Make a short list of your goals, achievements, interests, awards, organizations you work with, awards, or community activities.

Step 2: Write down some of your qualifications, skills and educational strengths.

Step 3: Create a short list of additional personal information that you feel relates to your goals, objectives, and personality. This might include memberships, volunteer work, current projects and hobbies.

Step 4: Ask your friends, teachers, or parents to give you some feedback. What do they see as your biggest strengths? Do they have any suggestions about information to add to the biography? Include that information in your brainstorming.

Some Pre-Writing Tips

Introduce Yourself

Begin the bio by introducing yourself, and always write in the third person. For example, write "Jane Smith is a seventh-grade student" rather than "I am a seventh-grade student." State your team or class affiliation. . . . "Jane entered Team Summit in 2015" and list any areas or special notes.

Education and Credentials

List your education after the introductory sentence, including the particular academic strengths or classes that you enjoy. If you have earned any academic honors, this would be a good place to mention them. You may also want to include different activities in which you were a participant.

Goals

Identify any specific goals or expectations that you have for the school year. These may include academic, extracurricular, or personal goals. Remember that this year we will be trying to connect our goals to the Vermont's Transferable Skills. Reference that document if necessary.

Citizenship/Principles and Values

You may want to include some of the citizenship characteristics that we discussed in class. Many of you identified character traits that not only are positive elements of the community but also are expectations you have for others. Identifying those that are important will help readers get a better sense of who you are.

Closing Statement

Conclude the bio by briefly stating any current or upcoming projects, such as a new activity you are taking up this fall. End the biography with a simple statement indicating your town of residence. You will note that most authors, in their biography, end with a similar statement.

Source: Montpelier Main Street Middle School, Team Summit, based on Lisa McQuerrey "How to Write a Short Bio About Yourself." *Chron*, June 30, 2018, http://smallbusiness.chron.com/write-short-bio-yourself-57289.html.

want to be a part of the Alzheimer's association because that is what I'm studying for my 8th grade challenge. Some other things people should know about me is I'm a really active person, I love all animals, and I consider myself a nice friendly person.

Storytelling

Stories are a particularly powerful part of human experience and inviting students to tell a story of themselves can take many forms. Lori Lisai and Joseph Murphy, educators at Lamoille Union Middle School in Hyde Park, created a Geography of Self series that includes a number of thoughtful ways to engage students in storytelling for identity exploration. In table 4.2, they ask students to compose "The Story of My Name."[13] Young adolescents are often intrigued by hearing parents or others tell stories of their younger selves. If they don't already know the story of their name, it's a terrific chance for them to start a conversation they may never have had with family members.

TABLE 4.2   **The story of my name: Lamoille Union Middle School**

The Story of My Name

To be human is to love stories. In stories, we see ourselves, learn about our world and learn how to make our way in it. One of your earliest stories is the story of your name . . .

READY . . .
For this project, you will be telling a story of your name. Read Sandra Cisneros' two short sketches from *The House on Mango Street*, titled "My Name" and "Marin." Notice how Cisneros captures intricate details about both herself and her friend Marin in these short pieces.

SET . . .
The story of how we are named is often interesting and complicated. It sheds light on your personal history as the first major decision about your identity. For this brainstorming, you will need to research the history of your name—both its roots as well as how it came to be yours.

> **What is the story of your name?**
> Why do you have the name you do? (Interview your parents or guardians.)
> How do you feel about your name?
> What is the meaning of your name, and what does it mean to you?
> If you could change your name, what would you name yourself and why?

GO!
Using your brainstorming, try to capture the power of Cisneros' writing in your own as you craft the 4-paragraph story of your name. After you have a rough draft, use *Notability* to incorporate images, video, audio, or any other digital embellishments to bring your story to life.

Source: Lori Lisai and Joseph Murphy, Lamoille Union Middle School.

Digital storytelling provides another way to capitalize on the power of story and multimedia. Digital stories combine videos, photographs, music, sound, text, and voice blended into multimedia presentations. Students can work individually or collaboratively to produce their digital stories, which are then easily uploaded to the internet to reach a broader audience.[14] Digital stories serve as an expressive alternative to the written product that we as teachers so often fall back upon. As educational researchers Cynthia Reyes and Kathleen Brinegar remind us, "Since not every student is a skilled storyteller when relying only on the written word, the potential of the digital story tool to document experience and emotion and elicit empathy due to its multimodal storytelling nature makes it accessible for understanding each other's stories."[15] Teachers we work with who bring digital storytelling into the classroom quickly realize why the work is worth the effort. Digital stories offer students the opportunity to work on a range of proficiencies at once, including writing, research, technology use, visual literacy, and critical thinking.[16] Reyes documented how, at Winooski Middle School, digital storytelling was a particularly powerful strategy for working with English learners, many of whom are refugees. Eh Man, a student from Thailand, used his digital story to tell his teachers and classmates what it was like arriving in a new country where he did not speak the language.[17]

> *Eh Man's Digital Story Script*
> My name is Eh Man.
> I am from Thailand.
> I am 12 years old.
> My family is from Burma.
> Our people are called Karen.
> I was born in 1997 on a farm.
> I have five people in my family.
> I have one brother and one sister.
> My family grew pumpkins.
> I moved from Thailand to American in 2008.
> When I first came to Winooski I didn't know English.
> I was scared and wanted to sleep all day.
> The next day I saw a kid riding a bike. He taught me to ride too.
> I went to Winooski school I learned some things about math
>   and reading.

I played sports in 5th and 6th grade.
My father works at Tiny Thai restaurant.
Now I like Winooski. I go fishing with my Dad.
It was hard at first but now I like my new life in Winooski.

Poetry

Students can use poetry to convey their identities to others and explore (for the first time in some cases) what informed those identities in the first place. Lisai and Murphy's Geography of Self series includes an option that does both of those things. As you'll see in table 4.3, the "Where I'm From" assignment is based on a well-known George Ella Lyon's poem that inspires students to consider their roots via various, often sensory, allusions. After the poems are written, students couple them with images and turn them into digital poetry using iMovie.[18]

TABLE 4.3   **Where I'm from: Lamoille Union Middle School**

Poem: Where I'm From

READY . . .
For this project, you will write a poem describing the geography of your life. To do this, you will need to think about your family, friends, home, community, state and country. After writing your poem, you will gather images and turn your poem into a digital story.

Start by watching the "Where I'm From" video by Digable Planets. Notice how their use of repetition gives the song momentum, propelling it forward.

Next, read George Ella Lyon's poem, "Where I'm From." Take note of his creative descriptors. Next, check out "I Am From," another example written by a California teen. Notice how both writers capture their roots in moments and objects rather than places.

SET . . .
Now, make four lists of adjectives and nouns describing the unique features, elements, objects and people in your life:

1. house/home
2. family and friends
3. town/village/community
4. state and country

GO!
Using the models provided, drop the phrase "Where I'm from" or "I am from" in front of each of your four lists to create your own "Where I'm From" poem describing the geography of your life. Experiment with rhythm and rhyme by changing or rearranging the words in your list. Repeat the phrase "Where I'm from" or "I am from" as many times as you find necessary.

When your poem is written and revised, begin searching for and saving at least one image for each line of your poem. Then upload your images to iMovie to create a digital poem.

Source: Lori Lisai and Joseph Murphy, Lamoille Union Middle School.

Movies

Moviemaking is another great way to invite young adolescents into learning and sharing about themselves. With relatively accessible technologies, students can convey powerful glimpses into their lives. Lindsey Halman, a teacher at Essex Middle School in Essex, created a "Who am I now?" movie project for her students to express who they are and identify their aspirations. In it, she invites them to consider how their identities at school and home may be different. In table 4.4, Lindsey also includes an assessment rubric that integrates both Common Core and local standards.[19]

Graphic or Symbolic Representation

Taylor, of Main Street Middle School, asks students to include relationship webs in their Learner Profiles.[20] Students identify and graphically represent the key relationships with family, extended family, teams, or other individuals or groups. With just a quick glance at these concise graphics, Taylor learns of the important people in each student's life. He's noticed that this activity, and the relationship webs it generates, fosters his students' relationships skills and promotes social-emotional learning. What's more, using Google Drawing provides learners with a nonverbal opportunity to express themselves. Table 4.5 shows how Taylor walks his seventh graders through the development of relationship webs within the context of the community page in their PLP.

Since Taylor works on a multiage team, students return to their relationship webs as eighth graders. They then identify which relationships have remained the same, which have changed, and which new ones have entered their lives. The experience becomes increasingly sophisticated as students reflect on what constitutes a healthy relationship and how relationships change over time as some relationships grow stronger and others more distant. Students at Williston Central School also use relationship webs to explore their identities. Figure 4.1 presents a web from Nora's PLP.

Identity Wheels, which take many forms and are readily available online, help students explore identity while emphasizing strengths and honoring each learner's life experiences, backgrounds, and interests. Figure 4.2 displays an example of an identity wheel, this format inspired by Oregon State University's resources.[21] The top part of the wheel hosts personal identities, where a student's distinguishing personal characteristics are featured. The bottom of

TABLE 4.4   **Who am I now? Identity movie project: Essex Middle School, Edge Academy**

Identity Project: Who am I now?
Who am I now? iMovies

TASK: Create an iMovie that shares who you are and your hopes and dreams for the future

Step 1:   Individual Brainstorm: Answer the following questions on your own.

- Who am I at school? _____
- Who am I at home? _____
- What do I care most about? _____
- What is/are my favorite thing(s) to do? _____
- Who supports me? _____
- What are my hopes and dreams for the future? _____

Step 2:   Partner Share and Storyboard Creation: With your partner, share your information and then create your own storyboard that includes:

- the information in the questions—take time to expand on this _____
- pictures _____
- multi-media _____
- creativity— transitions, music, cinematography _____

Step 3:   Record Identity Project: Work with your partner to record each other's identity project iMovies—you are the director of your own iMovie, but your partner is there to support you with recording, ways to improve your iMovie, etc.

RUBRIC:

iMovie	1	2	3	4
CCS.ELA.8.SL.5 Integrate multimedia and visual displays into presentations to clarify information, strengthen claims and evidence, and add interest.	Incomplete information from brainstorm. iMovie may be incomplete or lacking in evidence of who you are.	iMovie reflects most of the questions in the brainstorm and shows some evidence of creativity.	iMovie reflects all of the questions in the brainstorm and clearly communicates who you are in a creative and interesting manner.	iMovie demonstrates evidence beyond the brainstorm questions. iMovie uses transitions, music, cinematography, etc. to show a high level of creativity.
(EMS.Skills.3) Participates in class activities and discussions.	Does not participate in classroom activities or discussions.	Student participated in some activities and discussion, but not all.	Student was engaged throughout the process of creating the Identity Project iMovie.	Student was engaged in the entire project and offered new insights to the team to help move others forward.
(EMS.Skills.7) Takes initiative and is accountable for learning and achieving at a high standard.	Work is incomplete and no accountability was taken.	The work is almost complete, but some key components are missing.	All work is complete and done at a high standard. Student showed accountability for all aspects of the project.	The student took the project to a higher standard and showed an innovative approach.

Source: Lindsey Halman, Edge Academy, Essex Middle School.

TABLE 4.5 **PLP community page requirements:
Montpelier Main Street Middle School, Team Summit**

Team Summit
Personal Learning Plan
Community Page

LEARNING TARGETS:

CCSS.ELA-Literacy.W.8.2 Write informative/explanatory texts to examine a topic and convey ideas, concepts, and information through the selection, organization, and analysis of relevant content.

CCSS.ELA-Literacy.W.8.2a Introduce a topic clearly, previewing what is to follow; organize ideas, concepts, and information; include formatting (e.g., headings), graphics (e.g., charts, tables), and multimedia when useful to aiding comprehension.

CCSS.ELA-Literacy.W.8.2b Develop the topic with relevant, well-chosen facts, definitions, concrete details, quotations, or other information and examples.

****

Community Page Requirements

- **Definition:** Post your definition of a relationship at the top of the page.

- **Relationships Web:** Underneath your definition of a relationship, create a Google Drawing that shows your relationships.

- **Relationship Reflection:** Underneath your Relationships Web, please create a short, paragraph reflection that answers the following questions.

    - **Content Expectations**
      1. What is your strongest relationship? Why?
      2. What does that relationship provide for you? Friendship? Support? Safety?
      3. What values does that relationship represent? Trust? Loyalty?

      Here are some possibilities:
      friendship trust loyalty loving forgiveness hard work responsibility
      good listener caring brave sharing honesty smart brave respect

    - **Paragraph Expectations**
      1. Focus Statement
      2. Supporting sentences with details/evidence
      3. Transition words to link ideas
      4. Conclusion

- **Relationship Analysis:** Now reflect on these questions to complete the analysis below.

What is your strongest relationship? Why is it so positive?	What are the characteristics of this relationship that make it strong?
What are your best memories of this relationship?	How does this relationship help you set goals or meet challenges?

FIGURE 4.1   **Relationship web from Nora's PLP, Williston Central School**

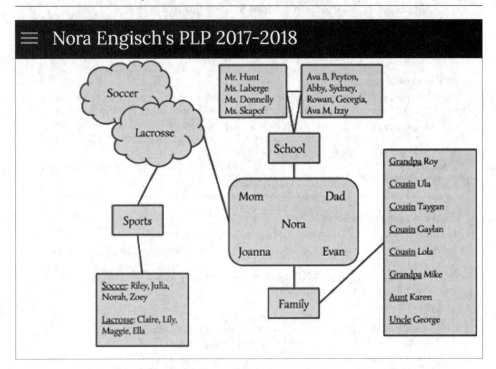

Source: Nora Engisch, student, Williston Central School.

the circle is where students characterize their social identities, including how others may perceive them. Understanding that identities can be fluid, with some expressed publicly and others hidden, can be an important outcome of this activity.

At Tuttle Middle School, teacher Christie Nold uses the Cultural Iceberg as a symbol for identity exploration (see figure 4.3).[22] She asks her students to imagine an iceberg, with 10 percent of it visible above the surface, and the other 90 percent under the water. She invites them to think about the visible 10 percent as what they believe people know about them and prompts them to share some of their "submerged selves" with each other.[23]

FIGURE 4.2   **Student identity wheel**

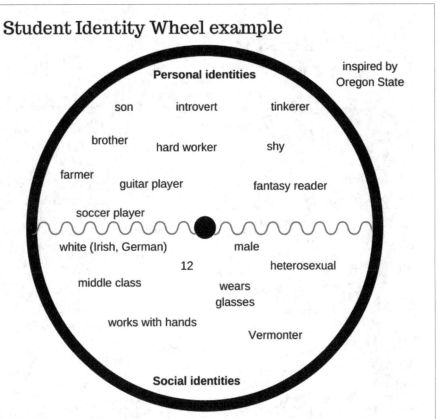

Student Identity Wheel example

Personal identities

inspired by
Oregon State

son   introvert   tinkerer

brother   hard worker   shy

farmer   guitar player   fantasy reader

soccer player

white (Irish, German)   male

12   heterosexual

middle class   wears glasses

works with hands

Vermonter

Social identities

Personal identities can include: a distinguishing characteristic(s) a person takes a special pride in; form a basis for the persons self-worth, individuality and distinction along with morals and values.
Examples: Volunteer, hard work ethic, daughter, brother, artist, chef , creative writer, poet, athlete, etc.

Social identities can include: ways we define ourselves and are perceived by others based on various physical, visible, hidden, regional, economic commonalities, or any other socially perceived commonalities we share with a group of people. Examples: Racial, ethnic and national identities, gender identity, sexual orientation, religion, ability, class, etc.

FIGURE 4.3   **The cultural iceberg model: A student's visible and submerged selves**

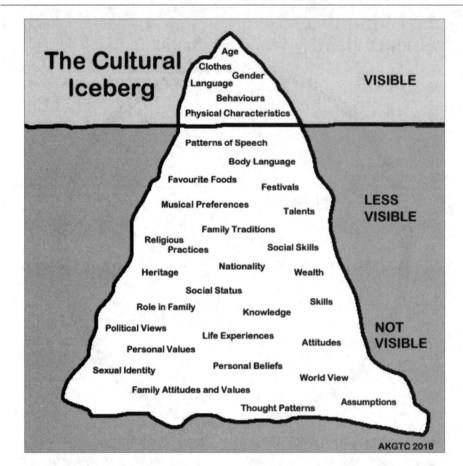

Source: "A Kids' Guide to Canada, If I Really Knew You (The Cultural Iceberg)," https://akgtcanada.com/if-i-really-knew-you/.

Photography and Augmented Reality

Another gem from Lisai and Murphy's Geography of Self series is the Self-Portrait, or Selfie. Table 4.6 exhibits how these teachers inspire students to play around with something many young adolescents already love to use in this era of Snapchat and other social media: the digital camera. To augment

TABLE 4.6 **The selfie self-portrait, Lamoille Union Middle School**

Self Portrait

A selfie, or self-portrait is a portrait of oneself, done by oneself. Although the concept is simple, there are many ways to capture oneself in a self-portrait. For this project, we will be using your iPad's camera to create a self-portrait.

READY . . .
Start by finding some self-portraits that you find cool. They might be funny, clever, inspirational, interesting, or just beautiful. Observe the portrait for lighting, camera angle, effects, and what it is that is being captured about the person in the portrait. Take a look at these examples:

Now check out the 19 photography tutorials here, and learn some techniques for making your photos stand out.

SET . . .
After gathering inspiration for your self-portrait, think about who you are, who you want to be, and what you want your portrait to say about you.

Your self-portrait should be a personal expression, inspired by, but not just a copy of something you've seen elsewhere. Use props, scenery, pose and lighting conditions to convey your personality.

GO!
Plan your shot. What will the shot look like? Where will you take it? Will you need assistance?

Take as many photographs as necessary, then use phixr to enhance your portrait. When your self-portrait is how you want it, upload it to ThingLink.

Source: Lori Lisai and Joseph Murphy, Lamoille Union Middle School.

the portraits hung outside their classrooms, students attached QR codes that launched viewers to a ThingLink, in which the online version of their portrait comes to life for visitors with embedded multimedia.

Engaging with family and community can also feed a student's profile. For instance, as part of a unit on immigration and family, students at Rumney Memorial School in Middlesex interviewed family members. They developed their own questions, recorded the interview, and compiled artifacts important to their family. Students shared the results with classmates and invited family guests. Some students used the StoryCorps app, which helped them frame their questions, record them, and archive them at the Library of Congress. This kind of family storytelling connects students to their families, their backgrounds, and their history at a time when students are often feeling disconnected. And a well-integrated unit like this generates entries for the Learner Profile, addresses plenty of subject area and transferable proficiencies, and puts students in an ongoing dialogue with their families about identity.

Students at West Rutland School undertook a similar exploration partnering with community members, which they named, "Who are We as West Rutland?" Aimed at creating community connections for seventh and eighth graders and deepening their understanding of themselves as part of a community, the project culminated in students sharing their work at an evening exhibition attended by parents and community members. Teacher Wendi Dowst observed, "Because the projects were community-based, parents became involved, and they saw extra value in what we were doing because the topic was close to them and their experience. One father made borscht with his son. The recipe was passed down through their family. . . . Now that the children have background knowledge about their community, they can gain access to these conversations with their families."[24]

The preceding examples are just a few of the more creative ways students in our partner schools have added to their Learner Profile. But creating the profile is not a one-shot deal. The Learner Profile, like the PLP overall, is most effective when it's visited and updated often. The Vermont Agency of Education declares, "the PLP should be seen as a 'living' document that can adapt as students develop over time and as their needs and ideas change. The honesty and commitment to this process by students and stakeholders, and the integration of the PLP into the learning environment by teachers and advisors, will determine the ultimate value of the Personalized Learning Plan process."[25] While there is obvious benefit in constructing its first iteration at the start of the year, young adolescent identities are in constant flux. To remain relevant, and to realize its capacity to support healthy personal and social development, the Learner Profile should evolve along with the student. That means revisiting it throughout the year.

SHARING THE LEARNER PROFILE

The student work featured in this chapter is the result of students investigating their current and future selves, and their individual and collective identities. Like Jamal from the chapter's opening vignette, they considered their strengths, identified their priorities for self-improvement, and shared their aspirations for the future. Along the way, they documented their journeys in their PLPs. While this positions them well for generating self-knowledge, students find great satisfaction in sharing about themselves, although it may take some nudging.

Sharing the Learner Profile component of the PLP is a powerful way to accomplish a number of goals. Making the time for students to explore each other's PLPs can lead to deeper relationships, mutual appreciation, and shared interest for collaborative learning. They may generate ideas for roles they'd like to adopt in or out of school. The class or team can establish a deeper sense of community and collective identity. Families can gain insight into their young adolescents at a time when they may be starting to pull away, one of a number of important purposes for student-led PLP conferences, as we'll learn in future chapters. The Humans of Burke and Who Are We as West Rutland projects mentioned earlier show how community members may gain new appreciation for the youth of their neighborhood, town, or city when identity activities are shared beyond the school. Perhaps most important, sharing PLPs in general, and Learner Profiles in particular, with authentic audiences can validate PLP work in way that assignments and deadlines simply can't.

Finally, let's not forget about students sharing Learner Profiles with their teachers. Eighth graders at Randolph Union Middle School assemble Learner Portfolios that they present to their new teachers at the beginning of the year to explain who they are as learners.[26] Teachers at Crossett Brook Middle School created a spreadsheet, broken down by team and teacher, in which they compiled links to students' profiles and recorded their observations (see figure 4.4). With this, not only could the student's advisory teacher learn from the profile, every teacher could. Teachers we've worked with have consistently claimed to know their students better, and in unexpected yet important ways, after dedicating ample time to Learner Profiles.

These examples remind us that including authentic audiences in our unit plans very often engage students and others in sharing more about themselves and their identities. These moments can help to break down the isolation some young adolescents experience. They can validate student strengths that may otherwise go unnoticed and unacknowledged. And they can go a long way toward dispelling the unfortunate myth too prevalent in popular culture that young adolescents don't care about anyone but themselves or that they've got nothing to contribute to their communities. We will revisit the role of authentic audiences more in future chapters, but for now simply keep in mind that

FIGURE 4.4   **Teachers shared spreadsheet with observations from learner profiles, Crossett Brook Middle School**

	B	D	E	F	G	H
1	Student Name	Link	What I learned	Type of learner	What I wonder	What this means for my teaching OR Other notes
2	######	https://	#### plays both Sax and Piano, with piano mainly at home and for jazz band.	He likes a distraction free zone in order to work and also likes hands on activities.	What type of subject matter is #### curious about?	#### is in the blue group which can get loud and crazy at times. He prefers less distractions. Keep up the hands on learning.
3	######	https://	#### chose to create a web site using WIX. This tells me that she is creative.	#### is an Eeyore — insightful, reflective, imaginative.	I would like to know more about what #### loves to do. I know she is into dance, but there was nothing about it on her About Me page. She only listed her learning styles.	#### has the ability to be reflective about her learning. She also likes to be creative. I think she could really be encouraged to do a killer Brainado project.
4	######	https://	#### loves to read	There was nothing mentioned about what type of learning works best for ####.	#### has many images of space on his about me page. Is this something he is also interested in?	#### also stated that he likes to tinker and be creative. This would bode well for more engineering design challenges.
5	######	https://	#### likes to Irish Dance!	Kinesthetic and creative learner.		Intrapersonal, likes to please everyone, and is sensitive. Important for me to work with her on putting herself out there musically!
6	######	https://	Creative, bright eyed and loves activity	Active		#### would be a great group leader
7	######	https://	Really liks student centered activities.	Kinesthetic.	What do you want to learn more about at CBMS?	More student choice!
8	######	https://	#### has a youtube channel and loves Google draw	#### needs to be calm to learn and has a fidget spinner that can help him during class.	I wonder what kind of an impact a mentor would have with ####. Someone who would listen to him, as he loves to share about his drawings and video games.	Working with #### one on one in study hall usually works well in order to review what he may have missed in class due to distractions or not being "calm" at that time. I will also keep providing opportunities for him to use Google draw any chance I get. He loves that!

Source: Crossett Brook Middle School.

the Learner Profile derives much of its power from being shared. Knowing that the PLP will have a real and relevant audience legitimizes the significant effort it requires. Preparing for a PLP conference drives critical dialogue between student and teacher, which is easily neglected in the fast pace of schooling.

LOOKING AHEAD: SCAFFOLDING LEARNING PATHWAYS

The Learner Profile is the launching-off point for using the PLP to know students well. Implemented along the lines described in this chapter, the Learner Profile contributes to three particularly important elements of effective middle grades education and responds to new demands placed on teachers in personalized learning. It frames important opportunities for students to explore their personal and social identities at a time when it's vital to their healthy development. Completing the Learner Profile also fosters a number of important teacher roles. As a Community Builder, you can help establish a safe, caring, respectful and productive learning environment that supports the personal and social challenges inherent in challenging, collaborative, and student-directed learning. The Learner Profile reveals practical insights into who your students are—personally, socially, and academically. And as Scaffolder and Scout, you can leverage this knowledge of each student and the learning community as a whole to craft and manage the engaging learning opportunities and flexible pathways at the heart of personalized learning environments. That's the task we take up in chapter 5: Designing Flexible Learning Pathways for Young Adolescents.

FIVE

DESIGNING FLEXIBLE LEARNING PATHWAYS FOR YOUNG ADOLESCENTS

It's 9:30 a.m. and time for math class. Jack is excited to see what they will work on today. He wonders what his professor will think of his 3D drawing of his dream home, with all the ratios done by hand, and the spaces he designed. Yes, this was extra. In fact, it was well beyond what was required, but he loved the assignment and the software he got to use. His mom had to tell him three times to go to bed last night, finally taking the computer from his room!

You see, Jack is taking calculus as a sixth grader. He's enrolled in an online class at Johns Hopkins University. Each session, he gets to video conference with his professor, but his favorite part is connecting with the other 12-year-olds from all over the country who are in the course and at a similar mathematical level. He collaborates with them on math projects online during class as well as in the evenings. And they've been great about giving him feedback on his dream home designs. On the math page of his PLP, Jack posts his regular work with Johns Hopkins, screenshotting problems, projects, exchanges with his peers and professor, and his reflections on his work. This is his second online course and it's added a lot to his school experience.

Jack grabs his laptop and earbuds, and heads to a table. Other kids mill about, gathering their own materials for their math groupings. He's often thought that, in other schools, his classmates might look at him strangely or think doing something like this during math time was weird. But the truth is, in this class, everyone seems to get what they need. It doesn't matter if it's reading, writing, math, science, social stud-ies, art, or music. All of his classmates have different interests, abilities, and options for how and where to learn. And they know that, for math, Jack moves to his station to get what he needs. He pops in his earbuds and clicks into his class. His mind feels a little fuzzy since he was up late drafting his dream home, but the math and design work were just so intriguing. He snaps to attention as his professor's face comes onto the screen and the next fifty minutes pass like nothing.

Ms. Duvay, Jack's homeroom teacher, provides regular support, encouragement, and troubleshooting as Jack engages with his course. But she's been up to a lot more when it comes to Jack. Her strategizing began when she sat in on Jack's final student-led PLP conference at his elementary school, which she tries to do for all of the students who will join her teacher advisory in the middle school the following year. Reviewing his PLP ahead of time, she knew she wouldn't really have the math chops, or the time, to create a custom curriculum to satisfy his obviously remarkable thirst for advanced math. But he immediately struck her as an interesting learner, a puzzle she'd need to solve. He struggled with his writing and despite his enthusiasm for learning, he hadn't yet blossomed into a child who could find much meaning in applying what he's learned. And after sitting through his conference, she knew she didn't want Jack to follow in the footsteps of previous middle schoolers who took a cab every day to the high school just to take advanced math courses. Those students missed out on too much else in their middle school life. It wasn't good for their development and it certainly wasn't good for her team's sense of cohesion and community. Meeting Jack's mother after that conference was encouraging; she shared that Jack had always been a self-motivated learner. That brief moment launched a strong teacher-parent col-laboration. It was his mom who'd found the Johns Hopkins course.

Now Ms. Duvay feels pleased that her strategic planning for Jack's pathway is paying off. The online calculus course has worked its magic for Jack the budding mathematician, especially after she asked the professor to set up a special chat room for the younger kids so they could be, well, kids together during the course. But more important, she's drawn Jack deeply into project work with his peers, including the sustainability unit they're currently engaged in. As she predicted last summer, once Jack understood the role of calculus in engineering and architecture, he leaped at the idea of joining the group working on sustainable living spaces. He's the group's lead architect, focusing on striking a perfect balance among cool-looking home designs, energy efficiency, and overall affordability. Others are becoming experts in building materials, the surrounding housing market, and the local building codes being hotly debated by the community. He's thrilled finally to be putting his math ability to good use, enough to finally give into Ms. Duvay's suggestion—very strong suggestion—that he write the script for the group's upcoming testimony at the town council's hearing on proposed efficiency guidelines for new homes.

After class Jack shuts his laptop and looks up. Ms. Duvay sits down next to him and asks how his session went. His eyes adjust to the classroom around him as she tells him that they should meet soon to discuss his next math course. She reminds him to add evidence and reflections from calculus, as well as from his upcoming work time with his sustainable spaces group, to his PLP so he can show what he knows in those areas as well. He's relieved when she tells him she's extending the work block to give everyone more time for reflection. He's pretty amazed at how much evidence is piling up as the town council hearing date rapidly approaches. And he can already imagine what artifacts he might use to show his growth across the targeted proficiencies. He knows his draft of the technical notes for the testimony will work nicely for "Integrate quantitative or technical information expressed in words in a text with a version of that information expressed visually." The writing part is harder for him, and it's a bit scary knowing it will become part of the town's public record. But he's interested in what he's seen in the playlist for Communicating for Advocacy that Ms. Duvay compiled for this unit. And his construction cost estimates make sense for the proficiency on Interpreting Categorical & Quantitative Data. He's feeling almost overwhelmed by how much evidence he has for "Apply scientific principles to design, construct, and test a device that either minimizes or maximizes thermal energy transfer."

Jack says suddenly, "Hey! Do you think my home design could count for art too?" Ms. Duvay smiles and encourages him to share his designs with his art teacher for feedback. She adds that he might also consider showing it to Ms. Davis, who teaches design technology, to see if he might make a 3D prototype of his design.

Jack is shocked and almost jumps out of his chair, exclaiming, "I can do that?"

"Yes," Ms. Duvay smiles. "You can do that." As she crosses the room to meet with another student, she sends a text to the art teacher: "Jack is coming re: architecture . . . isn't there a visual arts standard for designing places that meet a need?"

BUILDING YOUR RATIONALE: STUDENT ENGAGEMENT

Jack is clearly engaged in his work, and his involvement in the sustainability unit offered much of what he needed for that engagement. As educators, we know student engagement makes a big difference. The Schlechty Center, a private nonprofit educational organization, identified a set of five possible student responses to school-related tasks: engagement, strategic compliance, ritual compliance, retreatism, and rebellion. Only through engagement will students "learn at high levels and have a profound grasp of what they learn; retain what they learn; and transfer what they learn to new contexts."[1]

When a student is authentically engaged in learning, as opposed to merely being compliant, the student sees the task as personally meaningful; persists in the face of difficulty because of a high degree of interest; and finds the task sufficiently challenging to believe that she or he will accomplish something of worth.[2] And while teachers may achieve some success requiring students to be compliant, a far subtler approach is needed to get students engaged at this high standard.

The pursuit of engagement is further complicated by the developmental needs of young adolescents. As students move from elementary into the middle grades, student motivation and engagement often decline.[3] This is problematic on many levels, not the least of which is that engaged students are more likely to attend school, which in turn correlates with achievement and school completion.[4] While the causes are surely complex, Phillip Schlechty, founder of the Schlechty Center, posited that, "The reason America's schoolchildren are not learning what we want them to learn is that in too many instances they are being asked to do things they do not see as worth doing in order to learn things adults want them to learn."[5] Edward Brazee of the University of Maine similarly noted that, "The problem with middle school curriculum is that we ask students to give answers to questions they do not ask."[6]

Engaging learning needn't come at the expense of critical content knowledge and skills. The standards referred to in Jack's story come straight from the Next Generation Science Standards, the Common Core State Standards for Math and Literacy, and the National Arts Standards from the National Coalition for Core Arts Standards.[7] The difference is it's in the course of engaging learning that students see the immediate—and lasting—value in mastering content. Insights from neuroscience underscore this point. For learners to retain new information in the long term, it needs to both make sense and hold meaning. As David Sousa explains, "memory draws on the individual's past experiences to help it answer two questions: Does this new information make sense? and Does this information have meaning for me personally? When both sense and meaning are present, the likelihood of long-term storage is high."[8] Understanding the information is important but insufficient; a student must also find meaning within it.

As we construct learning opportunities for young adolescents, we need to consider, and inquire into, what students find engaging and meaningful. The Learner Profile, and the general emphasis of the PLP on knowing students well, provides a steady stream of critical insight we can leverage for learning. But in the course of designing learning pathways that are rich in engagement, both students and teachers begin to grapple with their new roles in a personalized learning environment. Recall from chapter 1 that, as they pursue flexible and engaging learning pathways, learners increasingly design challenging learning experiences based on their interests, aspirations, passions, and talents. They learn to self-direct how, when, and where learning takes place, as well as how to expand their learning environment.[9] To help students flourish in precisely these ways, teachers need to develop their roles as Empowerer and Scout.[10] As you'll see from the examples to come, there's ample evidence that students and teachers can successfully take up these challenges.

In this chapter's vignette, Ms. Duvay relied heavily on Jack's PLP and his PLP conference to quickly grasp who he was and what he needed. And while the Learner Profile captures critical information about a student, the PLP should also capture important artifacts and reflections from other rich learning opportunities. Teachers who benefit from reviewing a student's PLP owe a great debt to the teachers who came before them: For knowing their students well enough to craft engaging learning opportunities. For making time for students to document and reflect upon that learning in their PLPs. For what that does to foster more thoughtful, reflective, and self-directed learners. For sending along students ready to partner with their new teachers to design their next pathway. Integrating the PLP into the everyday course of designing and experiencing flexible pathways, where it can act as a barometer and catalog of engagement, greatly enhances its power in personalized learning.

CHAPTER OVERVIEW

We began this chapter with a vignette based on the flexible, student-directed pathways we've seen at several of our partner schools. It vividly conveys what it looks like when students are engaged in activities they view as personally meaningful, as students persist through challenges and setbacks because they see the work as worth doing and getting right.[11] It also depicts one possible component of a flexible pathway, taking an online course while targeting proficiencies aligned with individual academic strengths and weaknesses. Of course, Jack needed plenty of help from his teacher to craft such a pathway. And that's what this chapter is about. In it, we illustrate how students, in partnership with their teachers, can plan, experience, and document their own learning journeys. Because just as PLPs help us as teachers know students better, they can also help us manage meaningful and flexible pathways for learning.

We begin the chapter by identifying the purpose of flexible pathways and sharing what we've learned are particularly promising pedagogies for that purpose. The examples in this chapter present a variety of approaches to creating and managing flexible pathways. We illustrate how educators can work with students to design challenging learning tasks based on students' own questions, interests, and aspirations. And we consider the teacher's role as Empowerer and Scout along the way. Across these examples, you'll see how schools are integrating personalized and flexible pathways in various ways, including in discrete time blocks, within the core curriculum and as negotiated curriculum.

Above all, we hope you come away with the sense that you don't have to revamp your whole curriculum or risk the wrath of colleagues or administrators in order to appreciate the joy and enthusiasm of students engaged in work they deem worth doing well. Just as students benefit from flexible pathways for learning, so, too, do we as educators benefit from creating our own personally meaningful pathways in professional learning. And just as flexible pathways make possible more engaging and effective learning, your journey into flexible pathways will develop essential skills and dispositions that you and your students will need to fulfill your respective roles in a personalized learning environment.

JUST WHAT ARE FLEXIBLE PATHWAYS?

Like many concepts in education, ideas about what constitutes a flexible pathway abound. Before we share various models and examples, let's take a moment to consider some of them. According to the Vermont Agency of Education, flexible pathways "are any combination of high-quality expanded learning opportunities, including academic and experiential components, which build and assess attainment of identified proficiencies and lead to secondary school completion, civic engagement, and postsecondary readiness." These can include components such as blended and virtual learning; career technical education; service learning; dual enrollment; expanded learning opportunities; high school completion programs; and work based learning.[12] In other words, flexible pathways provide choices for learners that are rooted in their interests, skills, and opportunities. For many educators and families alike, it can be easier to imagine flexible pathways through high school. After all, students enrolling in a local college class isn't such a far-fetched idea. But what do these look like in the middle grades?

We think of flexible pathways for young adolescents in two ways. In the macro sense, students are charting a path through their education, unique to each, validating their life experiences, interests, and needs. In the micro sense, these pathways are steeped in the choices students encounter and make daily in the context of various learning tasks, projects, or assessments. For young adolescents in personalized learning environments, learning is ubiquitous. It's unlimited by the space and time constraints typically manifested in schools. Expanded learning opportunities become part of an engaging school curriculum, not relegated solely to after-school opportunities. Rooted in community asset, in this way, flexible pathways can increase equitable access to such rich experiences, open up the walls of the school, increase relevance, and broaden both youth and adult perspectives.

PROMISING PEDAGOGIES FOR ENGAGING AND EMPOWERING LEARNING

Flexible pathways are intended to promote engagement, but what *is* an engaging learning experience for young adolescents? Schlechty suggested that students are engaged in learning when they view the task as personally meaningful, persist even when the task gets hard, and believe they're accomplishing something worthwhile.[13] If this is what we're aiming for, how do we make it happen? How can teachers create the conditions for this level of engagement in the middle grades? The Association for Middle Level Education asserts that effective middle schools promote "active, purposeful learning" through a curriculum that is "challenging, exploratory, integrative, and relevant."[14] Research backs this up. When asked what types of learning activities they prefer, students this age often describe active, hands-on experiences over bookwork and lecture, and they appreciate the opportunity for an authentic audience.[15] They also tend to enjoy social and collaborative tasks, although they appreciate a balance of independent work. Many middle schoolers have an affinity for technology, which is not surprising given that thoughtful technology integration can respond to their needs for autonomy, responsibility, and competence.[16] And as we've discussed in previous chapters, the type of learning that helps them explore their identities and affords them a sense of agency can be particularly powerful, which is one of the reasons that service learning is a great match for this age group.[17] An important piece of one's identity is the ability to feel proud of something, to point to something at which you excel, or to be known as an expert about something and to feel that your work is making a positive difference in the world. Each of these aspects is a useful entry point into a wide and established swath of pedagogy that is fertile terrain for flexible pathways to personalized learning. And each is an important hallmark of personalized learning opportunities for young adolescents.

To summarize, as well as to help you consider which pedagogies will engage and empower young adolescents in learning opportunities, we offer the following questions. Reflect on your current approach or aspiration for teaching. Does the approach:

- build on students' own questions about themselves and the world?
- foster their basic needs for competence, affiliation, responsibility, awareness and an ethical sense of self?[18]
- honor students' developmental and cultural needs and identities?
- include opportunities for both collaborative and independent learning?
- respond to authentic and real-world issues?
- leverage technology to engage the local and global communities?
- maximize students' agency and ownership over the learning?

These questions can help you to select or refine powerful pedagogies in your classroom, team or school.

Fortunately, a number of teaching approaches activate many of these critical dimensions of young adolescent engagement. Some are likely familiar to you, such as project-based learning (PBL), service learning, design learning, deeper learning, place-based education, culture-based education, experiential education, expeditionary learning, and inquiry learning. Any one of these can serve as a useful starting point for rolling out flexible pathways in your own setting. Some may be uniquely suited to particular situations. Service learning and design learning, for instance, embark on solving real problems with others, focusing initially on empathy. Design learning then applies principles of engineering to prototype, test, and refine solutions, an ideal model for students developing products for use by others. But all of these pedagogies are grounded in inquiry and projects. And we encourage you not to get too caught up in semantics. As educators, we sometimes worry about implementing expeditionary learning exactly right, or we may wonder what the precise difference is between service learning and project-based learning. Instead, we suggest you explore them all so you can respond to your students' emerging interests and needs with flexibility rather than pedagogical dogma. Over the years we've learned to concern ourselves less with what an approach is called and more with taking advantage of what these rich and dynamic practices have to offer us and our students.

Let's take project-based learning, for instance. The Buck Institute for Education states that PBL enables students to work "for an extended period of time to investigate and respond to an authentic, engaging and complex question, problem, or challenge."[19] Some assert that project-based learning must be a collaborative effort, with teams working to answer a guiding question.[20] Others say PBL can be either an individual or group effort. Either way, learning of this nature can provide several essential ingredients for engaging and personalized learning: an opportunity for students to establish a personally meaningful direction for their learning; the chance to thoughtfully and collaboratively integrate real-world expertise; and the challenge to produce authentic evidence of accomplishment for a real-world audience. Each of these ingredients can be integrated into students' regular interactions with their PLPs.

In project-based learning, young adolescents and teachers identify a driving question they want to answer, and often work collaboratively to construct a solution or a contribution toward improving a condition. They focus for an extended period of time on their project, collaborate with local or global community stakeholders, and present to real-world audiences. Throughout the process, they regularly reflect and receive feedback and support from teachers and their peers.

You can see from table 5.1 the Buck Institute for Education's criteria for meeting their "gold standard" of PBL, that a project-based approach is a great

TABLE 5.1   **Buck Institute for education's gold standard PBL: Essential project design elements**

Key Knowledge, Understanding, and Success Skills	The project is focused on student learning goals, including standards-based content and skills such as critical thinking/problem solving, communication, collaboration, and self-management.
Challenging Problem or Question	The project is framed by a meaningful problem to solve or a question to answer, at the appropriate level of challenge.
Sustained Inquiry	Students engage in a rigorous, extended process of asking questions, finding resources, and applying information.
Authenticity	The project features real-world context, tasks and tools, quality standards, or impact—or speaks to students' personal concerns, interests, and issues in their lives.
Student Voice & Choice	Students make some decisions about the project, including how they work and what they create.
Reflection	Students and teachers reflect on learning, the effectiveness of their inquiry and project activities, the quality of student work, obstacles and how to overcome them.
Critique & Revision	Students give, receive, and use feedback to improve their process and products.
Public Product	Students make their project work public by explaining, displaying and/or presenting it to people beyond the classroom.

Source: Buck Institute for Education.

match for a personalized learning environment.[21] Because, regardless of what you call it, a personalized environment embodies a student-centered approach to student engagement and empowerment.

When project learning includes a service component, linked to a greater good, it intersects with service learning, which is "a method of teaching/learning that challenges students to identify, research, propose, and implement solutions to real needs in their school [or local] community as part of their curriculum."[22] Service learning occurs as students connect the curriculum, including skills and content, with authentic community needs. Educators often adopt a five-stage model to implementing service learning: investigating, planning and preparation, implementing the service activity, reflecting, and demonstrating and celebrating.[23] Despite this model, service learning doesn't necessarily follow a linear progression, and phases of service learning vary with different learners, projects, and contexts. It is important, however, that students deeply understand the central issues before embarking on a service experience, and that they have regular opportunities to reflect on their learning. One goal of service learning is to disrupt any existing biases through direct experience. Service learning that focuses on doing something *for*, instead of *with*, another group runs the risk of increasing stereotypes and biases. The concept of reciprocal learning is critical: that we learn with and from each other, and that everyone benefits. By integrating service into personalized learning, we can create shared experiences that connect students deeply to their communities, while increasing motivation, engagement and meaning.[24]

In their best expressions, PBL and service learning are both highly engaging pedagogies for middle schoolers. Many young adolescents have a strong desire to improve the world around them. Issues of fairness and justice can be paramount at this age. We encourage you to invite your students to think about how their projects might improve their communities. They might increase access to literacy skills by reading with younger students, teach elders how to use technology, or hold community forums on relevant and challenging issues, to name just a few ideas for integrating service into learning.

Of course, this kind of teaching and learning doesn't happen by accident. Mindful and strategic planning of any kind of project work is essential to success. As was the case with Jack's sustainable living spaces group, schools and teachers need to make time, structures, and protocols for this engaging learning to occur. A first step in planning project-oriented learning is to consider your access point. Will it be one unit, in one subject? Will it be a teamwide, integrated unit of study? Will you focus on a proficiency, standard, or transferable skill as a starting point in planning? Or will you select an overall content area? You'll see that many approaches share these central concepts, although they may have different names: a driving question, an entry event, teams of students researching and developing a product or presentation, frequent reflection, and an authentic culminating event where students share their work to a relevant audience.[25] When teachers create the conditions for students to ask and answer their own questions, as they do in service and project-based learning, they lay the groundwork for student empowerment.

In table 5.2, we share a template that captures the essence of these concepts and helps guide initial planning to building each into a project-based unit.[26] Note the similarities with Katy's Service Learning Planning Template (table 5.3).

TABLE 5.2 **PBL planning template**

PBL Planning Template by Katy Farber, Rachel Mark & Jeanie Phillips Tarrant Institute for Innovative Education, UVM Created from resources at Edutopia, Buck Institute and others	
Project Name:	Grade Levels:
Team/Teachers:	Content area(s):
Knowledge and Skills: Decide what content knowledge/performance indicators/proficiencies you hope to address with the project. Also, decide on which transferable skills you will teach and assess through the unit. List these below.	
Driving (or guiding) Question: Decide on a guiding question you would like students to consider. It should create motivation, sustained interest and a feeling of challenge. Examples (and guidance): ▪ How do the events of the civil rights era impact our society today? ▪ How does extreme weather impact different climate zones? ▪ How does probability relate to games? ▪ Why is science important and how can it help save people?	
Demonstration of Learning (what will students create?): Decide on what students will produce to authentically demonstrate their learning. Consider voice and choice within these products and the option to let students generate these ideas (books, videos, maps, websites, models, plays, etc.). *Examples*: Project search tool from BIE and examples from TIIE.	
Launch/Entry Event: Decide on an engaging entry event for the project launch. What will you do to spark student interest? Consider field trips, virtual field trips, dramatic skits by teachers, guest speakers, artifacts of meaning, etc. *Examples* and ideas here.	
Culminating Event/Exhibition: Decide on a community sharing event. Make it authentic and important. Who will be the audience? Is it authentic and motivating for students? *Examples*: here.	
Timeline: After you schedule the exhibition event, work backwards to create a timeline for the project (leave in an extra few days for rehearsing). *Example*: blank calendar, but any calendar planning tool will work.	
Learning Experiences and Artifacts: How will students acquire knowledge and practice skills? What will students create to synthesize knowledge and demonstrate skill? *Consider*: Community experts, interviews, creating scripts, research notes, plans.	
Scaffolds: What scaffolding or supports might be needed? List websites, readings, resources, and job roles that you think would work for your students. *Examples*: Padlet to curate resources with students; specific roles for students, text sets at various levels.	
Reflection: Design opportunities for students to reflect on their project work throughout the experience. *Examples* and ideas here.	
Assessment: Design assessments—these can be teamwork oriented, product oriented, and content oriented, or all 3! Think about what assessments will be formative and summative. *Examples* and ideas here.	
Project Evaluation: How will you and your students evaluate the project? *Examples/templates*: for students and for teachers?	

Source: Created by Katy Farber, Rachel Mark & Jeanie Phillips at the Tarrant Institute for Innovative Education from resources at Edutopia, Buck Institute, and others. For linked examples and more guidance, visit www.learninginthemiddle.org.

TABLE 5.3   **Service learning planning template**

Service Learning Planning Template
by Katy Farber Tarrant Institute for Innovative Education, UVM inspired by KIDS consortium materials and our PBL template

Project Name:	Grade Level:
Team/Teachers:	Content area(s):

Discover Strengths of Community (do these with students, but brainstorm your ideas first):
- List community assets.
- List community resources.
- Interview some community members from a strengths-based perspective (see these questions for inspiration).
- Consider diving deep into your community with a project to get to know it deeply, such as this one called Humans of Burke. This could also be a Flipgrid or documentary about your community.
- What will be your strategy for discovering the strengths of your community?

Discover Needs of Community:
- Explore relevant and interesting needs, issues, and problems facing the community using an engaging activity, such as a video, field trip, simulation, or thought provoking questions, quotes, or images.
- Use multiple resources: community members, media, student perspectives, websites, and data.
  - You can create curated text sets around different issues for your students.
  - You can create note-catchers or graphic organizers for these texts.
- What will be your strategy for discovering the issues facing your community?

Knowledge and Skills: Decide what content knowledge/performance indicators/proficiencies you hope to address with the project. Also, decide on which transferable skills you will teach and assess through the unit. List these below.

Investigate and Research Problems
- Have students identity problem areas they are most interested in.
- Group students by interest and other considerations.
- Teams begin researching the causes and effects of the problem.
- Teams begin researching possible solutions.
- Consider what scaffolds students will need for this research. What should they create?

Decide on a Project: Students will decide what they will create to address the community problem. This should be student-generated with teacher and peer feedback.
- Make sure the project is doable in the time period allotted. It should be ambitious, not impossible.
- Make sure students can access the materials they need for the project.
- How will your students share their projects and learning? On their PLPs, or another way?

Plan the Project:
- Students should create an action plan for the project with a timeline,
- Students should list out materials they will need.
- Students should list out possible community partners to help with their work and begin contacting them (with support).
- Students and teachers should identify the culminating event for the project and work backwards to create the project timeline and action plan.

(continued)

TABLE 5.3   **Service learning planning template** (*continued*)

Implementing Project: ▪ Students acting on project plans. ▪ Coordinating and leading planned events. ▪ Creating shareable items as evidence of learning. ▪ Completing regular reflections (weekly at least) about their learning.
Culminating Event/Exhibition: Decide on a community sharing event for the service learning projects. Make it authentic and important. Who will be the audience? Is it authentic and motivating for students? *Examples*: here.
Learning Experiences and Artifacts: How will students acquire knowledge and practice skills? What will students create to synthesize knowledge and demonstrate skill? *Consider*: Community experts, interviews, creating scripts, research notes, plans. Will they put these in a PLP? Website, or other location?
Scaffolds: What scaffolding or supports might be needed? List websites, readings, resources, and job roles that you think would work for your students. *Examples*: Padlet to curate resources with students; specific roles for students, text sets at various levels
Reflection: Design opportunities for students to reflect on their project work throughout the experience. *Examples* and ideas here.
Assessment: Design assessments—these can be teamwork oriented, product oriented, and content oriented, or all 3! Think about what assessments will be formative and summative. *Examples* and ideas here.
Project Evaluation: How will you and your students evaluate the project? *Examples/templates*: for students and for teachers

For linked examples and more guidance, visit www.learninginthemiddle.org.

TEACHER AS EMPOWERER: HELPING STUDENTS DESIGN CHALLENGING LEARNING EXPERIENCES

Students in personalized learning environments learn, over time, to "design challenging learning experiences based on their interests, aspirations, passions and talents."[27] As teachers, then, we need to create opportunities for them to learn the skills and develop the dispositions that will serve them well in this endeavor. For young adolescents, this starts by helping them pose meaningful and relevant questions.

Driving Questions

Driving questions invite curiosity, prolonged inquiry, and meaningful exploration.[28] They are often based on clear learning expectations and goals as outlined by adopted standards or proficiencies. They are best co-created with students to increase buy-in and relevance. They can be subject-specific or integrated with a wider focus. The key is that they connect to student experiences and curiosities. They invite students to wonder and learn. You likely have experience soliciting students' interests in a variety of ways. We've seen considerable success when teachers adopt a negotiated curriculum model.

Young adolescents are filled with questions about themselves and the world around them. Inviting—and giving time for—students to express these questions can be a powerful entry point into personalized learning and the PLP in particular. James A. Beane, noted democratic schools advocate, asserted, "Curriculum integration begins with the idea that the sources of curriculum ought to be problems, issues, and concerns posed by life itself. . . . Such concerns fall into two spheres: (1) self- or personal concerns and (2) issues and problems posed by the larger world."[29] In Beane's negotiated curriculum model, students are invited to ask questions about themselves and the world as a means of developing curriculum.[30] Of course there are lots of ways to invite students into wondering and posing questions. A number of Vermont schools have found negotiated curriculum to be a fruitful way to make learning more personal through honoring students' questions. Some, like the Alpha Team at Shelburne Community School, have used such questions as the basis for curriculum for more than forty years![31] Others have adopted the approach more recently. Either way, teachers increasingly recognize that students are a rich source of fertile questions for inquiry.

PERSONALIZATION IN PRACTICE Essex Middle School and
Shelburne Community School

Educators Lindsey Halman and Phil Young from Essex Middle School adapted Beane's process for their own setting (see table 5.4). On their team, students begin the process by posing questions about themselves, responding to two prompts: What do you want to know about yourself? And what questions do you have about yourself? Educators on the team model how to develop insightful questions and students have dedicated time during class to reflect and use a variety of media to develop and record their questions. At home, they share their questions with families and continue to reflect and refine them. The goal is for each learner to bring a solid list of thoughtful questions to class the next day. Students then work in small groups that represent as much diversity as possible,

TABLE 5.4 **Curriculum development process, Essex Middle School, The Edge Academy**

Phase I: Questions about Self

Phase 2: Questions about the World

Phase 3: Theme Development
- **Stage 1:** Small groups of students develop themes.
- **Stage 2:** Small groups present their themes.
- **Stage 3:** Independently, learners research, read and reflect on these proposed themes.
- **Stage 4:** "Dotmocracy" yields two themes connected to team mission and vision (e.g., Sustainability).

Phase 4: Theme Design
- **Stage 1:** Students and facilitators ask:
  - Where does sustainability come in? Community/global connections/partnerships? Technology? Arts?
  - What are some possible investigations/projects?
  - How are these investigations tied to our standards?
  - How can we use our local campus and outdoor classroom?
- **Stage 2:** What resources, activities, roles, responsibilities and evidence will demonstrate progress? How will we assess progress based on your standards/personal/community goals?
- **Stage 3:** Students discuss learning opportunities and assessment vehicles, and select different approaches for this theme, so that various learning needs are met.

Source: Lindsey Halman, Essex Middle School, Edge Academy.

sharing their questions with one another. Together, they seek commonalities that they then record on large paper and post in their classroom or hallway gallery. These small groups combine to form one or two larger groups, again looking for common themes across groups. These are also recorded and hung in a place for all to view. The students go through a similar process to consider the questions they have about the world, reflecting on two prompts: What do you want to know about the world? And what questions do you have about the world? Table 5.5 includes examples of self and world questions from students on Lindsey and Phil's team. You can imagine how these might provide helpful fodder for creating relevant and personalized learning opportunities.

After students have had a chance to pose questions in a negotiated curriculum model, they then work together to identify themes across the sets of questions. Using a process such as dot-voting or consensus building, the middle schoolers vote on the direction(s) their curriculum will take.[32] Table 5.6 shows how students on the Alpha Team at Shelburne Community School, working with teacher Meg O'Donnell and her colleagues, grouped their own self and world questions into the theme of conflict.

TABLE 5.5   **Questions about self and world: Edge Academy Students, Essex Middle School**

Questions about Myself	Questions about the World
What is my purpose in life?	Why do species go extinct?
Why do I look the way I do?	Does time repeat?
Would I be alive if my mom hadn't met my dad?	Will humans be able to travel further into space?
Why do I have a fear of heights?	When will the sun explode?
Why are my dreams so wacky?	How will technology advance?
What is my ancestry?	Will sicknesses ever be cured or evolve?
Will I always stay the same person?	What will happen with global warming?
Why do I have depression?	Why do people think it's ok to eat other animals?
Which job will I have?	What is it like to be someone else?
Which college am I going to go to?	How will politics change?
Why does food taste so good?	Will we ever find other life forms?
When will I die?	What happens after we die?
Why am I the height I am?	How will Earth change in the future?
Why do I have the color hair I have?	Will the Earth die out?
Why do I like my favorite color?	What made the Earth?
Is there anyone in the world who looks like me?	What happens after you die?
Why does my hair grow so fast?	What if there were no galaxies?
How long will I live?	What caused the big bang?
Why do I love reptiles?	If there was one thing on earth everyone could agree on, what would it be?
Why am I a morning person?	Is anything real?
Why do I need glasses?	
Why did I shave half my head?	
Why can I never finish an assignment on time?	
How would my personality be different if I were a different gender?	

These rich and relevant questions lead us to see how easily they could be explored through both personal and academic lenses, as well as how clearly connected they are to meaningful PLPs. The student-identified themes, such as conflict, become the driver of curriculum, a lens the team will apply in interdisciplinary and integrative ways. When students pose and answer their own questions, they engage in personally meaningful work and create collective meaning in a supportive and personalized learning environment.

Challenging Learning Experiences

Once fertile questions have been identified, teachers can partner with their students to determine how they will explore these questions and design the

TABLE 5.6 **Questions about conflict, grouped from self and world questions: Shelburne Community School, Alpha Team**

How does world conflict impact our daily lives?
How will war affect our future?
What would our world be like without conflict?
Will there be a WWIII? If so, when? What will be the cause?
How close are we to a major conflict with North Korea?
When will humans start to colonize other planets?
How have actions from the past changed my life?
Do I have anything in my past that affects me today?
Will the future weather patterns become more and more violent?
Does global warming play a role in the hurricanes?
How do we slow our consumption of the natural resources?
How does social media affect my friendships?
How can we prevent endangered species from becoming extinct?

ensuing work. Note that in *Phase 4: Theme Design* in table 5.4, students puzzle through the selection of resources, design of learning activities, and integration of goals and standards to ensure all students are successful. Their process, even in student-friendly language, is basically sound whether executed by students or teachers. Some teachers value an engaging entry event, those fun, exciting launches that kids remember forever. Perhaps a field trip to the landfill, putting a character on trial, running an election, or debating the merits of proposed legislation. Entry events jumpstart students' thinking about the driving question and topic. You and your students will also need to determine the various project tasks, as well as how students will acquire the skills and knowledge they need to be successful in those tasks. You'll want to consider the various ways students might demonstrate their learning. And create a culminating event grounded in authentic, real-world purpose and impact. It not only sets up an authentic audience for the learning, itself a strong motivation for students to own and vigorously pursue their learning, but it also drives clearer thinking about interim milestones and the activities, tasks, and just-in-time learning needed to meet them. It's up to you and your students to define each of these components of challenging learning. And referring to the essentials of any number of project-oriented pedagogies can provide a useful guide to keep things on track.

PERSONALIZATION IN PRACTICE Leland and Gray Union
Middle School

During their third PBL unit of the year, in collaboration with our colleague, professional development coordinator Jeanie Phillips, teachers at Leland and Gray
Middle School wanted students to craft their own challenging learning experiences based on their interests and passions, while also making a difference in
their community. Employing service learning as a model, students began by
investigating their school setting, using the categories of safety, environment,
beautification, community spaces, community-building, and school culture
to identify problems and opportunities that existed around them. In advisory
groups, they explored their campus and town, and they mapped their community, using a graphic organizer as a tool for recording ideas as they walked.
After returning to school and consolidating their list of possible problems to
address, they used dot-voting to select the initiatives they wanted to take on.
This resulted in four projects: creating a new outdoor classroom, painting com-
munity-minded murals, beautifying the campus through nature, and maintaining and renovating local trails. Using Google forms, students selected the one
they wanted to work on.

Having identified their projects, the work teams then engaged in common
or jigsaw readings to learn more about their topics. They generated action plans
including resources and a timeline. And they crafted grant proposals conveying
the purpose and importance of their project in order to obtain outside funding
for materials. It's remarkable what these young adolescents accomplished. In
addition to creating an outdoor classroom and new murals for the school community to enjoy, they rebuilt a bridge, cleared trails, added a welcoming arbor,
seeded the property with sustainable and noninvasive plants, and beautified
their school grounds with box planters tended with newly learned skills.[33] Along
the way, they learned about community development and mapping, horticul-
tural care, and project management. They honed their collaboration and leadership skills. And they acquired a host of skills transferable to many contexts.

Throughout the unit, the teachers at Leland and Gray provided ample time
for planning and they were careful to build in time for thoughtful reflection.
They regularly posed questions such as:

- What was satisfying about today's work? What was challenging?

- How did your plan support the work you did today? How might you improve your plan?
- If others wanted to do a project like this, what advice would you give them?
- What went well? What could be improved?

The teachers also made sure students had time to celebrate and demonstrate their contributions to the community. At a Project Showcase on their last day of school, students presented their projects to the broader community, giving tours and explaining their learning as they walked together. As one student wrote about the new outdoor classroom, "I think the classroom looks great and we worked really hard on this project. I think that people will use this classroom for many years including after we graduate!"

TEACHER AS SCOUT: HELPING STUDENTS EXPAND THE LEARNING ENVIRONMENT TO INCLUDE THE COMMUNITY

To be successful, the students and educators at Leland and Gray Middle School needed a wide array of resources. While they could access some of these at school, they also needed materials and expertise from their community at large. As students increasingly identify questions of personal relevance and engage in myriad ways of designing and solving problems, the need to engage outside of the school walls increases. As a result, teachers in these settings often serve as scouts, seeking out new forms of support and inspiration for their learners. In addition to materials, students might also require consultation with experts on topics teachers know little about. Teachers in personalized classrooms help students to "expand the learning environment to include the local and global community."[34] This means beyond the school walls, beyond the school day, and beyond their typical human and material resources. It also means opening up demonstrations of learning to new audiences, throughout the learning and at the end through culminating events, as with Leland and Gray Middle School's culminating Project Showcase.

PERSONALIZATION IN PRACTICE Cornwall Elementary School

At Cornwall Elementary School, our colleague and professional development coordinator (and then sixth-grade teacher) Emily Hoyler quite literally helped her students expand their learning environment. Fort building at recess was a long-standing tradition, awarded only to sixth graders as a privilege. Students at this school looked forward to earning that right as they entered the sixth grade. Unfortunately, concerns about safety led the school to revoke the privilege. The students who were in sixth grade at the time were learning about the United Nation's Sustainable Development Goals and were especially intrigued by the Global Goal for Equity.[35] They wondered how they might continue to enjoy this important part of their school experience in acceptable ways, bringing fort building back not only for themselves, but for all students at the school. Together with their teacher, the students posed the real and relevant question: How can we build a playground where students across ages can safely built forts together and engage in creative play? From this question, a project was born.[36]

Emily and her students began an ambitious project, rooted in place-based and project-based learning, to create a Loose Parts Playground at their school. Students wanted to create a space full of materials that they could use to build and play. They collaborated to write a proposal, gather materials, interview free play experts about risks and hazards, and reflect on their learning and progress along the way. They leveraged technology continually, as they researched materials, wrote the proposal, and composed posts to their community's email list service and school newsletter asking for donations. They also captured digital images during the project for documentation purposes.

As you might imagine, the project called for students to explore core content across many subject areas, such as learning about the safety of PVC to inform their decision about whether to include PVC pipes in the play area. Students created a video and website to tell the story of how the Loose Parts Playground came to be, working with several community partners, including representatives from the local cable television station who trained them in filming. They were invited as keynote speakers at a statewide educational conference, reflecting on their learning story and sharing the metaphor that teachers needed to let students "off the leash" in their own learning.

Learning was personal for these students in many ways. They cared about the work, as it was deeply relevant to their daily lives. They assumed roles that matched their interests, skills, and goals. For instance, one student had identified "uploading a video to YouTube" as a PLP goal. He became the project manager for the documentary and completed his goal in the course of the project. When asked about the experience, students were quick to state that it didn't "feel like it was school." Rather, the experience felt like a project lab, an entrepreneurial company, and a community workplace. Students felt a sense of purpose and agency. Perhaps the most important impact was one of legacy—these sixth graders left a playground for others as they departed their small community school to attend seventh grade in a nearby town.

PERSONALIZATION IN PRACTICE   Cabot School

The middle grades in Cabot, Vermont, are spread across two buildings (K–6 and 7–12) on one rural campus, resulting at times in a disconnect for the school's young adolescents. The middle school teachers wanted to bridge this disconnect. They were eager for all middle graders to feel involved, engaged, and affiliated with the middle school. They also wanted to promote student leadership and hoped to connect students to their community. Creating "Cabot Leads," a middle school leadership program based in service learning, was the teachers' answer to making learning more personal and engaging, while cultivating a strong community and sense of belonging.

Using LaunchPad, a project-based learning application that shares links, proficiencies, and learning experiences with students in an organized, engaging way, the teachers organized and structured the experience for students. In the program, middle school students identify a school or community-based job that connects with their interests and skills and meets a need in their school community. In the past, some of these jobs have included Tech Hero, Farm-to-School Coordinator, Culinary Assistant, Library Assistant, and School News Team member. Students apply for these jobs by writing and submitting a resume and cover letter and participating in an interview. Students then are matched with a job and a mentor and serve the school community for at least an hour a week throughout the school year. As the year progresses, each student creates a portfolio of the experience, including journal entries, photos, and work samples. Digital technology is heavily leveraged for this documentation and these artifacts gradually become part of students' PLPs, ultimately showcased at a spring exhibition of learning.

In their reflections, students often comment on their increased involvement and learning, noting their growing sense of purpose, identity, and belonging. And students appreciate their increased responsibility and independence, which are developmentally appropriate for these youth. Cadence, a middle schooler who works with younger students as a physical education assistant twice per week, noted, "I've learned to persevere when the kids don't listen, and try to get them interested. Being a gym assistant teaches me responsibility and makes me less shy. Having this opportunity is really important because this job or working in athletics might be something I would choose to do when I grow up. I'm learning time management and patience." Nialls, a culinary assistant, helps prepare food in the school kitchen every Tuesday. Echoing this sentiment of new learning, he explained, "I never thought that preparing the food for the school could be so much work! I get a voice in selecting new entrees for lunch and learning food preparation skills. I enjoy working as a member of the culinary team."

Cabot Leads validates all kinds of careers and learners. It offers flexible and diverse opportunities that extend far beyond traditional academic settings, such as helping to run the school's culinary program, work at a local goat farm, and staff the concession stand at sporting events. Students are encouraged to reflect on their own interests and talents and consider how these can be put to use to improve the school and community. In many ways, Cabot Leads brings together many facets of powerful and personalized learning in the middle grades: inviting student voice, cultivating new skills, offering authentic, real-world tasks, and fostering a sense of belonging.

PERSONALIZATION IN PRACTICE   Burke Town School

Recall Burke Town School? In this town of fewer than 2,000 people, most eighth graders attend the same small K–8 school for all nine years. Educators at the school noticed that many of these eighth graders were struggling to engage meaningfully in school, which in turn was impacting school climate. The team of middle school and related arts teachers decided the students needed a change. After discussing various ideas for increasing relevance and engagement, they settled on an integrated, long-term capstone project for the eighth-grade students, one that could be driven by community connections, student interests, and the United Nation's Sustainable Development Goals. The team began planning projects using LaunchPad, a project-based learning application, and curating resources for research via Padlet, an online sticky note organization tool.[37]

Earlier we described how these students explored their rural community's identity through a Humans of Burke block print project. Building on this, the students participated in a virtual reality experience, using "The Displaced" resources from the *New York Times*, to build empathy for immigrant and refugee populations and learn about the Sustainable Development Goals. These eighth graders then identified and targeted their own community issues, including poverty, food systems, health and safety, sustainable forestry, and clean energy. They partnered with community members to explore areas such as revitalizing the village infrastructure, as well as attending to water systems, business growth, and affordable housing. And they investigated traffic safety and trails, considering how to slow cars down and how to build a trail to connect East and West Burke.

Students worked at their own pace, with support and feedback from peers and their teacher, and with resources they selected for their own interests, needs and levels. Participating in carefully organized, project-based learning groups, the students forged connections with fifteen local organizations to embark upon their Projects for Hope. They worked out in the community, coming into regular contact with community mentors and student peers engaged in similar work. They connected with peer collaborators through regular Google Hangouts and presented their work at local school board and regional development meetings. Some, like the task force on a community garden, even proposed and earned grants, creating talks modeled on Ted Talks as part of the funding pitch. In each of these ways, the students experienced opportunities for real work with an authentic audience.

The learning from this project, and a learner's particular pathway through it, is another great example of personalized learning that can be documented in the PLP through weekly reflections, check-ins, photos, video, and assignments. The positive impact of Projects for Hope was multifaceted. The community benefited from the local projects the students pursued. Students benefited from the opportunity to demonstrate efficacy and responsibility. And the school benefited in many ways, not the least of which was that the school climate improved, as measured by parent feedback, community interest in partnering with the school, and a decline in behavioral referrals.

PERSONALIZATION IN PRACTICE The Dorset School

Of course, expanding the learning environment isn't only about contributing *to* the community. It's also about acknowledging how much we have to learn *from* the community that surrounds us. Communities are filled with rich human resources, individuals and groups who are often happy to serve as mentors, experts, and guides for our learners. As teachers help students expand the learning environment, they come to recognize that interacting with an authentic audience should not be relegated to the end of a project; it's beneficial much of the time.[38] In high-quality personalized learning, students work regularly with community mentors and partners to improve their work, reaching out via email and meeting virtually or in person to get feedback on their projects.

When the eighth graders at the Dorset School noticed that their cafeteria didn't serve local eggs from free-range chickens, they wondered if it might be possible to raise chickens at the school for this purpose. The students researched how to care for chickens and studied the conditions chickens require to be healthy and productive. As the students' work continued, it became clear that they would benefit from some insider knowledge. Visiting a local farm in the middle of this inquiry gave them invaluable experience from which to draw for the later stages of the project. They had the opportunity to handle the chickens and learn how to hold them properly and safely. They asked the farmer important questions, such as, "How do you keep the water from freezing?" "Can you keep the chickens warm when it gets cold?" and "How do you clean the coop?"[39] Could they have continued along with their project without consulting an expert? Probably. Was their work ultimately better for having expanded their learning environment to include the local farm? Quite likely. Are Dorset students now enjoying fresh eggs in the cafeteria that come from the school's own chickens? Most definitely.

LOOKING AHEAD: SCAFFOLDING FLEXIBLE PATHWAYS

Planning and carrying out engaging learning experiences with students always takes more time than you expect, especially as you and your students are acquiring the requisite skills to do so more efficiently. But the fact that students are acquiring the skills of designing rich and engaging learning opportunities, so central to their flourishing in a personalized learning environment now and in the future, makes it worth investing the time. They will get better at designing learning experiences, and you'll get better at guiding the process. By partnering as designers of learning, you're going a long way to eliminating the guesswork of creating engaging learning opportunities and ensuring that more experiences yield the deep and meaningful learning that sticks with students well beyond the final assessment.

We hope the various examples of personalization in practice have helped you to imagine how educators are using service and project-based approaches to personalize learning with and for students. Learning that sticks. You'll have noticed that many examples were rooted in students' authentic questions about themselves and the world. They offered hands-on and experiential opportunities for students to select among myriad pathways or to chart their own flexible approach to learning. And they provided students with chances to develop and demonstrate key aspects of their early adolescent development, such as independence, autonomy, competence, and responsibility. In chapter 6, we introduce you to more ways of supporting flexible pathways as we explore the role of scaffolding in this work.

SIX

SCAFFOLDING FOR EQUITABLE, DEEPER LEARNING

During his fleeting prep time, Mr. Williams heads down the hall toward his classroom. His teammate, Ms. Sanchez, breezes by at a rapid clip, holding large sheets of cardboard and some sort of wire, her balance focused but precarious. He smiles as they fly by one another. It was Ms. Sanchez's idea that sparked much of the work that shapes his own class today. Ms. Sanchez was the one who had heard first about Google's concept of 20 percent time and who suggested their students have a similar block of time to explore their own interests and passions. It seemed revolutionary just two years ago. The whole faculty took a leap of faith, planned ten one-hour sessions for Fridays throughout the spring semester, enlisted adult mentors from across the school and community and dove in. It was far from perfect that first year. But what they observed was convincing. They saw previously disengaged students now creating elaborate projects of their own design. They observed increased attendance on Fridays. They noticed new adult-student relationships grow, creating additional role models for students. And they observed a better climate overall.

Mr. Williams considers how those schoolwide passion projects have also offered the faculty a shared focal point and a shared commitment. They seem to help focus their efforts, personal discoveries and inspirations. And the learning opportunities across teams feel both more equitable and more sustainable now. The ball is *definitely rolling, he thinks as he reaches his room. Since the passion projects began, he's noticed, students have been adding to their PLPs much more regularly. He pops open his Google Doc on which all of his students' PLPs are linked. He clicks open Liza's and sees her identity page, featuring her piano with her cat stretched across the top, and her latest composition linked below it. Since the passion projects, Liza's PLP has revealed a whole world that Mr. Williams had known nothing about—her musical world. First, it seemed to him, Liza had needed to know that her musical life mattered, that it was important and valued. She'd also needed scaffolding to understand how to share her learning effectively. Once he had helped her to imagine possible types of evidence, Liza had been off and running, recording her music, sharing her composi-tions, and reflecting on her learning in various ways.*

Mr. Williams clicks on the Making link and sees Liza's latest work: a 3D sculpture that represents the theme of her latest piano composition: it is a mix of vinyl covered wire, aluminum foil, and an LED light, shaped into a scene of a turbulent ocean, and a blinking, tiny lighthouse. Her description is recorded via QuickTime and inserted directly below the picture. Mr. Williams marvels. When he went to school, there were only a few acceptable ways to show one's learning. Usually it was a written report or a test. Handwriting was a priority, and his was always rushed, leaning, and squished together. Oh, how that had mattered. He smiles, thinking about how his students now express themselves in so many ways.

After he had seen Ms. Sanchez give students so many creative options for reflec-tion, such as sketchnotes, Flipgrids, and VoiceThread, his own thinking about how to demonstrate learning expanded. Supported by the schoolwide passion projects, other teachers also began to try new approaches to student reflection. They experi-mented with various ways to scaffold reflection and had ended up creating a school-wide visual menu for students to use. In one sense, innovation had blossomed in the schoolwide passion projects, and the seeds traveled to each class. In another, innova-tion began in one teacher's classroom and had inspired the building. And just as Mr. Williams had learned much from Ms. Sanchez, so, too, are colleagues now are visiting his classroom to see how students lead their days, run morning meeting, support each other in class, and add evidence to PLPs they are proud to share. He muses about how the school now feels like a learning community for students and teachers alike. He appreciates learning from his colleagues and is glad to help them learn as well. These days, he better understands what engagement looks like and, importantly, how to support and scaffold students in that engaging learning.

BUILDING YOUR RATIONALE: FOSTERING EQUITY

Designing and sustaining flexible pathways taps the best instructional practices each teacher—and the whole profession—has to offer. And we haven't met a teacher yet who isn't relieved to find new practices they can adopt to address the ever-emerging demands of personalized learning. In the last chapter, we looked at many of these practices through the lens of Empowerer and Scout, critical roles in launching student in fruitful directions on their respective pathways. In this chapter, we shift to much of the nitty gritty of day-to-day instruction. Much will be familiar to you, but in most instances, you'll see even your favorite go-to practices in a new light. And you'll want to keep this light shining as you refine old practices and adopt new ones. That's how you'll stay true to your personal purpose for personalization. That's how you'll stay on the path to the unique opportunities for students promised by personalized and flexible pathways.

We want to introduce here, before you dive into the many instructional strategies our teachers have applied to flexible pathways, additional justification, motivation, and challenge for getting personalized and flexible pathways right. In the course of this work, you have an opportunity to right a long-standing wrong, and to focus on building a personalized learning environment that truly serves all students. This moment in education, with culture, science, technology, policy, and pedagogy so remarkably aligned, perhaps we can finally make significant headway toward truly equitable access to engaging learning opportunities. If we don't try, from policymaking on down to how we select, develop, and deploy our new strategies and roles, we will surely be more likely to replicate—perhaps exacerbate—existing inequality than to rectify it.

In their report on equity and deeper learning, Pedro Noguera, Linda Darling-Hammond, and Diane Friedlaender remind educators to "resist the tendency to teach all students in exactly the same way, or to make judgments about their ability based upon a few arbitrary measures of progress. Rather, our understanding of learning and development makes it clear that to really bring deeper learning to all, we need a student-centered approach."[1] As we consider our purposes and goals for personalized learning, research increasingly demonstrates that student-centered, personalized and proficiency-based approaches are a promising way to increase equitable outcomes, especially for African

American, Latinx, low-income students, and English language learners. In fact, underserved students in student-centered, personalized, proficiency-based learning environments have been found to outperform their counterparts in traditional settings on state assessments, showed increased graduation rates, and persisted in their college educations.[2]

As you proceed through this chapter, and reflect on previous ones, imagine the marginalized, the disempowered, and poorly served students in your midst. You learned in the last chapter a variety of ways to empower them to pursue issues of deep meaning to them. And being young adolescents, they are ready to engage with some of the world's deepest challenges regarding identity and justice. But they will not succeed in those inquiries, nor will success be experienced equitably, unless the extensive scaffolding needed in flexible pathways is built with those ends in mind.

CHAPTER OVERVIEW

In the opening vignette, Mr. Williams is fortunate to work in a learning organization. The teachers learn from one another, take healthy risks as they try new strategies in their professional lives, and support one another in this work. Along the way, they're modeling for students what it's like to try new things, to learn from mistakes, and to collaborate.

In this chapter, we draw on examples from individuals innovating in the interest of their students. We also illustrate how whole schools are experimenting together as educators. As in the case of Mr. Williams's school, we think both of these happening together is the hallmark of an innovative school, one truly embracing the path to personalized learning. Such schools recognize the power of individuals and small groups of teachers pursuing personally meaningful and immediately relevant pathways for their own learning. At the same time, these schools recognize that equitable access to personalized learning opportunities—and by that we mean equitable success as well—hinges on whole schools, with every faculty member on board, experimenting together with personalization. Most of us are all too familiar with "innovative" teachers or teams. They can be wildly successful, especially when they're guided by sound principles of teaching and learning. But far more often than not, they flourish—and sometimes languish—in obscurity, isolated in corners of a building, frustrated by local systems and policies, marginalized among their colleagues, and sometimes brought down altogether by influential parents or administrators who've had enough with the turmoil.

Throughout the chapter, we emphasize the critical role of scaffolding in personalized learning environments. We explore how teachers help students learn at their own pace. We consider how to help young adolescents develop the capacity to independently apply the innovative tools, strategies, and skills that are required for deep and challenging learning. As we do, we showcase the stories of teachers and schools integrating passion projects and genius hours, blended learning and maker-centered learning, playlists and badges, all toward the ends of engaging and equitable learning.

TEACHER AS SCAFFOLDER

Scaffolding, or employing various instructional techniques to move students toward deeper understanding and greater independence, has long been recognized as important to learning.[3] Helping students become self-directed learners calls for considerable scaffolding, as teachers provide instructional supports designed to develop the skills students need to reach the outer limits of their zones of proximal development.[4] A teacher's ultimate goal, however, is to gradually remove the scaffolds as the learner "internalizes the information and becomes a self-regulated, independent learner."[5] Two important ways that teachers in personalized learning environments scaffold student learning are (1) by helping students learn at their own pace and (2) by increasing students' independence in applying tools, strategies, and skills toward deeper and more challenging experiences. Let's begin with the first, by looking at pace.

Helping Students Learn at Their Own Pace

Although teachers know well that individuals learn at different paces, most schools group students by age, in grade-level classrooms, largely expecting teachers and learners to move through the same curriculum at the same pace. Personalized learning environments break out of this dilemma. And educators in these environments draw upon various strategies that help students learn at their own pace, despite the organizational or structural challenges schools present.

In a personalized learning environment, teachers provide learners with instructional supports (e.g., tutoring, peer collaboration, graphic organizers, tiered tasks) that are designed both to help students learn and to increase their independence. For instance, teachers we work with offer just-in-time mini-lessons—to students who need them—on finding credible sources online, paraphrasing rather than plagiarizing, citing websites, creating a bibliography, identifying and using primary sources, and respecting copyright laws. Teachers curate resources, suggest graphic organizers, or mandate specified research steps with planning templates. Scaffolding is essential as students embark on more self-directed, project-oriented learning. Add to that the multitude of pathways different students may choose to follow. It calls upon teachers to bring to bear just about every effective approach to instruction! Fortunately, for the most part, these strategies have been around for a long time and there are plenty of examples, trainings, and other resources readily available to help teachers add additional strategies to their toolkit. Some emerging designs leverage technology to extend the power of what we already know are effective strategies. Let's review a few of these, not to learn everything you need to know about them, but to appreciate how proven practices you, or perhaps a colleague down the hall, are already familiar with can open up the instructional landscape for personalized learning.

Direct instruction, small group work, and the workshop model
It can be hard to imagine personalized and flexible pathways leading to anything other than full-blown chaos. People worry that it means handing the classroom over to students to learn as they wish, providing no room for direct instruction and leaving no place for basic skill development or content knowledge. Educators who do this work know this isn't the case. In fact, teachers we work with often describe this work as closer, more personal, and more direct than when they taught whole-class lessons and lectures.

Students will show you, through your observations or their formative work (or sometimes with a direct plea!) what they need. Evidence in PLPs, such as writing samples from identity activities, along with test scores and traditional diagnostics, help you know a lot about a student's abilities and can convey their needs as even student-directed project work begins to take shape. And as more students engage in personalized learning, more often, and over more months in your classroom, your ability to anticipate their needs, to act as a Scout, will rapidly develop. And with knowledge of students' needs in hand, you can design the right response.

We appreciate international educator Andrew Miller's idea that teachers should create the what and the how (the scaffolding and instruction) to be ready for the when (the teachable moment):

> Activities and instruction don't disappear in a project—they just need to be used at the right time. PBL focuses on inquiry and student questioning: Once students generate their initial list of questions, teachers can be ready with appropriate instructional moves to support their learning. Instead of having a rigid calendar, you can keep a list of scaffolding and instruction that's ready to go when students are ready for it. They will continue to answer questions, ask new questions, and discover information and ideas, and you'll eventually need to provide that scaffolding and instruction.[6]

Counterintuitively, direct instruction is a critical part of personalized learning. Instead of providing everyone with the same direct instruction at the same time, however, direct instruction happens precisely when students need it—just in time for success in their engaging work—and in the format they need to successfully learn. For instance, grammar is a classic example of basic communication skills. When teachers lecture about comma usage without context, many students are understandably disengaged. The work lacks purpose. But if students are writing a letter to the principal about why the dress code is inequitable or to the legislature about why plastic bags should be banned in their community, they recognize the need for their writing to be compelling and correct. As with Jack preparing his town council presentation in chapter 5's vignette, students benefit from a genuine desire to convey their ideas accurately. Then they are ready to learn about writing mechanics. Then they have a reason to write powerfully. Their work has meaning and an authentic audience. It's not just an essay read only by the teacher.

Even when a skill is deemed essential for an authentic task, many more decisions need to be made. Sometimes all students will need to learn a skill at the same time, such as safety procedures before departing on a field trip. But in other instances, only a few students may need a particular skill, like Jack with architecture or his project team's need to grasp home energy use. You might think of this as a continuum of scale that can help you choose among instructional approaches. Acquiring different skills may require various levels of social support in order to master. Practicing certain math skills to full proficiency may require no social interaction, only the right online exercises; in other cases, such as with Jack's group, students may need to schedule time with peers to get feedback on their school board presentation. Think of this as a continuum of social support.

These are hardly novel ways of deciding how to proceed as teachers. We typically intuit a continuum of necessary structures when we design activities, from open discovery to scripted procedures, for instance. And we consider wherein lies the expertise, such as in a book, on YouTube, with a community member, or with the teacher. The point is, under many circumstances, a teacher isn't required for in-real-time, face-to-face, whole-group instruction. In the examples we just reviewed, perhaps only the safety instructions fits that bill. And with a full complement of strategies at hand, teachers can serve the needs of students while focusing their time on the students who need them most. After all, given Jack's reluctance as a writer, all the pressure he felt with his calculus work, and the impending stress of presenting to the council, perhaps it's best if his teacher scheduled a one-on-one consult about his script. We think they'd both appreciate being able to make that happen. That's what our teachers mean by discovering closer, more personal and direct instruction in personalized learning environments.

Effective personalization at times intersects with well-regarded systems of instruction. Differentiated Instruction, or tailoring instruction to meet individual needs, has proven an effective response to helping students proceed at different paces and levels of challenge. "Whether teachers differentiate content, process, products, or the learning environment, the use of ongoing assessment and flexible grouping makes this a successful approach to instruction."[7] Examples of differentiated instruction abound in high-quality classrooms: offering texts at various reading levels, including in audio formats; providing different levels of math problems centered on the same concepts; presenting material in visual and auditory ways; and meeting with small groups to teach and practice specific skills or extend learning.

Similarly, some of our partners have learned that a workshop model suits some instructional demands in personalized learning environments. Used by literacy teachers for years, the workshop model offers choice for students, time for individual, small- and whole-group instruction, and opportunities for all students to be engaged, regardless of ability level. It provides structured time for mini-lessons, group meetings, individual check-ins, progress monitoring, and independent work and reflection. The workshop model has a long and distinguished history as effective in just about any content area, so it's not surprising that our partner teachers are finding it effective as well in integrated, student-direct, personalized learning environments. Moreover, it was born in part out of a desire to treat students like emerging writers, on the same path as writers of any age, and deserving of a culture of collaborative support that any writer would appreciate.

We mention these two mainstream strategies as a reminder that there are any number of well thought out innovations to help us grapple with variations in student ability and the need to organize group work. But these and many other instructional strategies with great potential in personalized learning nonetheless developed and flourished in otherwise traditional classroom environments. And as a result, they require some updating to sync up with the fundamentals of personalization. Keep in mind the role shifts in personalized learning. The insights from differentiated instruction, for instance, can help us imagine how groups of students could come together, and be well supported, around a shared need for particular knowledge and skills. But if the teacher takes over the why, when and how of acquiring those skills, as is typical in many applications of differentiation, engagement and self-direction can suffer. And we can imagine the long-term impact on students for whom teacher-directed group work is the norm while their peers chart their own course. We believe teachers' wisdom about differentiation, or any other proven instructional strategy, can inform personalized learning without stripping students of their opportunity to choose topics of interest, align their learning to authentic and personally relevant needs, choose how they want to go about their learning, and select the resources they can connect with most meaningfully. But updating practices for personalized learning once again calls upon our constancy of purpose for why we're personalizing in the first place. How can we use that purpose and our vision of personalized learning so we aren't pulled off track by the legacy systems—and legacy instruction—we've inherited from a different time with often fundamentally different purposes? How can we learn from great instruction to inform our role as scaffolder? Let's begin with a scenario from a school relatively new to student-directed project learning and notice how they began innovating to manage flexible pathways.

PERSONALIZATION IN PRACTICE   Burke Town School

Burke Town School's Projects for Hope, described earlier, is a strong example of educators creating space and time for students to learn at their own pace. You can imagine how much teachers need to keep track of in such a complex, project-based design. They quickly discovered the need to structure the project time and reflection. They developed a schedule to scaffold this work for the young adolescents: 10 minutes of organization and self-assessment; 30 minutes of project work time; 15 minutes of reflection using a reflection menu; and 5 minutes share out one's progress with the larger group. Teachers also maintained a running log on a shared spreadsheet where they documented their regular check-ins with groups and individuals. Their goal was to consult with each group every two or three days, providing direct instruction, support, and guidance. The shared spreadsheet allowed them to see the work of other groups and advisors, and to maintain progress even if a teacher was absent. Figure 6.1 shows the menu students used to guide documentation, reflection and conferences with project advisors. These teachers scaffolded student-directed learning in an integrated way: adopting tools for project planning and curation; restructuring time to meet the needs of independent learners; adopting an intensive schedule to confer with individuals and small groups; and centralizing progress notes so all teachers could respond effectively to students engaged in personalized pathways.

Blended learning

Flexible pathways are frequently bolstered by blended learning, or when a student learns "at least in part through online learning, with some element of student control over time, place, path, and/or pace; at least in part in a supervised brick-and-mortar location away from home; and the modalities along each student's learning path within a course or subject are connected to provide an integrated learning experience," according to The Clayton Christensen Institute.[8] We agree with iNACOL that the most important component of this definition is the focus on student control, which emphasizes "shifting instructional models to enable increased student-centered learning, giving students increased control over the time, place, path, and/or pace of their learning pathways."[9] We have found that the tools used in blended learning environments can support personalized and flexible pathways in lots of ways, including

FIGURE 6.1   **Conferencing reflection and evidence gathering during project time at Burke Town School**

Conference With Your Project Advisor	PLP
■ As a group have a sit down meeting with your advisor. ■ Chat about progress, next steps, and challenges that your group has been faced with this week. — *This needs to happen at least once a week.*	■ Gather and upload evidence to your PLP. ■ Reflect upon the work that you've done this week. ■ Relate your learning to the transferable skills checklist. — *You need to do this at least once a week (but feel free to do it more often).*
Flipgrid	**What/Why?**
■ Record and share a flipgrid. ■ Similar to what/why; give us an update of what you've been working on and why you've been working on it. ■ This is a quick and easy way to share evidence of your work. — *You can do this multiple times per week.*	■ Take a moment to answer the day's What/Why question(s). ■ Be specific and answer either what you're going to work on or what you have worked on that day. — *You can do this multiple times per week.*

Source: Burke Town School.

through flexible pacing, differentiated instruction, immediate interventions, and anytime, anywhere learning.[10]

As they learn the skills for self-direction, particularly at the beginning, many students will need resources curated for them in advance. Educators know that simply saying "Google it" can lead to a scattering of low-quality websites with variable content, especially for students who are still learning how to evaluate digital sources. This is where some of the best of blended learning comes into play. You'll find yourself reaching for any number of blended learning tools to make this resource curation easier. In project-based learning, tools such as playlists, Google Keep, Padlet, open educational resources, and microcredentials can help students with their research and project design, as well as keep them motivated and inspired to accomplish the work.

As we addressed earlier, direct instruction is still an important part of personalized learning. Teachers in personalized learning environments sometimes need to look for ways to offload the day-to-day burden of direct instruction to meet the idiosyncratic needs of individuals and small groups of learners. Some have turned to blended learning, including playlists and micro-credentialing, to address knowledge and skills they are confident that at least some students will need in order to be successful. This frees up more time for needs that are harder to anticipate and require in-person support.

Playlists

Playlists are sets of experiences, activities or lessons, usually technology-based, that students move through at their own speed. They build on each learned skill and create individually paced opportunities for learning. You might think of them as self-paced, digital assignment charts. For example, in a math class, a teacher might have a playlist that includes a YouTube video, a way to communicate a concept visually, a set of problems, a Khan Academy video, and a way for students to reflect and show their learning. And a well-balanced playlist is created with a universal design for learning mindset, careful to solicit and honor students' different learning needs in general.[11]

Certainly, offering a wider range of learning activities to address important concepts is hardly new. Not only can it add to the interest level of students as they engage content learning in ways that feel fun or comfortable, but it's also essential for responding to initial failure to reach mastery. Both research and experience demonstrate that repeating the same learning activities rarely results in better outcomes. Further, preparing playlists, stations, learning packets or other examples of what well-known educational taxonomist Benjamin Bloom called "corrective activities" sets the stage for more immediately relevant, independent and collaborative learning about content.[12] Formative assessment, which we will discuss in considerable detail in chapter 7, has little impact without being followed by alternative routes to understanding. And alternative routes and flexible pathways are what personalized learning is all about.

With playlists, students are given "the unit plan, including access to all the lessons (in text or video form), ahead of time. With the learning plan in hand, students work through the lessons and assignments at their own pace. And because each student has her own digital copy of the playlist (delivered through a system like Google Classroom), the teacher can customize the list to meet each student's needs."[13] Of course, as education writer and innovator Tom Vander Ark reminds us, "The point of a learning list isn't to put students on autopilot, each with headphones and a computer, working without ever interacting. Rather, the clarity, access, and choice provided by a learning list creates opportunities to expand the roles of student and teacher in diverse, exciting ways that better meet individual student needs."[14] As a result, the responsibility for executing the learning plan shifts from teacher to student.

Of course, finding or generating quality content for playlists, or other forms of self-paced learning, can be a time-consuming endeavor. And it's just one of many important reminders of how essential teachers are in personalized learning environments. Fortunately, we have found open educational resources to be great resources in this work. Open educational resources are free online resources ranging from full courses to specific, targeted, stand-alone content such as tests, videos, and simulations. And they're all searchable by topic, discipline, age-range, and standard.[15] Teachers can draw upon these to craft personalized learning experiences for their students. And students can explore them based on their own interests for the proficiencies they need to master. Let's look at some of these in practice.

PERSONALIZATION IN PRACTICE Proctor Junior/Senior High School

Noah Hurlburt, a science teacher at Proctor Junior/Senior High School, structures his middle grades class with playlists. Hurlburt uses a Google Doc with links to activities his students move through at their own pace, guided by clear learning targets (see figure 6.2) and tracking their completion along the way (see figure 6.3). Along with the list of activities, students are given responsibility to collect evidence of meeting those targets, including the date collected (instead of a due date), and a place where Hurlburt offers feedback. Students also write the targets in their own words and answer the question, "How will I know when I've met the proficiency?" This helps to make targets explicit so students understand where they are headed and can be active participants in the assessment process.

Young adolescents who use playlists tell us that they appreciate the independence and responsibility it affords them. They are free to move along at their own pace, working with peers or individually, and getting assistance from the teacher as needed. In some cases, because they have more complete access to the content of lessons and units, a playlist empowers students to determine when they have homework. And importantly, playlists can distribute control of the learning environment, increasing students' ownership of their learning. (Hurlburt has even created a playlist for teachers on creating playlists![16])

FIGURE 6.2   **Noah Hurlburt's eighth-grade science playlist learning targets, Proctor Junior-Senior High School**

8th Grade Science
Independent Packet M

Name_____

MS-PS4-1 Use mathematical representations to describe a simple model for waves that includes how the amplitude of a wave is related to the energy in a wave.

MS-PS4-2 Develop and use a model to describe that waves are reflected, absorbed, or transmitted through various materials.

In this space, write a short explanation (in your own words) that breaks down the proficiencies above.

Chrome Music Lab- Take some time to play!

Learning Targets	Completion Date	Teacher Feedback
I can identify and explain the wavelengths that make up the EM Spectrum		
I can explain and demonstrate how wave frequency and wavelength combine to make up each different wave within the EM Spectrum		
I can know what the speed of light is, and how this speed is calculated		
I can identify, explain, and demonstrate how the EM Spectrum is utilized in daily life		
I can compare, contrast, and explain the similarities between visual light and sound waves		
I can design and engineer a smartphone amplifier that manipulates sound waves to increase music decibel levels		

How will I know when I have met the proficiency?

Source: Noah Hurlburt, Proctor Junior-Senior High School.

FIGURE 6.3   **Noah Hurlburt's eighth-grade science playlist tasks,**
Proctor Junior-Senior High School

Task:	Description:	Complete?
READ	CK12 Chapter Light waves reading/ questions Reading- reflectance spectroscopy EM Spectrum Review Notes Sound Waves Sound- Many Options	
PERFORMANC E TASKS	PT. 1M Light pre-test PT.2M EM Spectrum Inquiry Question PT. 3M Characteristics of waves - Springs Lab Formative PT. 4M PHET Animation- Lab Sheet PT. 5M Smartphone Amplifiers - 3D printing! Budget Sheet for mock up design Amplifier Rubric	
WATCH	EM Spectrum Song! EM Spectrum Interactive EM Spectrum Introduction Khan Academy - EM Spectrum Light is Waves What is Light? - Simple What is Light- Animation Style What is the Speed of Dark? What is the Speed of Light? Can We Go Faster Than Light? Would Headlights Work at Light Speed? What if You Run at the Speed of Light? The Transmission of Sound How Sound Works in Rooms Sound- Bill!! The Science of Sound Sound Waves- Khan Academy Physics of Sound, Amplitude, and Frequency	
CONFERENCE	*Check in with Mr. H with no less than all Performance Tasks, two successful formative quizzes, and complete model.*	

Formatives-
EM Spectrum Formative
Light Energy Formative

Source: Noah Hurlburt, Proctor Junior-Senior High School.

PERSONALIZATION IN PRACTICE   Peoples Academy Middle Level

In addition to Google Docs, teachers are finding other digital tools to be helpful in curating resources. HyperDocs, for example, not only offers a way to curate resources but suggests a flow for learners.[17] Joe Speers, a teacher at Peoples Academy Middle Level in Morrisville, has experimented with Google Keep to embed flexible pathways in his sixth-grade science class, substituting the teacher-directed, whole-class, lockstep pace with one where students self-pace and self-select paths through a learning sequence. In his blended classroom, Joe explained,

> I began transferring many classwork tasks to Google Keep that would generally involve whole-class instruction and then common work time. By issuing these assignments via Google Keep, we have the benefit of easy self-pacing, and we remove the thing fast workers hate: waiting for all of our classmates to be ready. As students finish each note's assignment, I share the next assignment's Google Keep. The next assignment is like the badge to indicate you finished and are moving on to the next task.[18]

PERSONALIZATION IN PRACTICE   Proctor Elementary School

When Courtney Elliot launched a project-based learning unit on Vermont history, she knew she'd need to do some significant scaffolding for her young learners. She chose Padlet, an application to create online bulletin boards with virtual sticky notes, to help her construct a blended learning environment for them. Padlets have been used in many ways in the classroom to support personalized, proficiency-based systems.[19] Elliot used the curation tool to curate resources and create pathways for her students, giving them choice on what they want to see and do before embarking on a project or performance task. She assembled resources for project ideas, the unit's driving questions, geography, history and climate resources, historic Vermont images, research videos, and whole-class questions. Students also used Padlets of their own to organize their research and task lists. They appreciate that it saves automatically and report that it keeps them organized, which, as we know, is a critical skill in self-directed learning.[20]

Micro-credentialing

Digital badges and micro-credentials are gamified way students can move through different levels of skills and concepts. As they demonstrate proficiency in a particular area of study, students "level up" and gain badges and credentials.

Badging, as it's sometimes called, exploits aspects of what Karl Kapp, professor at Bloomsburg University, calls structural gamification, in which game elements contribute to motivation and enthusiasm but the content itself remains separate.[21] Since it's the evidence of mastery that earns the badge, the learning activities that generated the badge, whether it be a lecture, collaborative group work, or selections from a playlist, can remain un-gamified. So, no, you don't need to teach like a game show host to use badges in your classroom. And you don't need to gamify all of your content materials. This makes badging particularly attractive in a personalized learning environment in which we encourage students to find their own, most fruitful route to mastering the content. In schools we've worked with, teachers have found micro-credentials particularly helpful with regard to broadly applicable skills—such as transferable skills, social skills, and routines—as gateways, passports, or licenses to take on new roles or responsibilities. Launching micro-credentials may require significant up-front work, which is justified if they relate to essential elements of the day-to-day life of a classroom or team. But even in their less-developed form, micro-credentials can bolster enthusiasm and channel learning in the contexts of units as well.

PERSONALIZATION IN PRACTICE   Lamoille Union Middle School

Chris Bologna, a seventh- and eighth-grade social studies teacher at Lamoille Union Middle School, took an interest in gamification to fend off what he calls "the onset of apathy" so common among young adolescents as they progress through middle school. Chris decided to try badging while pondering ways to further refine an expansive interdisciplinary unit he and his teammates had been teaching for a number of years. He and his team designed badges to ensure that all students had adequately immersed themselves into the cities and countries they chose to investigate. Each badge could be awarded only after completing a set of achievements, often referred to as quests. The Roaming Gnome badge, for instance, was awarded only after completing the following achievements: Multilingual, Danger Zone, Cartographer, Architect, and Bibliographer. Each achievement involved specific expectations, such as those below for Multilingual and Danger Zone:

- *Multilingual*: Using the native language, include five phrases or ten words and English translations you will need while visiting your city. If your country is English-speaking, look for five phrases using local slang or lingo, such as while visiting Thunder Road [Racetrack] in Barre, one might say, "Jeezum Crow!" when your favorite driver crashes.

- *The Danger Zone*: Describe at least five customs or dangers you need to be aware of while visiting your city or country. Write one clear sentence for each.

Other badges required for the unit included (along with their requisite achievements) Urban Planner, I Can Do This, and Stranded! Together, they formed a clear and shared set of core learning objectives for an otherwise complicated and largely self-directed unit.[22] Figure 6.4 shows a screenshot of how the team used Schoology to track students' progress as they completed requirements for the full range of badges.

FIGURE 6.4   **Tracking badges earned, Lamoille Union Middle School**

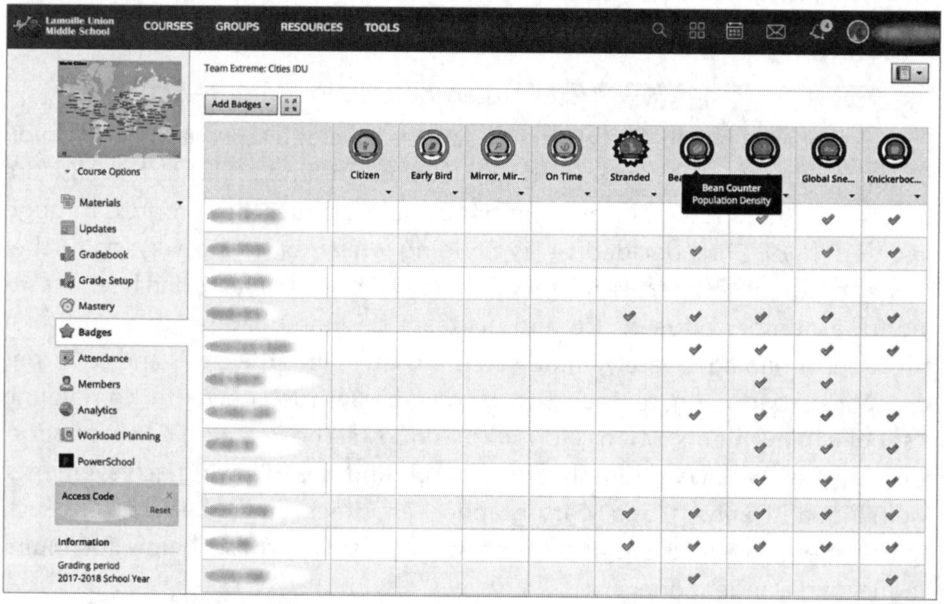

Source: Lamoille Union Middle School.

PERSONALIZATION IN PRACTICE   Peoples Academy Middle School

At Peoples Academy Middle Level in Morrisville, students in Stephanie Zucca-rello's sixth-grade class created a badging system to engage their peers more in working toward their personal goals. The school's weekly Opportunity Time was created as a chance for students to set goals and explore projects of interest. Stephanie and her colleagues realized their students would be more successful with self-directed learning if they first thought more concretely about themselves as learners. They tasked students with considering what they believed made them interesting. They then were challenged to select an adjective they aspired to become. Working with a peer, students created a Johari window, a technique that helps people understand themselves in relation to others.[23] They chose a word from a list of adjectives that neither they nor their peers saw in them, such as accepting, adaptable, extroverted, and ingenious. Then they developed a goal around that attribute, which they posted to their digital portfolios. Figure 6.5 illustrates Zuccarello's guide for students creating their personal interest goals based in part on the results of their Johari window exercise. A small student design group collaborated to build a badging system to help all students understand how to demonstrate evidence of "becoming" the chosen word and to share that growth with others through their portfolios (see figure 6.6).

Students used peer partners for a first round of feedback to see if their portfolios indeed demonstrated their growth toward their goal. Over time, earning the three possible badges helped them to feel confident about their growth and willing to share evidence of that growth with their learning community. As one student explained, "I need people to know about me, but I hate talking about myself. Creating an Identity Chart helped others to learn about me."

Helping students learn at their own pace is a fundamental building block of flexible pathways. The examples presented in figures 6.5 and 6.6 show how teachers can in many cases draw upon well-known strategies like direct instruction, group work, and the workshop model. But the compelling need to free up teacher time for what only teachers can do drove these educators to scaffold personalized pacing with innovations, often augmented with technology, such as blended learning, playlists, and micro-credentialing.

FIGURE 6.5   **Guide for creating personal interest goal page, Peoples Academy Middle Level**

Portfolios

Stephanie's Portfolios • Personal Interest Goal   11:50 AM

1. Title the Portfolio - *Personal Interest Goal*

Personal Interest Goal

2. Write your word under the title

Extrovert

3. Change the title picture to something that represents your goal

PORTFOLIO ITEMS

Updates
Info
Blog
Portfolios

4. Change your profile picture to a photo of you or an avatar

5. Begin adding evidence to your portfolio:
   ❑ Your Johari Window results
   ❑ Your KWHLAQ chart
   ❑ A screenshot of the comments on your chart proving that your goal was approved
   ❑ Any video, emails, designs that you have completed so far

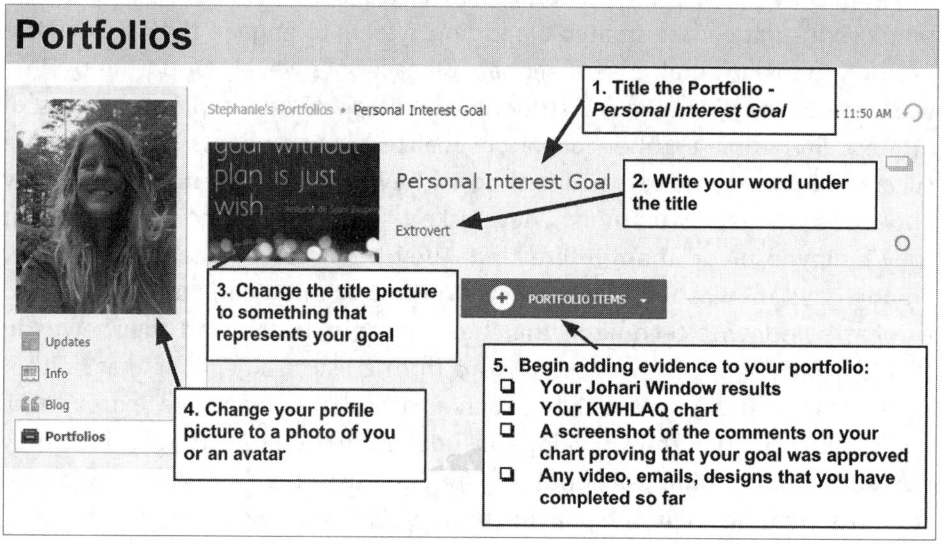

Source: Stephanie Zuccarello, Peoples Academy Middle Level.

Helping Students Independently Apply Tools, Strategies and Skills

Part of helping students learn at their own pace relies on growing the independence of young adolescents. Teachers as scaffolders support students' acquisition of new skills in various ways. In project-based learning, as students identify and plan their projects of interest, they inevitably encounter new challenges and face obstacles to overcome. Helping students select and apply innovative approaches to these challenges, particularly in solving authentic problems, is a key part of this work.

Passion projects and genius hour

We've observed many ways in which teachers help students gain independence as they apply new strategies. Some of the most illustrative have been as schools have adopted ambitious plans for passion projects and genius hours. In creating these opportunities for students to follow their curiosities, teachers step back from solving dilemmas for their students and instead allow students the freedom to iterate and reiterate as necessary.

FIGURE 6.6   **Student-designed badging system,
Peoples Academy Middle Level**

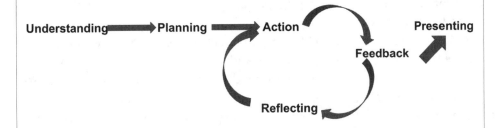

Badges

✓ You earn badges everytime you complete a step accurately.

✓ For *Action*, *Feedback*, and *Reflecting* you will have to earn a Bronze, Silver, and Gold badge. This means for each time you complete the Action - Feedback - Reflection you earn a badge; eventually getting a Gold!

Understanding ⟶ Planning ⟶ Action ⟶ Feedback ⟶ Presenting
Reflecting

Source: Peoples Academy Middle Level.

PERSONALIZATION IN PRACTICE   Crossett Brook Middle School

Teachers at Crossett Brook Middle School, in partnership with our colleague Life LeGeros, wanted to increase their students' engagement in learning. To that end, they launched a schoolwide effort in which students would explore their own interests, with support and guidance from teachers. The educators looked to the models of genius hours and passion projects and, with student input, created their own version that came to be called "Brainado." For the past three years, students have proposed, worked on, and presented a project of their own design and making, committing one hour each week for ten weeks, during the school day. Brainado projects are driven by students' interests, including what they choose to explore, how they explore it, and what they ultimately create. Students have learned to whittle, created backpacking meals with a food dehydrator, built a scale model of an earthship house, and apprenticed at a local mechanic's shop. Throughout the experience, the students iterate and problem solve, reflect, and provide feedback to their peers. The culminating event is a

"Sharenado," where students share their Brainado projects with the school and larger community.

Brainado is an all-hands-on-deck approach, with every educator available for mentorship and every space available for use. When needed, teachers help students find external mentors and community connections to help advance their learning. Through Brainado, students create meaningful projects to share in their PLPs. The school had gotten off to a rocky start with PLPs a few years prior, like many other middle schools in Vermont, because they launched them with an emphasis on goal-setting. By focusing first on engaging learning, educators came to appreciate how goal-setting, and other aspects of the PLP, could follow naturally. Instead of an isolated task, setting goals could become integrated into meaningful learning.

Students now view the PLP as a tool to tell their learning stories about Brainado, with reflections linked to photos and models of designs and plans. They use it to document their experience, from the conception of an idea, to the proposal, to the research and creation, to the revision and iteration, and ultimately to the presentation. The PLP tells the story of learning, including student passions and interests. It details what worked and what didn't, and highlights how students applied new strategies to solve the problem. Further, it validates learning inside and outside of school.

Brainado continues to evolve with more student leadership and input.[24] In fact, students were the ones who formally recommended merging Brainado and PLPs.[25] Overall, Brainado has become a touchstone for the school community as they strive to increase engagement and deepen learning. That collective success positions teachers and students to ask of each other questions such as, "How do we capture the energy of Brainado in our day-to-day classrooms?" or "How can Personalized Learning Plans be more like Brainado?"

PERSONALIZATION IN PRACTICE Flood Brook School

In partnership with our colleague and professional development coordinator Rachel Mark, the teachers at Flood Brook School first launched passion projects as a way for young adolescents to explore individual interests while learning the skills of self-direction. As the projects evolved, the teachers found the merging of students' passion projects and the PLP to be a fruitful route to student engagement. The students could optimize many of the core functions of the PLP through this student-centered work, including exploring their interests, designing their learning pathways, setting goals, and reflecting on their learning.

All students in the school's middle grades now conduct two independent passion projects per year, which conclude in a learning exhibition. This year, the audience for the exhibition—students in the lower grades, families, and community members—learned from these middle schoolers about topics such as building a trebuchet, a modular shelving unit, and a human-powered vehicle; coding in Scratch; and debating the dress code. One student, Vivian, studied guinea pig behavior, ultimately designing six mazes before she settled on the correct level of challenge. Vivian, like many of her classmates, was immersed in applying innovative strategies to a problem she cared about solving. Throughout the project-based passion projects, students learn about more than their chosen topics; they come to appreciate the power of iteration and revision in getting better results. Who knows how often their teachers may have tried to explain that basic life lesson? But owning their learning and caring enough about the outcome meant students finally lived the lesson for themselves. It's a good reminder, not lost on the Flood Brook teachers, of the power of project-based learning, an authentic audience and the engaging nature of student choice.[26]

Both Flood Brook's Passion Projects and Crossett Brook's Brainado, like their counterparts at other schools, are evolving and valuable strategies. Educators in both settings engage young adolescents in personal learning, while helping them apply tools, strategies and skills with increasing independence. And both approaches depart considerably from the traditional school world filled with textbooks and notebooks. In each, we see the need for different materials, hands-on approaches, and new creativity. For these reasons, maker-centered learning is a complementary approach that many schools have found useful.

Maker-centered learning

Maker-centered learning is a strategy that arose largely from the makerspace movement. Complementary in many ways with project-based learning, a makerspace is "a place where students can gather to create, invent, tinker, explore and discover using a variety of tools and materials."[27] It's also been described as "a unique learning environment that encourages tinkering, play, and open-ended exploration for all."[28] Others emphasize the collaborative nature of makerspaces, noting that they are "collaborative learning environments where people come together to share materials and learn new skills. . . . Makerspaces are not necessarily born out of a specific set of materials or spaces, but rather a mindset of community partnership, collaboration, and creation."[29]

This mindset of creation is at the heart of maker-centered learning, which need not be restricted to a particular space. It is both broader and deeper than the space itself and is connected to personalized and project-based learning in many ways. Agency by Design stresses that a primary goal of maker-centered learning is for learners to feel empowered to build and shape their worlds. This sense of "maker empowerment" is achieved, in Agency by Design's view, by helping learners develop three key capacities: looking closely, exploring complexity, and finding opportunity.[30]

You can readily imagine these rich capacities as a set of transferable skills that teachers might scaffold students to develop. Maker-centered learning can generate student questions, encourage students to discover and explore areas of interest, and enable flexible pathways for students to meet educational outcomes. For instance, maker-centered learning often invites students to identify and respond to a specific need by designing and prototyping a product. Both the student-identified needs and the ensuing products typically vary greatly, with a substantial part of the learning stemming from the process itself. From these pathways, maker-centered learning helps students create a rich and varied learner profile, and offers tangible evidence of proficiency, stemming from a purposeful context for developing skills and content knowledge. And maker-centered learning further bolsters the aims of personalized learning in its capacity to engage community partners.

PERSONALIZATION IN PRACTICE   EMMA

Testimony to the idea that maker-centered learning is more than just a location, many Vermont schools have been fortunate to access EMMA, which stands for Everyone May Make Anywhere.[31] EMMA is a mobile studio for creating and making. A van outfitted with items such as soldering stations, 3D printers, papercraft supplies, and laser cutters, EMMA travels to rural schools, bringing the opportunity for maker-centered learning to teachers and students alike. EMMA is the brainchild of long-time educator, Lucie deLaBruere, who helps schools leverage technology and other resources in their efforts to make learning personal.

At Crossett Brook Middle School, for example, students were working on the transferable skill of clear and effective communication. With a brief introduction to paper circuitry, these young adolescents were then challenged to use light to emphasize an idea they'd like to communicate at the end of a unit. Some students elected to underscore a theme of human rights; others focused on sustainability. Overall, the task of making served as a useful means to summarize and reflect at the conclusion of a learning task.[32] Lucie noted:

> While some students might stare at a blank piece of paper struggling with what they should write about, these same students quickly engaged with batteries, LEDs, and copper tape to create a paper circuit about something that "lights them up." For students who think with their hands, this 90-minute challenge provided a hands-on, minds-on way to generate possible focus ideas for their personal narratives.[33]

Our partners have discovered that even relatively brief exposure to making can spark students' leadership and design thinking capabilities. They then can become the drivers for change, asking for class activities to have a making component, helping other students learn the design thinking model, and becoming leaders in the use of technical tools found in a makerspace. After just one 90-minute session with EMMA learning to code with Scratch and use a Makey Makey invention kit, for example, fifth graders at Malletts Bay School decided to use their new skills to design and create an interactive display to be featured at their school's fall open house. Further enthused by this work, they accepted an invitation to share their work at a local Mini Maker Faire. Lucie recalled the process as far from smooth:

> The students experienced many points of failure. Some wires were too short. Some wires became entangled or undone as they moved around the project. They lost track of which wire went where and needed to come up with labeling systems. Audience members tripped over wires, so the students had to come up with safer and more secure ways to have the display survive many different people touching it.[34]

While Lucie was impressed by the resulting interactive display, she was particularly struck by how well the students demonstrated growth in creative and practical problem solving, one of the state's transferable skills. "Although I was impressed with the ideas and solutions they implemented in their audible garden, I must say that what impressed me even more was how they were able to 'Persist in solving challenging problems and learn from failure.'" Yet again, as we scaffold students' increasing independence, we are reminded of the power of iteration and of learning from one's mistakes.

LOOKING AHEAD: ASSESSING PERSONALIZED LEARNING

As presented in these past two chapters, teachers adopt a wide range of roles to support flexible pathways. At times, they empower students to begin with their own authentic questions as the basis for curriculum. Along the way, they help to scout fruitful paths, and material and human resources, to support the learning. And they apply a variety of techniques to scaffold the learning journey. As you recall your purpose for increasing personalization in your own context, remember that a deeply personalized school would include a variety of approaches, some classroom-based, some teamwide, and others at the whole-school level. Students might encounter something like Brainado, a makerspace, project-based service learning, and playlists—all in the course of a day! How, then, are we to assess all of this rich and personal learning? In chapter 7, we will explore how a proficiency-based approach to assessment can help you, your students, and their families to understand this personalized learning on a new level.

SEVEN

PLPS AND PROFICIENCY-BASED ASSESSMENT

Clara heads out to the small greenhouse. Because two of her classmates cleaned the glass, she can finally see the tiny plants through the door window. She opens the door and hauls in the watering can. The morning chill settles around her, and she pulls her sweatshirt sleeves down a little lower.

She pours a slow trickle of water onto the tiny, bright green plants. The small basil, tomato, oregano, and carrot shoots are dainty and reaching. She thinks about how, just four months ago, this greenhouse was a shack, filled with random junk from all over the school.

Clara, along with her classmates in the Local Food taskforce, wrote a grant to the Rural Education Partnership for funding to restart the gardening program at their school. After presenting their grant proposal to teams of adults and other students, they received the funds to make the greenhouse usable again. It took them several days just to clear out the space, then several more to clean it up, and then even more to organize it. At times it felt like they'd never finish. It was really hard work. Finally, though, they were able to order their seeds, tools and containers, and set it up for this growing season. They coordinated with a local gardening organization to get the garden (full of grass and weeds!) tilled and mulched and worked for hours with several master gardeners on preparing the space.

It's been a long road, for sure, but Clara feels like she has a lot to show for it. And she's been able to make it work for her PLP. She recalls a conference early in the fall with her teacher advisor, Mr. Nuñez, who's the math leader on her team. He encouraged her to be the chief financial officer on the project. Clara was tempted—she'd be good at it—but she also knew she'd already generated plenty of evidence of her mathematical modeling ability from previous projects. The proficiency report she'd generated just prior to the meeting made it clear: she's got to focus on science, and the greenhouse seemed a great match for experimenting with the role of environmental and genetic factors in the growth of organisms, and certainly the role of photosynthesis in the cycling of matter and the flow of energy. And when she showed her progress charts to Mr. Nuñez, he agreed, and so did her mom.

That began her first real project collaboration with the team's science teacher, Ms. Bailey, and Leticia, a senior in agriculture at the state university. They both helped Clara focus on designing experiments and gathering evidence that applied directly to her target proficiencies. Clara loved using Ms. Bailey's playlist on the science of gardening, especially the videos tagged to organism growth and photosynthesis proficiencies. And seeing the lab Leticia works in made setting up her experiments so much easier. Plus, Clara muses, Leticia's just cool and really nice. Leticia said she was really impressed with how much evidence Clara uploaded into her PLP, like the time-lapse videos showing the side-by-side growth of different tomato varieties and the data log from light, water, moisture, and temperature sensors. And even the video of Clara's presentation when they pitched their grant proposal. Leticia said she's even gotten some new ideas for her own senior thesis! Pulling up all that evidence quickly convinced Clara's mother that the project was well worth all the time Clara was spending in the greenhouse. If everything goes as planned, Clara hopes the findings will help determine which varieties will be most economical for the food program.

Clara's anxious about deciding when to transfer the plants from the greenhouse to the outdoor garden. All of her research and several expert gardeners told her not to plant those warm weather crops too early. The morning chills confirm her thinking. "Patience, I just need patience. And this is not an area where I'm strong," Clara reminds herself, chuckling. Just waiting for her little sister to pull on her socks is painful enough! Clara and the other students on her team check the weather station every day, looking for the right conditions to transfer the plants. They chart the weather on a graph, and average the temperature changes each week. At the end of the month, they will present the results of their task force to the Rural Partnership at a conference for rural students and teachers. They'll also share these with the school board, advocating for the importance of continuing this program once Clara and her classmates are off to high school. A small jolt of expectation, of knowing she will be presenting this work, multiple times and to real audiences, and then moving on to high school, blooms in her chest.

Clara pulls her phone from her pocket and snaps some photos of the tiny plants in their little square containers. She likes the symmetry, their potential, and is proud that they are safely in a space that she created. Quickly, she pulls up her notes app on her phone and writes:

> *tiny seedlings*
> *i see you*
> *full of potential*
> *full of opportunity*
> *waiting*
> *waiting*
> *for the right temperature*
> *for the right place*
> *to unfurl*
> *to uncurl*
> *to be free.*
> *Just like me*

She quickly uploads the photo and this poem to her PLP using her mobile app and wonders how to tag it. "Oh, why not?" she thinks, and chooses "communicating scientific information." She then brushes off the dirt from her hands, grabs the empty watering can, and heads back to class, pulling the squeaky greenhouse door closed.

BUILDING YOUR RATIONALE: FOSTERING COMPETENCE

As they experiment with increasing independence, it's not unusual for middle schoolers to feel unsure of themselves and their skills at times. This can be further complicated by what child psychologist David Elkind described as "the imaginary audience," or the tendency for students this age to feel as though they are constantly being observed and judged.[1] Take these feelings of uncertainty, add their concerns about being judged, and introduce assessment and evaluation into the mix, and you could end up with the perfect storm! This is one reason why nurturing competence—and, importantly, an accompanying *sense* of competence—in young people is an important aim of middle grades education. Assessment matters, perhaps more than ever in personalized learning environments.

Clara's story illustrates how proficiency-based assessment can bolster rather than threaten a student's sense of competence. It was the body of evidence regarding her mathematical modeling ability, not an ambiguous grade in seventh-grade math, that gave her the sense she was already competent in project budgeting. And it was her lack of evidence regarding organism growth and energy systems that prompted her to focus her next endeavor on these specific science proficiencies. This evidence-based focus on proficiencies, conveniently tracked and reported by teachers and students, also empowered her to advocate for herself as a learner, with her teachers, and with her mother. That system gave her the tools to bolster her sense of competence as a self-directed learner as well. And that system provided her teacher, Mr. Nuñez, with the assessment tools to responsibly oversee her overall learning plan. It also established much-needed focus for her greenhouse project on specific learning outcomes. That focus helped framed his work as an Empowerer, Scout, and Scaffolder.

Let's return briefly to the three pillars of personalization. At its core, the strength of the first pillar—the PLP—lies in its ability to help us as teachers to know our students well. It provides a window into students' lives and identities, offers a clear framework that places the student in the driver's seat for learning, and creates a platform for engaging families and community members. The second pillar—Flexible Pathways—helps us to establish authentic learning opportunities based on this knowledge of students. It invites and honors learning of personal and social significance while promoting proven pedagogies such as project-based, place-based, and service learning. And it values anywhere, anytime learning, leveraging the power of ubiquitous technology and blended learning to embrace the many ways students are acquiring new knowledge and developing new skills of immediate and lifelong value. It is the third pillar—Proficiency-Based Assessment—that takes on the challenge of assessing learning that is personalized. By using a proficiency-based approach, we value students' learning from wherever it happens and whenever it occurs, honoring authentic evidence of mastery and removing a reliance on seat time or Carnegie units. In keeping with the emphasis on student ownership, the third pillar increases the responsibility of the learner to monitor progress. As a result, it also increases the emphasis on transparency and formative assessment.

Vermont's Agency of Education asserts that, in an effective proficiency-based system, assessment is a learning experience for students. The students receive timely and differentiated support and feedback based on their needs, while having voice and choice in assessment options. Importantly, students' progress is based upon demonstration of proficiency rather than accumulation of seat time, and "learning is the constant and time is the variable."[2] These tenets of proficiency-based assessment are precisely what makes it such a strong match for personalized learning environments, given that in such a system, "students take ownership of their learning and assessment, students collect evidence of their learning over time through personalized learning plans, and students' personalized learning plans reflect opportunities for flexibility in where, when and how they learn."[3]

Proficiency-based assessment is indispensable to personalized learning. It emphasizes formative assessment grounded in specific and standards-based feedback, authentic and portfolio assessment, and targeted tracking of progress. As you'll read in this chapter, the comprehensive set of features in proficiency-based assessment, many of which are pulled straight from well-established best practices in assessment, brings the full power of assessment to the unique context of personalized learning environments.

CHAPTER OVERVIEW

This chapter explores the role of proficiency-based assessment in a personalized learning environment and in relation to the PLP. We review formative and summative assessment practices and dive into many facets of proficiency-based assessment, exploring the role of clear targets and success criteria, the importance of practice, the role of regular and specific feedback, the tracking of skills, and the reporting of learning. Along the way, we provide examples of student and teacher products to illustrate this challenging and rewarding work. Of course, effective assessment is inherently complex and requires extensive training, practice, and refinement to reach fruition. We can only offer an overview of proficiency-based assessment here. What we offer that may be otherwise difficult to find, however, are the fruits of regular teachers using proficiency-based assessment in the context of simultaneous efforts to personalize learning opportunities for young adolescents. They've embraced the premise that a new assessment system can and should serve the unique demands of engaging, relevant, and student-directed learning.

ASSESSING PERSONALIZED LEARNING

How do we assess learning that is personalized? While the value of the PLP resides in its ability to reflect an individual student's identity, aspirations, and widely ranging evidence of personal growth, this same value presents interesting challenges for assessment. Whereas traditional assessment principles prioritize some degree of reliability (students take the same test, respond to the same text, complete the same essay, or perform the same experiment), assessing personalized learning prioritizes validity by valuing authentic evidence of knowledge and skills derived from real-world challenges.[4]

Let's imagine, for a moment, three students and their final grades in a traditionally assessed science class. The first student misbehaved in class and was repeatedly penalized for chronically late work which, when averaged with his surprisingly strong grades for quizzes, labs, and tests, dragged down his final average from a B to a C. The second student tried hard, sought extra credit, but struggled academically and bombed the final exam, resulting in a C for the course. The third student, whose troubles at home led to lots of absences, a missed lab, and poor quiz grades, rallied with an A on the final, but that was barely enough to raise his average to a B for the semester. What do their final grades really say about their knowledge and skills in science? What do they tell us about these students as budding scientists? Not much, especially on a transcript without each student's backstory.

Sorting out this assessment quandary is a key impetus for proficiency-based assessment. The Great School Partnership defines proficiency-based learning (and its synonyms competency-based, mastery-based, outcome-based, performance-based, and standards-based education) as "systems of instruction, assessment, grading, and academic reporting that are based on students demonstrating that they have learned the knowledge and skills they are expected to learn as they progress through their education."[5] Notice the focus is on what students can do, not on what they can't do, or their grades or rank or how many courses they have "passed."

A proficiency-based approach can untangle the dilemma of assessing the actual science abilities of our three students above. Transparent and specific performance criteria for the science that these students were engaged in would tell the story of what they really knew and could do. Separating the assessment of those criteria from their other behaviors, eliminating penalties, percentages, and averaging would have further sharpened our understanding of their abilities as scientists. As the Great Schools Partnership describes it, proficiency-based assessment can "more accurately reflect a student's learning progress and achievement, including situations in which students struggled early on in a semester or school year, but then put in the effort and hard work needed to meet expected standards."[6]

This last point is particularly salient in the broader picture of personalized learning, in which students are expected to take on authentic and inherently messy challenges as they go about their learning. The New England Secondary Schools Consortium asserts:

> Failure is nearly always encountered on the path to understanding and success, and proficiency-based approaches to grading allow teachers, students, and parents to focus on the end goal—learning the most important knowledge and skills—rather than the struggles or mistakes made along the way. Proficiency-based grading helps students see failures as opportunities to learn and grow—not as sources of shame.[7]

But disentangling proficiency from traditional grading practices is just an entry point to the ultimate power of proficiency-based assessment in personalized learning. Acknowledging and dispensing with the shortcomings of traditional grading means we can jettison many of the teaching traditions and routines it spawned, many of which have little backing in the literature on student achievement. In their place, proficiency-based assessment offers up a set of assessment practices proven to advance student achievement even in traditional settings. There are several central shifts in the grading progress within a proficiency-based approach. Rather than one grade or entry earned per assignment, for example, students earn a grade or entry for each goal or proficiency, regardless of how many assignments or learning tasks supported that goal. Instead of being based on a mix of achievement, effort, and behavior, a proficiency-based approach measures and reports on achievement and separates out habits of work. Whereas traditional grading calls for everything to be recorded in the gradebook, in this circumstance only selected assessments are used for grading purposes. Finally, rather than averaging all scores, regardless of when the work was completed, teachers in proficiency-based settings report only the most recent or advanced evidence of learning.[8]

Proficiencies happen to be ideally suited to personalized learning as well. As CompetencyWorks describes it, "A competency-based structure enables personalized learning to provide flexibility and supports to ensure mastery of the highest standards possible. With clear and calibrated understanding of proficiency, learning can be tailored to each student's strengths, needs, and interests and enable student voice and choice in what, how, when, and where they learn."[9] Students need regular opportunities to demonstrate to themselves and others that they can succeed. What better way for teachers to create these learning conditions than to make assessment criteria transparent; be clear about what success looks like; provide multiple, low stakes, opportunities and ways to practice; provide regular and specific feedback regarding not only where a learner is in relation to the target but also what is needed in order to move closer to it; and report out that progress in meaningful, accurate, and descriptive ways? That's the essence of proficiency-based assessment.

Making Assessment Criteria Transparent

Being clear about what success looks like is a crucial first step in proficiency-based assessment. As students set out to develop a new skill, they need to know what they're aiming for. What is the learning target? What are the criteria against which they will self-assess and be assessed? Proficiency scales and targets help answer to these questions.

Learning scales "promote clarity by supporting transparent learning progressions for students, structured feedback from teachers, and differentiated student-driven learning experiences"[10] They are similar to rubrics, but different in three important ways. First, they're written specifically for students to understand. Second, they're focused on what a student can do, rather than what they can't. And third, words are used instead of numbers, in order to reflect growth toward proficiency. For these reasons, many teachers use learning scales that begin with "I can" statements. By focusing on what a student can do, educators promote hope and emphasize potential, the belief that students are competent and will be successful. The learning target is the specific level on the scale at which proficiency is met.

PERSONALIZATION IN PRACTICE Peoples Academy Middle Level

Phoebe Slater, a reading interventionist at Peoples Academy Middle Level, distilled key district standards for reading fluency into specific language accessible to her students (see table 7.1). In Phoebe's case, students used "I can" statements to guide and evaluate their efforts toward fluency in reading. To inspire the students in the work and to provide an authentic audience, the project culminated with students reading station identification messages on air for a local radio station.

PERSONALIZATION IN PRACTICE Shelburne Community School

Like Peoples Academy, Shelburne Community School uses "I can" statements within its learning targets. One group of the middle school's students was learning to identify, explain, and evaluate causes and effects as part of the transferable skill, Informed and Integrative Thinking. Their social studies teacher, Sam Nelson, began this work by introducing students to the learning scale for this proficiency (see figure 7.1).

TABLE 7.1 **"I can" statements on reading fluency**

Domain: ELA: Reading: Key Ideas	**Graduation Standard:** Comprehend, interpret, analyze, and evaluate a wide range and level of complex literary and informational texts.				
Performance Indicator:	Read with sufficient accuracy and fluency to support *and demonstrate* comprehension				
Learning Target(s)	Read grade level texts with sufficient accuracy. Read grade level texts with sufficient fluency. Demonstrate comprehension of grade level texts.				
	Proficient with Distinction	**Proficient**	**Basic Proficient**	**Making Progress**	**Getting Started**
Important Components ▪ accuracy ▪ expression ▪ automaticity (rate or pace) ▪ phrasing	I can use this skill in other settings, reading various types of texts with accuracy and fluency.	I can read grade level texts with sufficient fluency—using all of the components of fluency.	I can read grade level texts using several components of fluency.	I can explain the different components of fluent reading. I can demonstrate some of the components in practice exercises.	I can identify fluent reading when I hear it.

Source: Phoebe Slater, Peoples Academy Middle Level.

FIGURE 7.1.   **Learning scale for informed and integrative thinking, Shelburne Community School**

Cause + Effects				
Informed+ Integrative Thinking: Identify main and supporting ideas, patterns, trends, clues, and relationships in sources of information.	I can list causes and effects.	I can list the causes and effects related to an event.	I can explain in my own words how the causes and their effects relate to an event.	I can evaluate the causes or effects. I can defend how the causes or effects had a positive or negative impact.

Source: Shelburne Community School.

Sam decided to model for his students what it looks like to demonstrate progress on the learning scale by examining a critical event in his life: becoming a teacher. Figure 7.2 depicts how he mapped a think-aloud on his whiteboard to demonstrate that he "can list the causes and effects related to an event." In figure 7.3, he shows how he can move along the scale and "explain in [his] own words how the causes and their effects relate to an event" (his becoming a teacher). With these two examples, students could then experiment with applying the learning scale and determine what it means to demonstrate two different levels of proficiency on the same skill.[11] And perhaps most important, and in stark contrast to typical rubrics, Sam wrote this scale to be independent of a specific product. He chose to express his understanding with concept mapping. But this scale could as easily be applied to an essay or a story captured in a podcast or video.

Providing Multiple Opportunities for Practice

Skills worth knowing take plenty of practice. Consider learning to drive, for instance. In most cases, we first learn the rules of the road, including street signs and traffic patterns (knowledge). We practice driving (skills) with coaching and support from a trusted adult (teacher). Of course, many of us struggle with parallel parking and hill starts, benefiting from more practice and more feedback. Eventually we take the driver's test (performance assessment) and

FIGURE 7.2   **Modeling a cause and effect think-aloud,
Shelburne Community School**

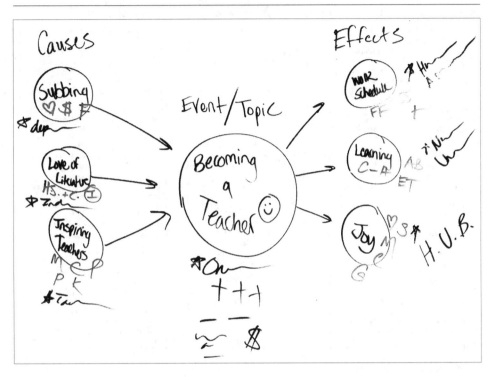

Source: Sam Nelson, Shelburne Community School.

hopefully pass (demonstrate proficiency). If we don't pass the first time, we continue to hone our skills and try again. Practice is key to learning. Proficiency-based assessment draws from these real-life experiences with learning. Learning scales are meant to scaffold multiple opportunities for practice by sharpening teacher and student understanding of what progress looks like.

PERSONALIZATION IN PRACTICE   Shelburne Community School

Sam's students also have multiple opportunities to get it right. In figure 7.4, Sam has evaluated a student's work against the cause and effect scale. He expects the student to resubmit an improved product in order to advance to the next level of proficiency.

FIGURE 7.3   **Cause and effect diagram, Shelburne Community School**

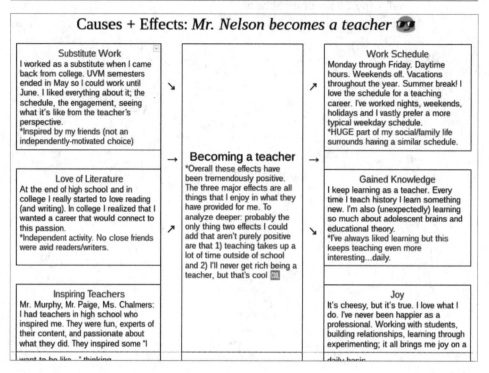

Source: Sam Nelson, Shelburne Community School.

Offering Regular and Specific Feedback

Proficiency-based assessment relies on formative assessment strategies to ensure that students receive ongoing feedback that is specific and targeted. With properly introduced learning scales, students should have a clear sense of the assessment criteria, a vision of what success looks like. As they undertake the process of learning over multiple opportunities, they need clear feedback on where they are in relation to the target, and what they need to do in order to move closer to it.

Unlike summative assessment, which is intended to measure outcomes after instruction is completed, formative assessment is ongoing and occurs while the learning is in progress. It's rooted in brief snapshots of a learner's

FIGURE 7.4   **Student product evaluated on cause and effect scale**

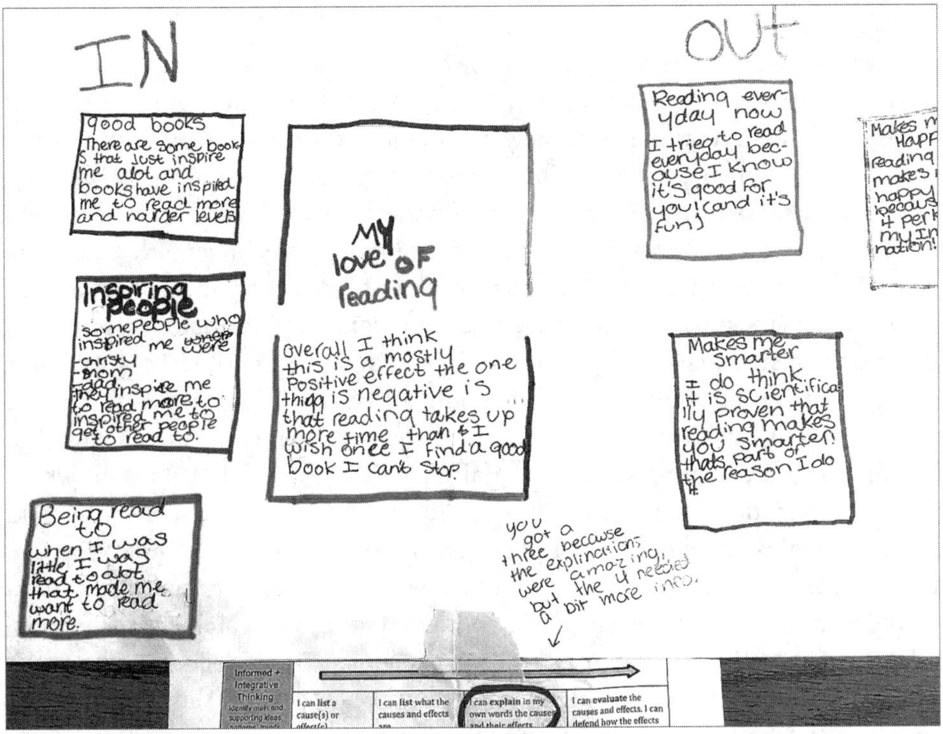

Source: Student group, Shelburne Community School.

comprehension, learning needs, and progress. The Association for Middle Level Education identifies just such an approach when it calls for "varied and ongoing assessments (that) advance learning as well as measure it."[12] Formative assessment tasks are intended to promote student learning, illuminate how learners are progressing toward a goal, and inform next steps. And there's a compelling case to be made for spending time on formative assessment. Students who participate in formative assessment perform better on a variety of achievement indicators than their peers do; furthermore, when learning objectives and assessment criteria are clear and transparent, students' self-assessment abilities improve, which in turn improves learning outcomes.[13] What's more, the accessible language of proficiency-based assessment, conversations about targets and scales, and technologies that help us share (and in some instances, gather) granular and just-in-time data all contribute to new and more powerful opportunities for formative assessment.

Formative assessment might take the form of questions, exit tickets, graphic organizers, discussions, self-assessments, observations, and any number of other check ins on students' understanding and readiness. And they needn't be teacher-designed. Fodder for formative assessment also emerges organically from students' self-directed work, which nonetheless can be examined related to learning scales. Formative assessment helps reveal concepts learners are struggling to understand or skills they are having difficulty mastering, as well as what learners know and can do. Frequent (even daily) formative assessment can catch misunderstandings early, before they are cemented in a learner's mind. Take it from Noah Hurlburt, science teacher at Proctor High School, who said, "I'm catching misconceptions at the source, instead of waiting until the final test and saying 'Oh, gosh! Half the kids really didn't do well, where did I miss it, what was I not getting?'. . . So I design it with misconceptions in mind."[14] Noah's extensive use of playlists to promote self-paced and independent learning, which we highlighted in chapter 6, frees him up during class to have the individual or small group consultations to catch these misconceptions. Formative assessments inform a teacher's daily decisions about the just-in-time instruction, resources, and groupings—the scaffolding—as well as how best to adapt time, space and roles to the evolving needs in a personalized environment.

The use of formative assessment needn't be limited to proficiencies alone. Take for example this quick check in from Burke Town School. Teachers used the tool in figure 7.5 to obtain a snapshot of students' emotional and logistical status in the midst of project-based learning. They then used the results to inform adjustments to their schedule and plans.

Monitoring and Tracking Growth

A high-quality learning management system (LMS) or other tracking tool amenable to proficiency-based assessment can help students, parents, teachers, and administrators continuously track student progress on key proficiencies. And there are several good reasons to do so. First of all, providing teachers with access to graphic displays of their students' growth on formative assessments has been associated with increased student achievement.[15] What's

FIGURE 7.5   **Project check-in form, Burke Town School**

How are you feeling about your Global Goals Project today? (Circle one)

What questions do you have?

_____
_____
_____
_____
_____
_____
_____

What point are you on in this project?

❑ Deciding on a project idea.
❑ Researching the idea.
❑ Creating a timeline.
❑ Finding funding.
❑ Contacting community partners.
❑ Researching how to create the project.
❑ Beginning to build the project.
❑ Revising my idea.
❑ Revising my timeline.
❑ Working with community partners.
❑ Building the project.
❑ Finding ways to make the project sustainable.
❑ Completing the project!

Source: Burke Town School.

more, because a digital system can manage evidence of learning from a variety of sources, teachers can be more responsive and targeted in their feedback, regardless of the contexts in which students are pursuing their learning. And with appropriate systems and platforms in place, these tracking data can be made available to multiple parties, including mentors, community partners, families, and students themselves, removing a wall standing between collaborators in a student's progress that before now was nearly impenetrable.

A growing number of LMSs are incorporating tools to help manage and track student progress toward proficiency. Figure 7.6 shows how teachers on Team Extreme at Lamoille Union Middle School assembled resources for an interdisciplinary unit on cities using the Schoology learning management system. Schoology makes it possible to establish achievement levels with its Mastery Settings function. These can be tied directly to school or district learning

FIGURE 7.6 **View of interdisciplinary resources and activities for an integrated unit on cities, Lamoille Union Middle School**

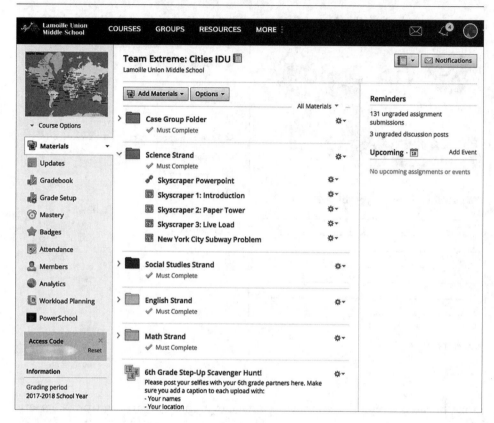

Source: Team Extreme, Lamoille Union Middle School.

scales. Progress toward mastery can be reviewed at the student level using Schoology's Objectives Report which summarizes proficiency-specific achievement across all related learning opportunities and evidence (see figure 7.7). Teachers can quickly review the status of an entire class across a range of proficiencies and drill down to get tallies for the number of students at each level on a specific proficiency (see figure 7.8) as well as see how an individual student performed on multiple opportunities working at a specific proficiency (see figure 7.9). Figure 7.10 graphically summarizes full class performance. Handy

FIGURE 7.7   **Teacher view of individual student progress on statistics proficiencies by learning activity, Lamoille Union Middle School**

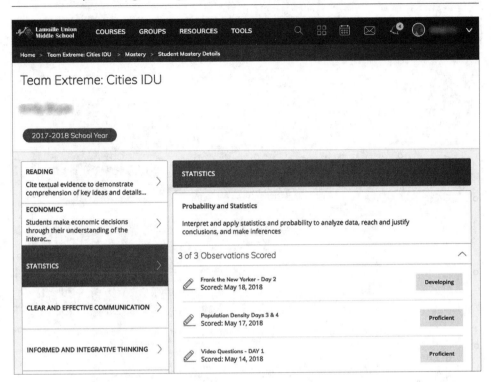

Source: Team Extreme, Lamoille Middle School.

functionality and user-friendly color-coding aid teachers wanting to leverage these large records of proficiency for just-in-time decisions about grouping and differentiation.

LMSs are making great headway toward a previously unimaginable reality: an efficient approach to personalized learning grounded in authentic and formative assessment. Key to the sustainability is students taking responsibility for compiling evidence, tagging it to proficiencies, and reflecting upon progress. Taking on this new role deepens their own experience while taking on often time-consuming work of teachers. Combined with monitoring and reporting functions of a proficiency-oriented LMS, we can begin to imagine a

FIGURE 7.8   **Whole class view of student progress on proficiencies, Lamoille Union Middle School**

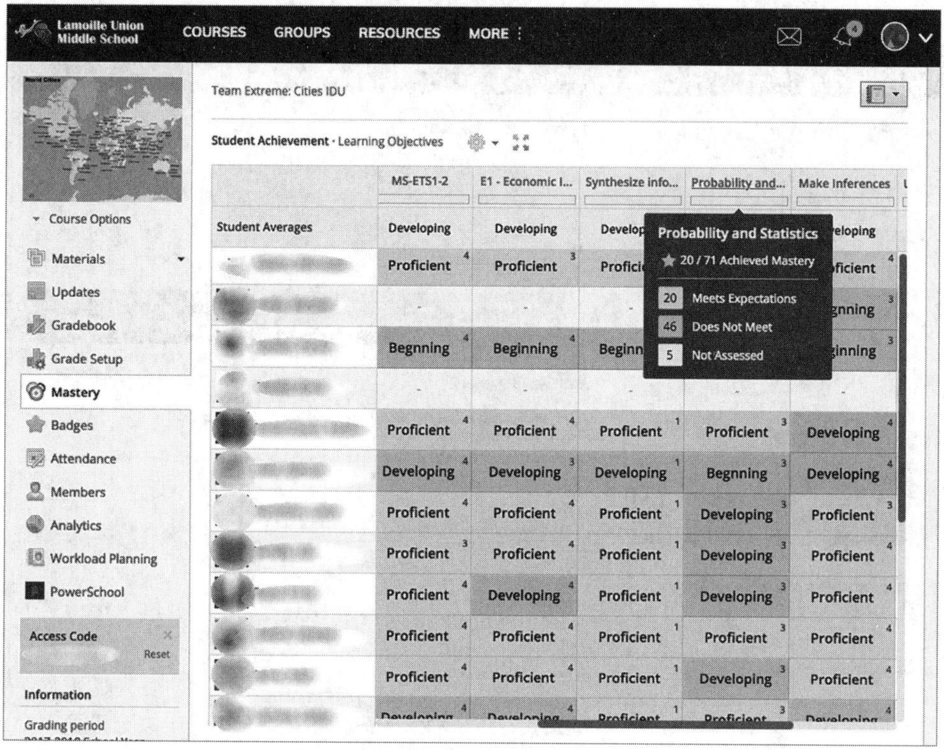

Source: Team Extreme, Lamoille Middle School.

truly powerful—and sustainable—assessment scheme for personalized learning environments. As Marzano summarized, "When it comes to using classroom assessment to enhance student achievement, having students track their progress using rubrics is a hidden gem. This strategy involves multiple types of assessments, increases interactions between teachers and students, and provides students with clear guidance on how to enhance their learning."[16] When students track their own progress, the gains are even greater than those realized when teachers track them.

It's worth considering why proficiency-based educators increasingly are moving away from numbers to represent the quality of student work in

FIGURE 7.9   **Whole class progress indicating activities associated with score, Lamoille Union Middle School**

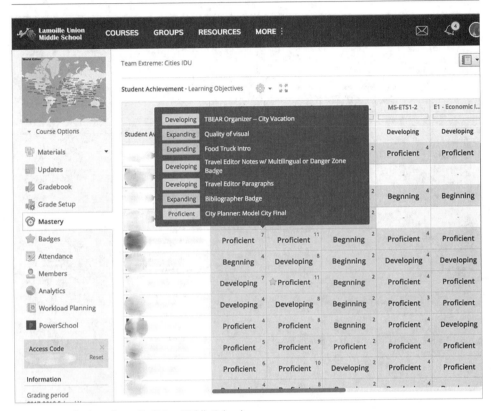

Source: Team Extreme, Lamoille Union Middle School.

learning scales. First, associating numbers with each level of proficiency (e.g., beginning, developing, meeting, and exceeding) causes them to be frequently misinterpreted as equivalent to grades A, B, C, and D by students, families, and even teachers. This simply replicates many of the problems we've experienced with traditional grading. Yet we would anticipate a student's early progress toward a proficiency might align with language at the lower ends of a learning scale. In proficiency-based assessment, a student wouldn't be punished with a 1 or 2 any more than a D or C for beginning a new learning journey. Instead, proficiency scales use language to provide students with the detailed

FIGURE 7.10   **Box and whisker analysis of class performance by proficiency and activity, Lamoille Union Middle School**

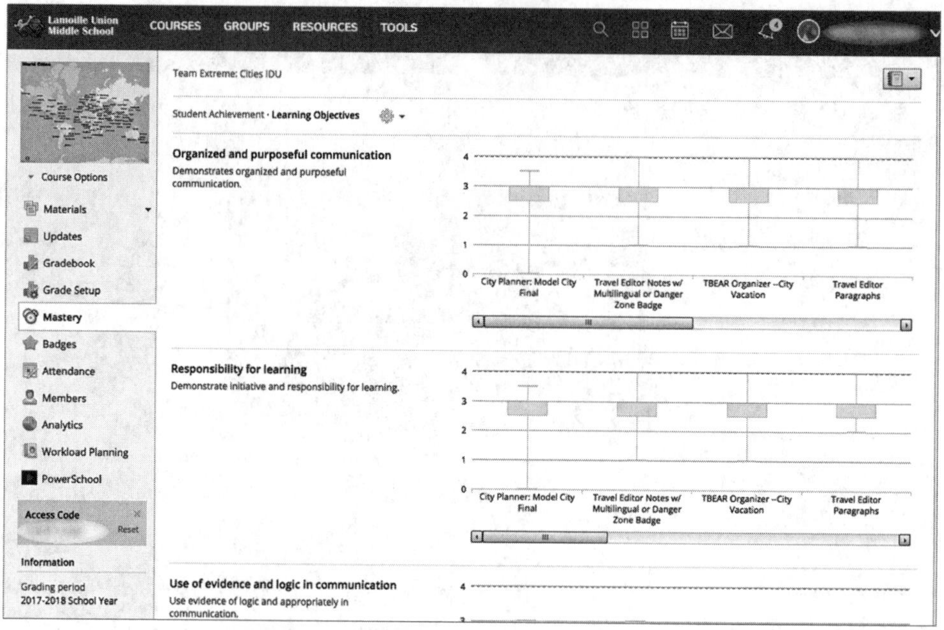

Source: Team Extreme, Lamoille Union Middle School.

information they need to assume greater control over, and responsibility for, their personalized pathway.

PERSONALIZATION IN PRACTICE   Shelburne Community School

Kelly Spreen, a physical education teacher and Lauren Goracy, a special educator, launched their own version of Shelburne Community School's new emphasis on Personal Interest Projects. Their plan synthesizes many facets of the personalized and proficiency-based approach. Students consider avenues toward fitness they want to pursue, select one, and develop a detailed plan aligned with district PE proficiencies and related transferable skills. Table 7.2 represents middle schooler Lindsay Beer's plan to "Strengthen my core, legs, and arms to help increase speed and endurance." Notice especially the emphasis on tracking

TABLE 7.2 **Personal PE plan, Shelburne Community School**

What I hope to learn during my PE PIP 2017–2018			
Goal **1. I want to . . .** Strengthen my core, legs, and arms to help increase speed and endurance	**Steps To Completion:** 1. Use weight room to strengthen muscles. 2. Run on the treadmill and practice increasing speed quickly and running for extended amounts of time. 3. Practice putting it all together, speed, strength, look for improvements, look for areas of improvements needed and then repeat the steps for that part. 4. I can use my parisi training workouts. **Workout 1** ▪ Lap around field ▪ 10 pushups ▪ Pigeon stretch ▪ Plank 30 sec. ▪ Butt kickers ▪ High knees ▪ Hold the knee (forward) ▪ Hold the knee (Backward) ▪ Repeat 5 times **Workout 2—Parisi** ▪ 10 of each, squats, jumping jacks, seal jacks, flings, ▪ Hip bridges, dual leg and single leg ▪ Iron cross ▪ Prone hurtlers ▪ Push-ups ▪ Chin Ups ▪ TP Deadlift ▪ Lunges	**Evidence of achievement:** 1. Photos 2. Videos 3. Workout Routines 4. Health App, Phone	**How it will be tracked:** 1. Pictures 2. Videos 3. Fit Bit 4. 100 chart **Anchor Task** **if I forget my materials or weather doesn't permit:** My activity doesn't require any equipment from home and is indoor or outdoors at the school. Therefore I can work in any situation.
What Type of Goal is This? _Y_ **Cardiovascular Endurance** _Y_ **Muscular Strength/Endurance** _Y_ **Flexibility** _Y_ **Sport Performance** _Y_ **Skill based**			
Why is this goal important to you? I think by increasing my speed and strength I can become more able to support my ankles and knees and avoid the pain that I currently have. It is also very helpful for sports and other physical activities. **What Equipment or resources do you need?** Weight Room at school, my phone			

Source: Lindsay Beer, student, Shelburne Community School.

evidence of learning and the clear alignment with goal-setting in the far-right columns. And again, the straightforward, student-friendly "I can" language is used in the proficiency scale that accompanied the plan (see table 7.3). Their planning template demonstrates a powerful convergence of project-based learning, student choice and self-direction, and proficiency-based assessment.

Helping students track their progress using tools in proficiency-based environments helps students understand what and how they are learning and subsequently set goals based on accessing and using their own data.

Integrating Summative Assessment

Summative assessment also plays a role in a personalized and proficiency-based approach. Yet, while *students* learn from formative assessment, it is the *system* that learns from summative assessment. While formative assessment occurs while the learning is happening, summative assessment occurs at the end of the learning; it's intended to assess a student's mastery after instruction is complete. The tasks typically occur at the culmination of a specific curriculum. Summative assessment need not be limited to a test, however. In a proficiency-based system, these tasks often are performance based. Performance tasks ask students to demonstrate their understanding and skills: they conduct an inquiry-based lab; they write a letter to the editor or legislator about a real and relevant issue; they solve an authentic engineering or mathematical problem. When students complete a performance task that is meaningful and rigorous and combines content knowledge with transferable skills, they demonstrate much more than the memorization of facts on a multiple-choice test. Each of these is meant to determine if students have mastered the intended learning outcomes. They are often used as an accountability measure, either for the school, as is the case with demonstrating Adequate Yearly Progress, or for the learner, such as a grade on a report card or transcript.

The role of summative assessment in a personalized learning environment is to plan and report student progress toward those proficiencies. In project-based learning, it's often the final products—the models, speeches, videos, proposals, or sculptures, for instance, that represent the culmination of the deep learning during the project. Summative assessments are usually tied to learning scales or rubrics which, at their best, help evaluate evidence of authentic learning against required proficiencies. And if a student falls short of a particular targeted proficiency, there is no reason this summative assessment

TABLE 7.3 **Personal PE plan proficiencies: Shelburne Community School**

LEARNING TARGETS FOR MY PE PIP					
Transferable Skill					**Alignment with District PE Target**
Self-Direction	With support, I am encouraged to exhibit a positive attitude and actively participate.	I am beginning to exhibit a positive attitude and actively participate.	**My positive attitude and active participation demonstrates that I value physical activity for my personal health and well-being.**	My positive attitude and active participation encourages others and fosters a growth mindset.	CVSD PE: SHAPE 5: Participation
Informed and Integrative Thinking	With support, I can begin to understand the knowledge and skills needed to achieve and maintain a health-enhancing level of physical activity and fitness.	I am beginning to understand the knowledge and skills needed to achieve and maintain a health-enhancing level of physical activity and fitness.	**I can demonstrate the knowledge and skills to achieve and maintain a health-enhancing level of physical activity and fitness.**	I can demonstrate and apply the knowledge and skills to achieve and maintain a health-enhancing level of physical activity and fitness through self-directed learning and activities.	CVSD PE: SHAPE 3: Personal Wellness

Source: Kelly Spreen and Lauren Goracy, teachers, Shelburne Community School.

couldn't be used formatively, informing the next steps on that child's journey toward proficiency. After all, a proficiency-based approach to assessment is a natural complement to personalized learning environments for young adolescents because it's intended to build competence. That means retakes aren't just OK, they're expected.

Contrary to the common refrain that "final" exams prepare students for the harsh realities beyond school, the adult world offers unlimited retakes. The bar exam, for lawyers, for example. Take it as many times as you like. NCLEX too (nursing), NREMT (EMT/paramedic), PRAXIS (teaching), FAA (pilots), CPA (accountants), MCAT (medical school), LSAT (law school), and ASE (mechanics) exams. Even your driving test! You can just keep taking the exam until you pass. And after retaking any of these exams, your final result is the only result that counts. You know what they call someone who passed the bar exam on the fifth try? An attorney. But in our students' world, if there's a chapter 7 science test on Tuesday, they usually only get one pitch and a swing to get it right.[17]

Instead of planning for a bell curve or broad distribution of grades, we want *all* students to succeed. And, in a proficiency-based system, we craft learning opportunities accordingly.

Anticipating Concerns from Families

One of the most common concerns about proficiency-based assessment pertains to students' applications to higher education. Families may worry that, without traditional assessment, their children will be at a disadvantage as they apply to colleges and universities. As the shift to proficiency-based assessment is introduced to communities, you can almost see the wheels turning inside of parents' heads. One of their first questions is, what about the high school transcript and applying to college? And, often second, what about the GPA? How will the school determine the valedictorian? Because it is such a massive shift from their own school experience, this can often be unsettling and difficult to understand. And most of us can appreciate these very real anxieties. At the same time, we've learned some useful lessons from schools as they make this transition.

Let's start with the first concern. How will colleges perceive this new, proficiency-based, report card? While it looks different from the traditional one, it can provide a much wider lens on a student's journey through secondary school. And it turns out that this is a lens that colleges actually appreciate. Sixty-seven elite colleges in New England, such as Harvard and MIT, have voiced their support for proficiency-based learning, asserting that "students with proficiency-based grades and transcripts will not be disadvantaged in any way."[18] Furthermore, "according to some admissions leaders, features of the proficiency-based transcript model shared with the group provide important information for institutions seeking not just high-performing academics, but engaged, lifelong learners."[19] Many parents don't know that colleges are accustomed to receiving different kinds of transcripts, such as those from home-schooled and international students. In fact, they have done so for years. As long as the sending school's information is clear and comprehensive, students are not disadvantaged in the college admissions process. Many universities themselves are considering moves to proficiency- or competency-based systems.

The second concern—what about GPA and valedictorian?—is also common. Families often assume that calculating a GPA is impossible in a proficiency-based system, which is concerning given that the GPA is one piece of evidence that many colleges still expect. However, schools using proficiency-based assessment often compute grade point averages precisely for these purposes. In fact, they are part of several new proficiency-based report cards being used in Vermont. While we believe converting proficiencies to numeric scores for a GPA is problematic in that it doesn't reflect the strengths-based, developmental approach of high quality, personalized learning, schools can—and often do—provide this evidence to colleges in the application process. Further, because GPAs are still determined, class rank can be as well, and the tradition of awarding a valedictorian can be continued as well, if chosen by the school system. While we would debate the effectiveness of using students' numerical scores to convey learning and growth, it is a myth that students at schools using proficiency-based reporting lack evidence that colleges and universities require.

Proficiency-based report cards look different from traditional ones. As with any educational change, a solid plan for informing and involving the school community is vital. Stakeholders need to make sense of the new reporting system and to provide feedback on it. Family nights, forums, video introductions, screencasts, and brochures are all ways schools can help students and their parents or guardians manage the shift to proficiency-based report cards. The process is rarely easy, but when decisions and actions are supported by research and experience, educators can stay the course and build understanding along the road to personalized learning.

Anticipating Concerns from Colleagues

Families aren't the only ones who sometimes struggle with a shift to proficiency-based assessment. Educators are also justifiably wary of new practices, and more experienced teachers have seen the pendulum swing many times over the course of their careers. So it's understandable that some might opt to sit this latest one out. While the implementation of proficiency-based assessment varies from state to state and school to school, however, it is unlikely that education will return to a one-size-fits-all approach anytime soon. For one thing, social and economic change are significant forces behind personalized learning, exhibiting themselves in many ways, including home-schooling, online learning, and the proliferation of charter schools. Those forces aren't likely to abate, and nor will the pressures they exert on traditional and public schools. But there are purely educational pressures as well, particularly the need to come up with diversified assessment systems that help teachers serve all students better. As Noguera, Darling-Hammond and Friedlaender argue, "The current high-stakes testing environment has inadvertently reinforced long-standing tracking systems that deny students of color and low-income students access to a thinking curriculum, instead relegating them to remedial, rote-oriented, and often scripted courses of study."[20] When educators recognize the promise of proficiency-based assessment to drive engaging learning *and* address long-standing inequities, they are less likely to view this educational shift as just another fad. So, while even some personalized practices undoubtedly will change over time, and the pendulum will certainly continue to swing, we've found that the educators we work with are hopeful, rather than disdainful, about this dramatic yet purposeful shift.

Teacher as Assessor: Helping Students Showcase Evidence of Learning through Exhibitions

Many young adolescents crave an authentic way to demonstrate their hard work and learning. When students know from the inception of a project that they will be sharing it with an authentic audience, many feel excited and driven. Inviting a real audience into school to witness student work brings a sense of purpose to the students. After all, it's exhilarating to talk about your thinking, your successes, and challenges with real humans from beyond your classroom; most kids are used to sharing only with the teacher or perhaps the class. Helping students showcase evidence of their learning to a broader audience by bringing an audience into school—or taking the work to an audience outside of it—can motivate students to shine and do their best. It helps kids to feel important and know that people care about their work.[21] Moreover, the evidence that emerges from these moments is often the richest of all.

Culminating events often take the form of a learning fair or exhibition at the end of the unit, but they don't have to. They can also take the form of film festivals, poetry slams, performances, simulations, digital sharing, school board presentations, conference presentations, art exhibitions at a local café, or community events. Regardless of the form, however, a culminating event should be an authentic way to share projects to a wider community, in which the students present their work publicly and see the value in doing so. Students need to understand how their work is connected to their society and the audience should be one that is important to the students.[22]

How will your students share their work? Students are often more motivated when their work will be seen by more than just the teacher, completed solely for a grade. Students need to present to an audience that matters to them, such as their peers, family, community, special interest groups, or leaders. What follows are just a few examples of culminating events we've seen our partner schools host successfully.

- *Learning Fairs or Schoolwide Exhibitions.* In the Learning Fair, students set up stations and present to small groups of people about their projects. Educators at Manchester Elementary-Middle School designed their School Exhibition Night to bring families together to learn about learning. Students even shared the (working!) wind turbines they created, among many other innovations.[23]
- *School Board Presentations.* School boards often want to hear directly from students about what is happening in the classroom. At Proctor Elementary, students tested the school for sound challenges and energy loss. The students reported back to the board about their findings, which then informed the board's decisions about the next year's budget.
- *District Board Presentations.* Eighth graders at Burke Town School presented to their supervisory union board about their PBL unit: Projects for Hope. They shared what they learned from participating in project-based learning, what they thought could be improved, and their opinions on whether or not other schools in their district should do project-based learning.
- *State or Local Organizations.* Depending on the topic and presentation medium, local organizations can be a great audience. One group of middle school students created a play to exhibit their learning and invited members of the local college's thespian club to give them feedback on their play at the end of their unit.
- *Film Festivals.* Students can create films, documentaries, public service announcements, newscasts, trailers or other films, and host a film festival where they invite local filmmakers, media personnel, and community members. Ottauquechee School had a recent public service announcements film festival, where they debuted their PSAs on wind energy. And Compass School hosts an annual student film festival to which they invite

their alumni who work in film and media to provide feedback on the films to the current students. In addition to providing an authentic audience, it's a great way to stay connected with former students.

- *Community Meals.* Students can plan and serve community meals, where they can show all sorts of learning: meal planning, culinary skills, intrapersonal serving skills, among others. The students of Cabot School made pizza for all participants in a learning fair about their yearlong service learning project called Cabot Leads.

- *Presentations of Learning.* In these more formal presentations, students lead a group of important people through their portfolios and projects. The audience often includes peers, family, select important adults, and educational leaders who then provide feedback and decide if the student has met the expectations for the project. The PLP conference, one type of presentation of learning, is featured in greater detail in chapter 8.

These are just a few of the many types of culminating events we've seen hosted successfully. Your students are sure to offer more.

Many teachers are understandably fearful about sharing student work with the community. They think that everything has to be perfect and meet adult standards to be shared. It's helpful to remember that, despite the excitement of the culminating event, project-based learning really is about the process of learning.[24] The end product should not be viewed as the only evidence of learning. At some point, teachers may need to let go of any perfectionism or insecurity and help students the best that they can for a public audience. Overall, educators we work with find that, while planning and hosting such an event can be time consuming, the power of students sharing their learning with others makes it all worthwhile. As our colleague Rachel Mark concluded:

> School exhibitions take work. They take work to organize, schedule, promote and pull off, and they can feel overwhelming from the teacher side. But they also provide a very specific opportunity for students to stand proudly next to the results of all their hard work and say, "Yes. I did this." And that can be the best time and place for families to hear the pride in their student's voice.[25]

LOOKING AHEAD: SUSTAINING THIS GOOD WORK

We're aware that this might seem overwhelming. After all, personalized learning suggests that students should have access to flexible pathways based on who they are and what they need. Formative assessment is most effective when it's ongoing and results in rich feedback grounded in clear and transparent learning targets. Students need access to their assessment data so it can inform their personalized planning and self-direction. And today's families increasingly demand access to progress data, which is hard enough to achieve even when only reporting numbers and grades. At first glance, the challenges may seem insurmountable. But the reason for doing so is clear. As a student from Lamoille South Supervisory Union said, "Getting a good grade is no longer a mystery. The learning scales spell out what you need to do well." This student's observation captures much of the purpose for our efforts toward proficiency-based assessment.

Proficiency-based assessment is grounded in knowing students well through their PLPs and focuses on students' personalized and flexible pathways while cultivating student competence. Now that we've examined each of these three pillars, let's look at two key components that underscore their interdependence. In the next chapter, we explore the use of goal-setting and student-led PLP conferences, positioning both practices as key strategies for making learning personal and powerful.

EIGHT

PLPS, GOAL-SETTING, AND STUDENT-LED CONFERENCES

Karen pulls up a chair to the table of three other teachers. She's rushed from the bathroom after making sure her student with a bloody nose made it to the nurse's office. Their common planning time period always goes by so quickly that Karen is inclined to jump right in and get started with student-led conference planning, but she forces herself to stop, take a breath, and ask, "How is everyone doing?"

Her teammates welcome her in readily and, after few moments of pleasant conversation, everyone feels grounded and ready to go. This team has focused on building trust and relationships since day one. They created shared norms that they regularly refer back to, and those help keep the team on track. Not only is it much more pleasant to work on this team than others she's been on, Karen reflects, but it feels much more effective because it's grounded in an awareness that their work matters and that their common planning time yields positive results for their students.

"OK," Karen begins. "We need to finalize plans for the upcoming student-led conferences." She refers the team to their PLP and student planning document in their shared folder on Google Drive. "How are you both doing in terms of our workflow? I know time is tight this time of year and it can be stressful to fit everything in! Has everyone had their students upload recent evidence, especially the final projects from last week, and the reflections?" Another teacher, Emily, nods. Allison, a newer teacher, shakes her head no.

"I just haven't found the time for them to reflect yet. I know I am running out of time." She taps her foot anxiously. The team is quick to encourage her that she still has time. Together they look at her schedule to see how they can help out. Allison nods as they find a time for reflection and Emily offers to come in and assist. Allison is visibly relieved by this support.

"OK, next on the plan is for us to hold individual conferences with students about their PLPs, and for students to practice their student-led conferences with their PLP partners. How do we want to schedule that?"

The team continues this way, until they have a clear plan with benchmarks of progress leading up to the student-led conferences. Teachers will have a chance to confer one-on-one with each student to give feedback, and students will have several practice sessions with peers.

Karen offers one last item before the meeting closes, *"Remember we are going for 100 percent participation here—if a family member or family friend can't come in, try to schedule a Google Hangout or Skype sometime that works for them. If this is impossible, let's make sure that student presents to a school staff member they feel close to. Emily, can you create a table for that so we can set it up?"* Emily nods, *"No problem!"* and quickly adds this to their planning doc in Drive. The team jokes around, chatting about their upcoming weekends as they pack up their laptops and head back to class.

BUILDING YOUR RATIONALE: FOSTERING EFFICACY

The teachers on this team are clearly planning with young adolescents' needs in mind. As they look toward the launch of the student-led conferences, these educators are careful to ensure students have had several experiences in preparation for the big event. They've intentionally built in time for students to update their latest work to their PLPs, as well as to reflect on that work. They've scheduled individual conferences with each learner for the purposes of teacher feedback. And they've made space in the busy school day for students to practice leading these important learning conversations with peers. What's more, they've anticipated the very real possibility that not all students will have a family member available to come to school at the time of the conferences. As a result, they have two strong options planned: holding a virtual student-led conference or having another professional in the building stepping into the role of trusted adult.

With each of these acts, the teachers create the conditions in which young adolescents can feel efficacious. Stevenson proposed five components to describe middle schoolers' personal efficacy needs: competence, awareness, affiliation, ethical sense of self, and responsibility.[1] By carefully scaffolding the PLP conference in these ways, the teachers ensure students have a real chance to feel competent, demonstrate responsibility, and experience affiliation and belonging. They set their students up for success.

The teachers on this team are also planning with their own needs in mind. You may also have noticed how these teammates support one another in their work. They're careful to check in on the others' personal needs before jumping into the business at hand. They inquire if their colleagues need assistance. And they quickly strategize to provide that backing when it's needed. In addition to promoting students' self-efficacy, they're creating the conditions for teachers to feel efficacious, as the relationship between support and teacher self-efficacy is well documented.[2] What's more, collegial support of this sort also plays a vital role in enhancing teachers' job satisfaction, professional growth, and commitment to teaching.[3]

Shifting the ownership for communicating one's learning to students is not a new idea for middle grades educators, who have long advocated for student-led conferences as a developmentally appropriate and empowering replacement for the more traditional teacher-parent conference.[4] In an SLC, "the student is in charge of the academic conference with the parents. The teacher simply serves as a discussion facilitator when needed. This increased accountability moves the student from passive—and frequently second-hand—recipient of information shared between teacher and parent to active participant in a three-way interaction among parent, teacher, and student. Students assume 'equal partner' status in discussions concerning their academic progress."[5] The use of this alternative conferencing format has been linked to a number of positive outcomes. In settings where SLCs have been adopted, students report being more likely to revise and edit their work, as well spend more time on it overall; teachers report planning lessons with greater intent; administrators report increased family participation; and parents report a preference for the SLC over the traditional conference format.[6]

CHAPTER OVERVIEW

It might sound simple, but one way to make high-impact change like personalized learning and student-led conferences more manageable is by constructing a timeline and a to-do list. We have learned that teams are well served by viewing the student-led conference as an important milestone that helps launch the rest of their year. By backward planning from these student-led conferences, teachers identify ways to leverage the conference for all sorts of smart moves in the first three months of school, including when to implement any number of the identity development and norm-setting activities we referenced earlier in the book. In this chapter, we explore the planning process for personalized learning in greater depth. We'll briefly introduce you to some strategies our partners have used to bring order to the implementation of Learner Profiles. They've then applied these same planning principles to later stages of developing personalized environments. It's useful to see how a thoughtful plan for Learner Profiles can yield the benefits to student development, classroom culture, and an engaging launch of PLPs.

PLANNING THE PLP CONFERENCE

SLCs are a natural fit for developing and sharing PLPs. Indeed, they are widely seen as an all-but-necessary strategy for bringing student, family, and teachers to the same table for the purposes of planning, evaluating, and communicating the process of personalized learning. And they provide a number of opportunities for an authentic audience for students and their Learner Profiles, including their PLP partner, teachers and families, as well as community mentors who may be invited into the conference as well. We've started calling them PLP conferences, or PLPCs, but many folks have simply retained the more familiar term SLCs. Conferences are rich but rather complex affairs, but as you'll see in the following examples, the planning is remarkably straightforward and the preparation tools others have created are widely available, transferable, and adaptable.

PERSONALIZATION IN PRACTICE   Peoples Academy Middle Level

As with the team in the opening vignette, Maura Weiler and her colleagues on Team Apollo at Peoples Academy Middle Level in Morrisville were careful to scaffold the PLP conference to help it run smoothly. They provided specific resources for students and families alike. Students benefit from clearly outlined agendas, ideally that they've helped to construct, as well as the chance to practice running through this important exhibition of their learning. For some, this will be the first time talking with their families about themselves as learners in a formal way. Table 8.1 features the agenda the Peoples Academy Middle Level teachers developed to help students share their growth with their families.

This team offered families guidance, as well, on what is often a new role for them. Table 8.2 conveys some of the advice this team provided, which included sample questions family members might pose during the conference. Families also benefit from knowing that the PLP conference is not intended to be an in-depth meeting with the teacher and that they are welcome to reach out at other times for those purposes. The focus here, however, is on the connection between the learner and the invited audience.

PERSONALIZATION IN PRACTICE F.H. Tuttle Middle School

Christie Nold, a teacher at Tuttle Middle School in South Burlington, uses tools like those used by Team Apollo, and then approaches the conference itself as a performance assessment for students. Table 8.3 illustrates how she conceptualizes the task and prepares students to confidently conduct the PLP conference with their families.

TABLE 8.1 **Student-led conference agenda: Peoples Academy Middle Level**

Student-Led Conference Agenda
▪ Welcome Statement   ▪ Includes sharing your "About Me."

▪ Launch Presentation
  ▪ Share Academic Goal
  ▪ What do you think will be most challenging?
  ▪ Why is this goal important to you?
  ▪ How can your parents help?

▪ Share the negotiated curriculum theme for the year - Creativity!
  ▪ What are the possible projects you may want to work on?
  ▪ What are some topics that are connected to this theme?

▪ Share academic successes in Keynote:
  ▪ What have you been learning about in all of your classes?
  ▪ What about the specific piece of evidence you selected made it a success for you?

▪ Include a closure.   ▪ Thank your family for coming

Source: Team Apollo teachers, Peoples Academy Middle Level.

TABLE 8.2 **Student-led conference guidance for families: Peoples Academy Middle Level**

HINTS FOR PARENTS FOR STUDENT-LED CONFERENCES

- Express positive interest and anticipation about the upcoming conference.
- Listen and respond to the student.
- Express pride in growth and progress.
- Ask questions.
- Be positive, offering to help in areas where improvement is needed.
- Recognize that students need to develop independence in communicating progress—the teacher will be there to facilitate and answer specific questions but will not take charge of the conference. There may be two conferences happening at the same time—the teacher will be in the background.

POSSIBLE QUESTIONS TO ASK DURING THE STUDENT-LED CONFERENCE

- Can you explain this to me?
- How did you come up with this idea?
- How have you grown in this area?
- How can you improve in this area?
- How can we help you at home?
- What was important to you about this?
- If you could do this work over again, how would you change it?
- Have you thought about future goals?

Source: Team Apollo teachers, Peoples Academy Middle Level.

IMPLEMENTING LEARNER PROFILE TASKS: WHERE AND WHEN?

As you can see by Maura's and Christie's examples, a successful PLP conference does not happen by accident. Clearly, these teachers are scaffolding the tasks required of students and families for successful conferences. Supporting learners like this demands a great deal of forethought, planning and preparation. Research on SLC implementation often identifies streamlining paperwork and finding adequate preparation time as primary dilemmas.[7] While the digital format helps somewhat with the former challenge, the latter requires adopting schedules that reflect the importance of this work. Some suggest three phases of student-led conferences: preconference preparation, conference, and post-conference evaluation.[8] Others advocate for a six-stage process to encourage wider acceptance and implementation of the practice.[9] Regardless of how you break down the implementation, it's worth planning it out in advance. Let's look at another example to help imagine what this planning would yield in practice for the teachers involved. What does it take to get to the thoughtful

TABLE 8.3 **Student-led conference performance assessment, Tuttle Middle School**

Transfer Goals
Students will be able to independently use their learning to:

Disciplinary Outcomes: Content Area Proficiency Based Graduation Requirement (PBGRs)
▪ Indicator(s): Content Area PBGRs: Social Studies 1: Inquiry
   ▪ B: Students analyze information to develop reasonable explanations that support inquiry
   ▪ C: Propose solutions to problems based on findings and ask additional questions
Cross-Disciplinary Outcomes (Transferable Skills):
▪ Indicator(s): T1: Clear and Effective Communication
   ▪ B: Use appropriate evidence and logic in communication
   ▪ E: Demonstrate effective, expressive, and receptive communication, including oral, written, multimedia, and performance

Essential Questions: ▪ How can students play a central role in their learning? ▪ Which habits of mind and essential skills lead to success?
Enduring Understandings Students will understand . . . ▪ Claim statements must be supported with evidence and reasoning ▪ Reflection and goal-setting can contribute to success
Students will keep considering . . . ▪ How to set a SMART goal connected to specific actionable steps ▪ The difference between formal and informal communication ▪ How to identify evidence connected to a claim
Performance Task
How will students demonstrate their understanding (meaning-making and transfer) through performance? Intro/Overview: Students will lead their conference in which they will share their reflection of self as a learner, evidence of their reflection, SMART goal, and actionable steps to achieve their SMART goal. G (goal)—Students will communicate their learning to family and teachers R (real-world role)—Students will serve as the facilitator A (real-world audience)—Family and teachers S (real-world situation)—Conference (traditionally, parent-teacher—now, student-led) P (real-world product/performance)—Conference S (standards)—Assessment of T1: B&E (clear and effective communication); PBGR 1 (inquiry)

(continued)

moments illustrated earlier in the book by Cassandra and her father? Or by Jamal and his mother?

PERSONALIZATION IN PRACTICE F.H. Tuttle Middle School

Teachers at Tuttle Middle School begin their planning by agreeing on their intended outcomes and how some of the big pieces fit together. Table 8.4

TABLE 8.3   **Student-led conference performance assessment, Tuttle Middle School** (*continued*)

Learning Plan
Lesson #1
Model: Identification of self as a learner—creating a claim statement with supporting evidence. (Video analysis)
Guided Practice: Create a claim statement together, assess what evidence could be used to support the claim
Independent Practice: Per individual assignment on Google Docs
Formative Check: Shared Google Doc (share link in NEO) for Claim Evidence and Explanation (CEE format) in gradebook
Instructional Next Step: Setup for evidence
Lesson #2
Model: SMART (specific measurable attainable relevant time-bound) goals from evidence ▪ Smartboard filled out sheet with moveable reveals and underlying ideas/words
Guided Practice: Narrative where they develop SMART goals and objectives ▪ Self-select based on proficiency of understanding (narrative vs partially done) ▪ Students work in small self-selected groups to create SMART goals based on the information that was provided ▪ Full-group share of the developed SMART goals, including demonstration of thinking
Independent Practice: Development of own SMART goals and objectives ▪ Top of Google Doc developed from evidence
Formative Check: NEO submission
Instructional Next Step: Check for gaps and understanding
Lesson #3
Guided Practice: (Fishbowl share to model) Partner, Share and Evaluate using Rubric for Transferable Skills
Independent Practice: Revise based on partner feedback (evidence gathering, reformatting, etc.)
Formative Check: Script and/or Video—Voice Text (google tools)
Instructional Next Step: Parent-Teacher Conference / Google doc share via link in email

Source: Christie Nold, Tuttle Middle School.

captures their view of the intersection between the Learner Profile of the PLP (in their case, the About Me, Goals/Plans and Portfolios sections) and their student-led conferences. In it you'll see how the faculty clearly identified student outcomes for both the PLP and the accompanying student-led conference. Moving on to table 8.5, you'll notice how they carefully outlined a clear timeline, as well as common expectations to be shared by all teachers across the several middle school teams in their building. They also identified a list of critical decisions that would be determined by each team individually (see table 8.5), which is an important consideration for schools with multiple teams.

TABLE 8.4   **Outcomes and components to align learner profiles with student-led conferences: Tuttle Middle School**

Student Outcomes for PLP process	PLP Section
Learn about and share who they are as a learner.	About Me (Identity Project)
Gain skills and habits of goal-setting or planning.	Goals/Plans
Develop ability to highlight growth.	Portfolio
Student Outcomes for Student-led Conferences	**SLC Components**
Learn to effectively communicate about your journey as a student and take ownership of your learning.	Tour of key portions of PLP
Ability to reflect on challenges, invite support, and consider how to address in the future.	What I need to work on
Build the disposition to celebrate your own successes and recognize growth.	What I am proud of
Make connections between your perspective and the expectations of school.	Throughout—relate to Transferable Skills or other expectations

PERSONALIZATION IN PRACTICE   Williston Central School

With years of experience with PLPs and SLCs behind them, teachers on the Swift House team at Williston Central School have developed a timeline for both, including an extensive list of links to resources for them to use along the way. This one-stop shop to help everyone stay on track is an example of thorough planning that pays off amid the time pressures of day-to-day teaching. Exploring table 8.6 is a great way for you to leapfrog over much of the time you might ordinarily devote to developing practiced vision and developing resources.

ASSESSING THE PLP CONFERENCE

PLPs draw their power from hosting collective conversations about three fundamental underpinnings of reaching and teaching young adolescents: knowing who they are, how they learn, and why it matters. PLPs, through the Learner Profile, can capture what students hold most dear about who they are and who they want to become. How we as educators facilitate and respond to the Learner Profile goes a long way to defining how seriously we take our relationships with

TABLE 8.5 **Calendar of agreed-upon milestones and necessary decisions: Tuttle Middle School**

	Common Expectations	Team Decisions
About Me (Sept-Nov)	"What is important to know about me to help me learn?" Every student's project is reviewed. Students get a response individually or as a group.	▪ How do we launch the Identity Project? ▪ When will students work on it? ▪ How do we support it? ▪ How will teachers review students' projects? ▪ How will teachers respond to students? ▪ How might students share their projects?
Platform (Dec-Jan)	Every student will have a PLP Platform that includes the three sections (titles and formats TBD by teams).	▪ What platform will we use? ▪ How will we introduce to students? ▪ When will we add the Identity Project? ▪ What aspects of platform will we allow students to choose and customize? ▪ What sections will students start with on their PLP?
Goal-Setting (Jan-Feb) OR	Every student will engage in goal-setting and/or planning for a personalized project. Students will document their goals/plans, record progress, and reflect on the outcome and process. Students will have time during school to pursue and reflect upon their goal / project.	▪ What goal-setting process will we use? ▪ How should we frame the goals—Transferable Skills, content areas, academic rather than personal, etc. ▪ When will students work on their goals/projects? ▪ How will we introduce this process? ▪ How will we involve parents?
Project-Based (Jan-Feb)		▪ What are the requirements of the project? How and when will we launch it? ▪ How will students document their goals/planning and project progress? ▪ How will the project be assessed? ▪ How will we share projects? With what audience? ▪ How will we involve parents?
Portfolio (March)	Every student will curate some of their work to highlight growth and learning.	▪ How will students select work to include? ▪ What kinds of final reflection to include?
SLC (April)	Every student will engage in a Student-Led Conference in the spring. (For students whose families do not attend, an alternative audience will be provided.) Students will use their PLPs as a source for the conference.	▪ How will the conference be formatted? ▪ How will students present? ▪ How will students be supported with time and guidance for selecting work, creating final reflections, and practicing leading their conference?
Reflection and Planning (May-June)	Every student will reflect on Student-Led Conferences and wrap up their PLP for the year. Teachers will begin planning Project-Based Learning units to be delivered 2017-18 school year (individually or in teacher teams).	▪ How should students reflect on their PLP? ▪ How to wrap it for the year? Should students share anything with peers or parents? ▪ How can we take what we learned this year and apply it to the development of Project-Based Learning units for next year?

TABLE 8.6 One-year plan for coordinating PLPs and conferences teamwide: Williston Central School, Swift House

Month	Task	Task Resources	Additional Resources
September	▪ Create PLP site: ▪ Identity, academic goal, personal goal, high quality work, reflection, 8th grade challenge tabs ▪ Complete identity work: ▪ Autobiography (Google presentation/doc) ▪ Relationships Web (Google drawing) ▪ Executive Functioning Skills Survey ▪ 8th Grade Challenge-Put plan into tab ▪ Email EA/WL teachers when PLP sites/Protean is live	Autobiography Relationship Web Pick One Executive Functioning Survey (form) or Executive Functioning Survey for Students (doc) 8th Grade Challenge Project Plan (doc to embed)	Smart but Scattered Survey Book link Executive Functioning Survey Teen Version Executive Function Presentation to review with students after survey if wanted
October (10/20 Conferences)	▪ Principles/Values Reflection ▪ Create academic and personal goal based on transferable skills ▪ 1 evidence per goal ▪ Complete 8th Grade Challenge kick-off form (house specific ideas—insert picture into PLP site under 8th Grade Challenge tab) ▪ Research identified executive functioning skill-present findings ▪ Create doc-definition, what does this look like in your life? ▪ *September & October tasks to be completed before conferences ▪ Email EA/WL teachers when PLP sites/Protean is live	Note: The Executive Functioning Results from the survey should drive either the personal or academic goal (or both). Ex. perseverance (EF skill and goal) is the goal and the ways they worked toward this is through their evidence. Personal Goal Setting Academic Goal Setting Executive Functioning Prompts	Transferable Skill Goal Ideas Transferable Skill PBGR WL add family tree project to identity tab
November	▪ Add new evidence that connects to each goal (under goals tab) ▪ 8th Grade Challenge Journal/Reflection #1 ▪ Personal & Academic Goal Reflection (under reflection tab)	Goal reflection doc	
December	▪ Add new evidence that connects to each goal (under goals tab) ▪ Executive Functioning skills reflection-strategies (What's working well? What evidence do you have of this?)	Goal reflection doc	Reflection examples from Tarrant post 8 methods for reflection
January	▪ Add new evidence that connects to each goal (under goals tab) ▪ Personal & Academic Goal Reflection (under reflection tab) ▪ 8th Grade Challenge Journal/Reflection #2	Goal reflection doc Principles/Values Reflection	

(continued)

TABLE 8.6   **One-year plan for coordinating PLPs and conferences teamwide: Williston Central School, Swift House** (continued)

Month	Task	Task Resources	Additional Resources
February	▪ Add new evidence that connects to each goal (under goals tab) ▪ Personal & Academic Goal Reflection (under reflection tab) ▪ PLP screencast	Goal reflection doc	Screen Cast Example Example of Script
March 3/23 Conferences	▪ Add new evidence that connects to each goal (under goals tab) ▪ Personal & Academic Goal Reflection (under reflection tab) ▪ Share goals, evidence & reflection at parent conference	Goal reflection doc	
April	▪ Add new evidence that connects to each goal ▪ Personal & Academic Goal Reflection	Goal reflection doc	
May	▪ Add new evidence that connects to each goal (under goals tab) ▪ Personal & Academic Goal Reflection (under reflection tab) ▪ 8th grade—Spin on "Who Am I/executive function" letter/reflection ▪ 7th grade— Brainstorm 8th grade challenge ideas ▪ 8th grade assembly kick off	Goal reflection doc	

For linked examples and more guidance, visit www.learninginthemiddle.org.

students. Through their vivid documentation of learning, PLPs also make plain our commitment to authentic learning, whether or not we are truly committed to designing—or at least permitting—learning opportunities for each student that are sufficiently engaging to have a deep and lasting impact on who they become as people. In capturing the complicated stories of student growth through a language of achievement that reveals the outcomes most valued by students, teachers, and community alike, PLPs embrace rather than hide from schooling's highest calling: our welfare, indeed our democracy's future, depends upon all children learning what matters, about themselves and about the world around them.

The full impact of PLPs, like so much else we've discussed in these chapters, may depend on having an authentic audience. A good Learner Profile cultivates relationships, but only if it is shared with teachers, families and others to inspire those relationships and the learning that stems from them. PLPs can capture vivid representations of authentic learning opportunities but must be shared in order to be anything more than a media-rich personal diary. And proficiency-based assessment provides a powerful system to guide, track, and report growth, but unless the data inform rich conversations among students, teachers and families, its real potential is lost.

Many have struggled trying to make each of these things happen independent of each other. Some have tried pulling them together into a PLP. But authentic audience for the PLP as a whole—the all-important force behind so much of personalized learning—cannot be built into the PLP as a document. As we've suggested throughout the last several chapters, it's in PLP conferences and all they entail that PLPs are legitimized and put to the test. By placing the PLP in a social context, the PLP conference is its moment of actualization as a pedagogical tool. It drives activities and conversations that otherwise are too easily neglected in the mad dash that is day-to-day schooling. How do we know when these conversations are worthwhile? Sometimes it's as easy as consulting the primary stakeholders: students and families.

PERSONALIZATION IN PRACTICE Lamoille Union Middle School

An English teacher at Lamoille Union Middle School in Hyde Park, Katie Bryant conducted action research as her team tried out both PLPs and PLP conferences for the first time.[10] Katie wanted to learn how leading a conference would affect her students' engagement in the PLP process and, in particular, she wondered if students would be motivated by the fact that they had to make a presentation to their parents about their goals. The objective for this very first PLP conference, just eight weeks into the school year, was straightforward: students were to share a personal goal, an academic goal, and something they were proud of from each of their core classes.[11]

In order to explore her question of student engagement, Katie surveyed her students before and after the SLC. Prior to the conference, most of the seventh and eighth graders reported that they were nervous. They elaborated with comments such as, "I have never talked in front of my parents and teachers before, and I'm a little nervous." One student described a conference experience in a prior school, "When I was in Michigan, parents had a conference with your one teacher, and you sat outside of the room when they talked about how you were doing in school and what you needed to work on or any behavior issues. The meetings ran for about twenty minutes and never did the student get to talk to the teacher and parents at the same time, and after the twenty minutes were up your parents came out of the classroom and said, 'good job' or 'I am disappointed in you.'"

Katie and her teammates helped prepare the students and their families for the experience, providing letters home, scripts, and templates for the process. On the day of the conferences, Katie's team observed an increase in family participation, as have others who have transitioned to student-led conferencing.[12] Seventy percent of students and their families took part in the PLP conferences, as opposed to less than 40 percent the previous year when they used the traditional parent-teacher model. And, in some cases, the school's 1:1 iPad program enabled students to conduct the conference at home in the event that parents were unable to attend at school. Parents and guardians commented about how much they appreciated the new format:

- "The best part was hearing about my son's goals that he has set for himself. Hearing him talk about what he wants for his future and the path he has taken to make sure he can reach his goals."
- "The best part was being able to use technology to participate remotely and share the material."
- "The best part was watching my son taking control of his own education."[13]

In fact, of the 70 percent of families who participated, 100 percent said they preferred the student-led version to the traditional model. Katie surmised that, "Some, I think, were maybe a little uncomfortable coming in, and then they stayed and loved it."[14]

Conscious of the anxiety that students expressed prior to the conference, Katie and her teammates were delighted and relieved that students also shared largely positive feedback on their post-conference surveys. After leading the meetings, students' comments included the following:

- "The best part was having my parents be proud of me and letting me tell my parents how I felt like I was doing in school and how I felt about my grades and teachers."
- "I liked getting to present what I do well and what I would like to see myself do better and compare it to my teachers' and parents' ideas.

- "The best part was that I got to lead it and it helped me talk about what I'm doing well and what I need help with. Plus it made me feel good to get feedback on my work in that very moment."
- "The best part was getting to show your parents what you're proud of and getting to interact with your parents and teachers at the same time. I also think that it was nice to have your parents and teachers make a goal for you and to have them know what you're doing in school so they can help."

Because Katie was conducting action research, she gathered considerable data to inform her team's work on PLPs and conferences. Most schools can benefit from gaining greater insight into family perceptions, however. It needn't be tied to a formal research project. Figure 8.1 features the family survey administered by Team Infinity at Lamoille Union Middle School after the conferences have been completed. You can see it's easily adaptable to your own context and the results are useful for informing future conference protocols and plans.

DEVELOPMENTALLY RESPONSIVE GOAL-SETTING

As students reflect on their learning during the PLP conference, sharing their goals with their families can be an important part of that experience. Yet, when asked if the student-led conference helps them focus on their goals, students' responses are often mixed:

- "Not really, but I am trying more this trimester than last one."
- "I think it made me more aware of my goals and more likely to start taking them seriously."
- "Definitely, because it gives you something to work toward, and makes all these hours in school not seem pointless."
- "I think the SLC makes more people aware of your goals and more people help you try harder to reach them."[15]

Goals can be tricky. It would be nice to outline a simple cycle, or even a spiral, but the reality is that you and your students will experience learning pathways that lead to new goals just as often as the goals may lead to new learning pathways. We know that helping students set their own meaningful goals is important to developing high-quality PLPs and motivating students

FIGURE 8.1   **Student-led conference family survey, Lamoille Union Middle School**

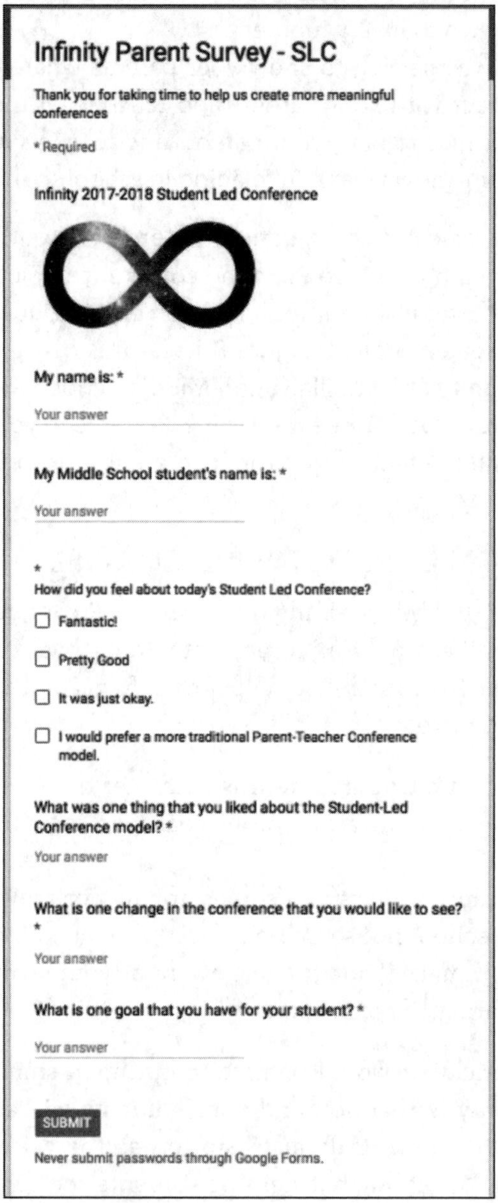

Infinity Parent Survey - SLC

Thank you for taking time to help us create more meaningful conferences

* Required

Infinity 2017-2018 Student Led Conference

My name is: *

Your answer

My Middle School student's name is: *

Your answer

*
How did you feel about today's Student Led Conference?

☐ Fantastic!

☐ Pretty Good

☐ It was just okay.

☐ I would prefer a more traditional Parent-Teacher Conference model.

What was one thing that you liked about the Student-Led Conference model? *

Your answer

What is one change in the conference that you would like to see? *

Your answer

What is one goal that you have for your student? *

Your answer

SUBMIT

Never submit passwords through Google Forms.

Source: Team Infinity, Lamoille Union Middle School.

to work toward meeting proficiencies. Our research has also taught us that this process is most effective when it's co-designed with students and reflects student interests.[16] But all too often, goal-setting can fall short of the meaning, relevance, and reflection necessary to be a powerful learning tool within a proficiency-based system.

It's perhaps no surprise that, over the years as we've collaborated with middle grades teachers to create personalized learning environments, we've encountered a number of obstacles. Some we've managed to jump over, some we've maneuvered around, and some we've hit straight on. But each now provides an opportunity for you to learn vicariously, thus avoiding making the same mistakes. We offer here several recommendations for setting goals with young adolescents in developmentally responsive ways. We have found that these approaches can root the students' goals in greater purpose and relevance, while connecting them to the proficiency-based assessment system.

Begin with Engaging Learning

Many organizations advise starting students on their personalized learning journeys with goal-setting. It makes sense, after all, to establish a goal—or choose your destination—before embarking on a journey. However, most students and teachers know little about the destinations that are possible when students are charting the course, driven by their curiosity, a sense of purpose, and a search for personal and social meaning.

Without plenty of direct experience with where this kind of learning can lead, students are far more likely to parrot back to their teachers the goals they've been trained to value most for the work they do in school. "I want to get all my homework in on time." "I want to get Bs or better in all my math quizzes." "I want to read fifteen books this year." They may even express some genuine enthusiasm for staking a brave claim on what they're capable of accomplishing. But these are not the goals that will sustain students or teachers on the challenging path of personalized learning. Nor do they reflect its promise. So how do we start, then? We start with engagement.

We have learned over the years that jumping into a powerful learning experience before setting goals can be a more effective way to engage young adolescents in their PLPs and personalized learning. This is precisely why we've waited until chapter 8 to discuss goals in greater depth. When students become immersed in deeply engaging learning, they start to identify things they *need* to know or be able to do. When students care about what they're learning, acquiring new skills and knowledge becomes a matter of urgency. And who wouldn't want students to feel a positive sense of urgency about learning? That's precisely the time to focus on goals.

Cultivate a Wide Range of Student Interests

Goal-setting on topics of interest makes sense in theory. Much of personalized learning is predicated on the idea that individuals have their own interests that excite them. And, in fact, most definitions of personalized learning note an intent to address students' interests. In practice, however, not all students arrive at school knowing what they want to learn about. Certainly, lots of young adolescents have things they care deeply about. But many students need support to help them consider their range of interests. We, along with a number of schools in Vermont, made the misstep of expecting young adolescents to come to school already knowing what they wanted to learn about. And we expected them to be inherently excited about it. Instead of assuming everyone will arrive at school with a clear passion, help cultivate a wide range of student interests. Consider how you can create ways for students to discover new passions through a series of identity and interest exploration activities. These can include the surveys, identity maps, and reflective activities about purpose and backgrounds laid out in considerable detail in chapter 4. Starting the year with many of these tasks can give students a fertile place to begin projects that are grounded in their own experiences, identities, cultures, and interests that they've had a chance to meaningfully explore and share.

Couple Goal-Setting with Meaningful Action

Even if students do arrive at school with a passion to learn computer programming, for instance, setting a goal to learn to code changes little about their school experience unless they actually get to spend time learning to code in school. Don't equate goal-setting alone with personalized learning. Setting goals and then continuing on with school as usual, while expecting students to pursue their goals solely as homework, does not make learning personal. Many young adolescents have already made up their minds how they feel about school, and the idea of getting (or having) to set a goal doesn't necessarily change that. Schools that took this misstep early on overemphasized goals and underemphasized action. Students set goals, but that act alone didn't change their daily experience of school. Instead, you'll want to make sure that students have a chance to make learning personal during their in-school time. In addition to increasing engagement, it can help elevate equity for students whose out-of-school access to learning opportunities may be more limited. In addition, if students are inspired at school, many will carry this enthusiasm over to the home environment and be motivated to continue learning there.

Invite a Wide Range of Goal Types

It's an unfortunate reality of middle school that not all young adolescents care about academics as much as their teachers might wish. Restricting goal-setting to what one might consider "academic" or "core" subject knowledge and skills is not necessarily an engaging prospect for middle schoolers. When some Vermont schools first required students to set goals, they were not always personally meaningful. "Despite the best efforts of educators, students asked 'How can this be personal if I don't care?'"[17] Instead of overemphasizing academic goals, remember that the PLP is also vehicle for identity exploration, demonstration of personal learning and self-reflection. Instead of forcing students to set academic goals that may feel inauthentic, invite students to lead the way. After they've been immersed in truly engaging learning, they will be better positioned to tell you what skills they want to work on, how they want to improve personally, and what they want to explore. Trust the process. The academic content will emerge from the learning experiences when fueled by genuine student interest, motivation and relevance. It is then that your students will "desire to do things they cannot do unless they learn."[18]

Scaffold the Goal-Setting Process

Although goals are a commonly accepted component of a PLP, many young adolescents may experience goal-setting as alien or forced. In fact, the idea that they have a degree of choice in what and how they learn may be quite unfamiliar to some students. Even as adults, we don't always set goals when we set out to learn something new. When just starting out with personalization, some schools did not provide sufficient scaffolds to support students in learning what constitutes a reasonable and achievable goal. This misstep is easily rectifiable. Providing clear modeling and organizational tools for students can be helpful. Like any learned skill, students need to see it in action, need to practice it themselves, and benefit from guidance along the way. Luckily, there are a number of simple goal-setting structures, such as WOOP and SMART, that are appropriate for youth in the middle grades.[19]

. . . But Not Too Much!

On the other hand, too much scaffolding can feel stifling. You'll want to avoid over-schoolifying the process. When students are required to follow lots of steps and complete various forms simply to identify a goal, the detailed process may not feel relevant or worthwhile. In fact, it may seem a lot like what they're already asked to do too much of in school. In this early misstep, some schools required an abundance of worksheets for students to complete when setting their goals. Instead, provide support to students at the moment they show they need or want it. Allow students freedom in the format they use, the tools they apply and even the wording of their goals. When they need help, provide just-in-time scaffolds.[20] The students will be more receptive, and often even welcome it. And always keep in mind, we all need practice figuring out how life skills like goal-setting work best for us. The best practice for goal-setting is establishing your own learning plan; the more opportunities students have for personalized learning, the better they'll get at setting goals.

PERSONALIZATION IN PRACTICE   Shelburne Community School

Eric Brunvand, an English language arts teacher at Shelburne Community School, described the soft entry into formal planning that he and his colleagues used with their students' Personal Interest Projects. His words underscore the idea of focusing on engagement first, coupled with a stealth approach to just-in-time scaffolds.

> We did not require students to create more than one or two action steps. Instead we asked them to jump into their projects as soon as possible and then to set next steps as they went. I looked at it as you would a household project . . . you normally end up heading out to the hardware store more than once as you figure out exactly what the task entails.[21]

By integrating planning with goal-setting, these teachers provide structure that students can find useful, rather than stifling. Notice that, in their Personal Interest Project planner (see table 8.7), the term "goal" is not even included![22]

TABLE 8.7 **Personal interest project planning guide: Shelburne Community School**

I want to LEARN how to _____	
How am I going to share my learning in a public exhibit?	These are my possible ACTION Steps 1. 2. 3. 4. 5. 6. 7.
I HAVE the following resources: I NEED the following resources:	

PERSONALIZATION IN PRACTICE Williston Central School

It's not always easy for young adolescents to think of goals or to put them into words that easily convey their meaning. Whereas Shelburne Community School took one approach to that challenge, the teachers on the Swift House Team at Williston Central School took another. They offer students a set of goal statements taken from Vermont's Vital Results and Transferable Skills (see table 8.8). Learners can select from these straightforward statements to help identify and set goals for the quarter, semester and year. They also invite students to self-assess using their Life Skills Learning Scales for Goal-Setting and Reflection (see table 8.9).[23]

PERSONALIZATION IN PRACTICE Fayston Elementary School

Teachers at Fayston Elementary School also used Vermont's Transferable Skills as the basis for goal-setting. Knowing students benefit from unpacking the meaning behind a standard or proficiency, Amy Jamieson, a speech-language

TABLE 8.8 **Academic/personal goals based on Vermont's transferable skills: Williston Central School, Swift House**

Transferable Skill	Sample Goals
Communications (listening, vocabulary use, reading; organization and purpose within writing and speaking; clearly express ideas via writing, speaking, or technology)	I develop writing with a clear focus, strong evidence and analysis, and command of writing conventions (grammar/usage/mechanics). I read consistently at home and at school (at least one book per month beyond my assigned reading), expanding my knowledge of genres and authors that I find enjoyable.
Creative and Practical Problem Solving (generating a variety of possible answers or strategies using evidence, asking genuine questions, problem solving, perseverance, risk-taking, making predictions, making generalizations, using models to show thinking)	I demonstrate clear understanding of a problem by showing all of my thinking (e.g., using models, words, symbols). I consider, test, and justify more than one solution.
Informed and Integrative Thinking (using evidence and reasons to support ideas; summarizing information; evaluating the usefulness of informational resources; applying learning across content areas)	I apply knowledge from various classes to other situations. I demonstrate understanding of new vocabulary by creatively applying it to new content.
Self-Direction (taking initiative and responsibility for learning, setting goals, making informed decisions, taking healthy risks, demonstrating a growth mindset and persevering when challenged)	I develop and apply strategies for persevering in the face of challenges and obstacles. I manage time effectively to help myself avoid stress and create high quality work.
Responsible and Involved Citizenship (participating and collaborating effectively and respectfully to enhance the learning environment; taking responsibility for personal decisions and actions; demonstrating respect for differences; demonstrating a commitment to community)	I regularly accept opportunities to take on leadership roles and act as a positive role model. I offer help and assistance to those in need.

pathologist, leveraged language arts classes to increase the relevance of the sophisticated terms. She asked fifth and sixth graders to put the less familiar terms into their own words. Jordan provided the student perspective on this process:

> I'm in sixth grade at the Fayston School. At the beginning of the year we did an activity to learn about transferable skills, and the transferable skills are clear and effective communication skills, citizenship, problem solving,

TABLE 8.9   **Life skills learning scales for goal-setting and reflection: Williston Central School, Swift House**

Life Skills Learning Scales				
Goals	**Getting Started**	**Making Progress**	**Got It**	**Transfer**
Goal-Setting and Evidence	I am learning what goals are and why they are important. With help, I can set short-term goals and use strategies that help me meet them.	I can set short-term goals. With help, I am starting to set longer term goals that are appropriate for me. I am learning strategies to help me manage my time, collect evidence, and meet my goals.	I can set short and long-term goals that are appropriate for me. I can manage my time and I use strategies that help me collect evidence and meet my goals.	I regularly set goals, both in and out of school. I manage my time well and use strategies flexibly to collect evidence and meet goals.
Goal Reflection	I am starting to understand how to reflect on a goal and why it is helpful to have goals.	With help, I can reflect on my goals and make changes to help me be successful.	I can reflect on my goals and adjust them as needed based on my reflection	I regularly reflect on my goals and adjust them based on my reflection.

Date: _____

Why did you score yourself where you did? What evidence do you have that supports your self-assessment?

self-directed learning, creativity, and informed and integrative thinking. First, we worked by breaking into small groups. Each group had a transferable skill. We took the big words and put them into our own words that we could understand better. We then made posters to put on the walls of our classroom that we could look at through the school year when we think about our learning.

Amy also reflected on the success of that activity:

Here are the posters that the kids created, during their language arts class. As a team . . . we thought, "Wow, look at these crazy words. 'Self-direction, problem solving, citizenship.' What do these really mean to fifth and sixth graders?" So they had the chance to break them down, and put them in their own words. And in each classroom, they remind the students about their daily learning. "How did I use problem solving today? What did I do that was self-directed?" The kids refer to them a lot, and they're more meaningful because the words are broken down into language they can really relate to.[24]

LOOKING AHEAD: SUSTAINING INNOVATION

As the examples in this chapter convey, rounding out the personalized learning plan with meaningful goals and a student-led conference can be a powerful combination. Each takes considerable forethought to make happen, particularly when planning with student efficacy in mind. And there's nothing like a date on the calendar for student-led PLP conferences to drive students, teachers, families, and plenty of others to meet their commitment to personalized learning.

To coordinate the implementation of the various innovations needed to make learning personal, our partner teachers have come to appreciate and rely upon comprehensive plans. We encourage you to visit www.learninginthemiddle.org, where we share a list of critical planning and implementation steps for one important milestone on the path toward personalized learning: the student-led PLP conference.[25] The sample plan first presents the list organized by the purposes the practices serve, and then by an implementation timeline that conveys a logical implementation sequence, exploiting how the practices can support one another and sync up with the calendar of schools. Look it over with your own context, goals, and timeline in mind. It can help you translate ideas into action, deepen your understanding, dramatically increase your likelihood of success, and reveal to your colleagues and your students, the power of personalized learning environments.

Students carry the greatest load in this endeavor, collecting and organizing, reflecting upon, and presenting their growth to the people they care about most. Teachers make the tough choices to make the time, scaffold the work, consult one-on-one with each student about their PLP, and facilitate the event of the conference. And families make the time, risk a new kind of conversation with their child, and for too many, brave entry into a building that may signify personal sorrow, anger, perhaps even humiliation, given their own personal histories with school. Yet the power of student-led PLP conferences is derived from all that goes into them, particularly when coupled with goals that students care about because they genuinely believe they'll accomplish something of worth. And perhaps more reliably than any other similarly demanding educational strategy, PLP conferences reward everyone's investment in them. As you reflect on your purpose for making learning personal and consider various strategies that may work in your classroom, team or school, chapter 9 offers several specific ways to help you build on these milestones to sustain this important work.

NINE

SUSTAINING INNOVATION IN YOUR CLASSROOM, TEAM, OR SCHOOL

M*s. Phillips rubs her eyes and settles in on the couch. She smiles as she remembers how she used to say to her mom as a teenager, "You are so boring! You just sit there on the couch at night and drink tea!" Well, here she is, settled on the couch, steaming cup of tea at her side, and fighting off the fall chill with her favorite blanket across her lap. With her two kids tucked in, the fleeting hours to herself, before her eyes close on their own, are now hers.*

She sips her tea and thinks about her day. Miles and his group are almost ready to present to the school board tomorrow night. Ms. Phillips knows they are nervous, and she wonders how she can help them feel confident and ready tomorrow as they practice for their peers. She snaps open her computer a few minutes before her favorite weekly Twitter chat. She loves that she can be in her yoga pants and wool socks, sipping tea, and connect with educators from all over the world. As she sits back and searches the hashtag, she sees the flow of conversation. This week, the topic is Design Thinking. She clicks on the hashtag to see what folks in this global professional learning network have to say about this topic.

Right away she sees an image linked by an educator she follows from Indiana. He posted a photo of the phases of Design Thinking: Empathize, Design, Ideate, Prototype, and Test. She knows her technology integrationist, Jenna, has reviewed these with her students in the design process of their projects. Then she ponders, could this be a framework for presenting to the school board? Certainly, empathy as the first step in a makerspace or STEM project is a powerful way to frame the work and could engage the board in understanding why the community might need a nature trail. Also, for the students who still might be having trouble seeing why all of this matters, the empathy step can have a big impact. Another teacher offers a template for students using the steps in Design Thinking, and she quickly downloads that, adding it to her drive to consider modifying for use tomorrow.

Ms. Phillips taps her fingers on the side of her cup. She knows that Miles's team had to re-do some of their 3D printed models, including a bridge model that broke. She wonders what resources exist for deepening this learning and understanding. Was the bridge designed with engineering concepts in mind? She doesn't remember seeing that team research bridge designs and engineering concepts. She opens her Hyperdoc that is full of playlists for each group. She sees tomorrow she has a link with presentation tips, reflection activities for group work, and a guide for providing peer feedback. She clicks another hashtag, one that often lists open educational resources, and pours through links—what might help her students consider bridge design features to tweak their model, or to share at the presentation? After a bit of looking she finds a resource: a learning module about bridge design created for middle level students on an engineering website. It looks like it takes about thirty minutes to complete. She adds this to the playlist for tomorrow, hoping they can fit it in around practicing their presentations.

She sits back, sips her tea. It is amazing, she thinks, how she can tap into this river of resources, and find helpful tools, ideas, and links that connect deeply to her practice and are responsive to her students' daily needs. Sometimes, if she is struggling with a student, she will jump into Twitter chats among educators she knows are focused on socio-emotional learning and growth. Other times, she follows and connects with educators from vastly different schools than her own, making sure she is surrounding herself with educators from a variety backgrounds, ethnicities, school types, and communities so her resources are not insular or from an echo chamber. At times she will even post a question to crowdsource resources, gain a different perspective, and find inspiration. How she even taught before she used Twitter this way, she can't imagine. Truly, it gives her several educational communities to connect with. Support, guidance, perspective, and resources, all in yoga pants.

For tonight, though, she is done. She clicks over to her favorite late-night comedy show for a laugh before heading to bed.

SUSTAINING INNOVATION

The work of personalizing learning can be both challenging and invigorating. The teachers in this book, along with so many others, put in very real effort—emotional, intellectual, even physical—in pursuit of educational change. This journey is perhaps all the more extraordinary in an era too often characterized by initiative fatigue.[1]

As he grappled with the implementation of PLPs, Kevin Hunt at Williston Central School reflected on the challenge of confronting too many initiatives:

> It seems whenever there is a paradigm shift in education it is always accompanied by the response "give it a few years and this will pass too." I haven't been in the field long enough to confirm this, but I have been in plenty of meetings and have attended several conferences where I've heard veteran teachers mutter these disparaging words. I've always done my best to remain optimistic and look at change in education as something exciting and refreshing, but at the same time, I often try to empathize with those with decades more experience than I have and think to myself, would I be saying this too if I've lived through so much change that felt meaningless?[2]

We believe Hunt is on to something here. As longtime educators, we recognize the oft-uttered sentiment that, "This too shall pass." We agree that, if change feels meaningless to teachers, many will abandon it.

We also believe that if change feels purposeful, and is defined by a *self-identified* purpose, it can become transformative. Recall chapter 2 for a moment, when we invited you to consider your purpose for this work. What is it that you're trying to accomplish? Why are you interested in personalizing the learning of the students in your classroom or school? Are you looking to allow students more control over their learning or to make the learning opportunities more equitable? Are you hoping to create a safe space for them to explore their identities? Or maybe to assess students' growth more meaningfully? Perhaps you're seeking a way to deepen your family engagement strategy. Or possibly it's that you're excited to bring students and their communities more closely together. We've learned that, when change initiatives align with a deep sense of purpose, they are more likely to succeed. And regardless of your purpose, we're confident that closing the gap between the learning students do for school and who they are as people is key to students' engagement, efficacy, and success.

The stories and voices of teachers who do this work make it clear: although they often regard the work of personalization as some of the most challenging of their careers, it's of a sort they are unwilling to abandon. This may be the most hopeful finding from our work. Teachers observe changes in students who feel respected for their interests, honored for their struggles, and heralded for the new roles they find themselves in among their peers and community. Teachers describe gaining strength by hearing about a parent's newfound respect for their child and what they're doing in school. Such testimonies are a powerful inspiration from which to launch PLPs and personalized learning.

Throughout the book, we have emphasized the importance of taking meaningful yet manageable steps toward implementation. To bolster your chances of success, we've offered you a path for adopting PLPs. Successful innovation, however, demands more than just strategic planning. It also requires developing and sustaining the personal motivation and collaborative culture necessary for the long-term work of meaningful change. You need a support system to help you sustain these steps through the multi-year, iterative work of personalizing classrooms and schools. And these initial steps must complement each other, to ensure that students and teachers see in the work immediate rewards rather than just another reform to be resented. The shorter-term rewards are milestones you can look to, with colleagues, students, and families, as evidence of your collective efficacy. It's that sense of efficacy that will keep you going when things get tough.

How have educators in Vermont found ways to persevere, to continue the work well after the novelty wears off, to move forward despite lagging momentum or looming obstacles? Hunt also mused about this in relation to the challenge of remaining positive:

> I've recently been thinking about what an appropriate response would be to those who are skeptical about personalization, PLPs, negotiated curriculum, etc. How do we remain positive, and where do we start? It's not always easy going against the grain, and it's even harder when you feel like you are alone in embracing change. One of the most common questions I hear from educators around the state is "How do I start?" The buzz around Act 77, PLPs, personalization, PIPs, negotiated curriculum,

PBL—and every other acronym that is trending right now—can seem foreboding and overwhelming. But if we are doing these things for the right reasons, the payoff (in the form of student engagement and love for learning) is completely worth it. I found that when a paradigm shift happens for the right reasons, with students' best interests at its core, then it will not merely go away over years, but rather evolve into a system that best serves the learner.

How can we remain positive? We have witnessed teachers adopting many strategies to support their personal growth throughout the implementation of PLPs, whether on a team or as a single teacher braving the cutting edge more or less alone. These educators have found a range of useful strategies as they strive to remain positive while evolving and sustaining a system for personalizing learning in their classrooms and schools (see table 9.1). As you read through some of the examples that follow, consider what might work for your context and personal priorities.

Expand Your Learning Networks

One way educators in Vermont have found to sustain themselves and this challenging but rewarding work is by expanding their professional networks in order to learn from others. Finding other educators who have similar goals can be a powerful motivator, particularly if you're feeling isolated in your school. With so many online communities now available, it's easier than ever to find like-minded colleagues. Various Twitter chats and blogs focus on personalized learning and related pedagogy. And, of course, the opportunities aren't strictly virtual. Teachers point to attending institutes and conferences or visiting other schools as helpful in connecting with like-minded teachers, particularly when they find themselves isolated in a more traditional setting, facing unique challenges, without collegial support within their schools.

What's more, if you can't find the right match for your needs, you can always create your own network. When the Vermont legislature first mandated personalized learning plans, for example, some teachers in the state launched their own online community as a way to support one another and share ideas for maximizing the potential of PLPs with middle grades learners. PLP Pathways, as the online community is known, offers a monthly webinar and a blog in which teachers regularly discuss their successes, challenges and progress

TABLE 9.1   **Sustaining innovation**

Helpful Ways to Sustain Teaching Innovation	
Expand your learning networks	Seek out new colleagues to learn from Find or establish new online communities
Share your work with others	Write for social media Present at conferences
Study your work	Conduct action research Explore appreciative inquiry
Partner with students	(Re)Design school structures Co-create learning opportunities
Assume leadership roles	Join the teacher leadership committee Consider teacher coaching positions
Build personal and collective efficacy	Create opportunities to reflect on successes Collaborate with colleagues
Plan and establish milestones	Plan for and embrace observable moments of impact Highlight evidence of success

with the wider educator audience.[3] Another group of educators started a collaborative blog to share thoughts and resources for helping students think about future careers. Focused on developing and scaling the concept of career advisory, the Vermont Flexible Pathways Collaborative explores models for supporting students as they clarify career options and pathways. The group also investigates partnerships between traditionally siloed institutions and organizations to promote collaboration toward these ends.[4]

Share Your Work with Others

In much the same way as broadening your professional learning network, sharing your work with others benefits them and helps you get feedback, discover new ideas, or celebrate a success. Leveraging any number of social media outlets to disseminate your—and your students'—work can help sustain innovation and positive momentum. Writing for blogs like PLP Pathways is a great, low-barrier-to-entry way to begin. And if you enjoy writing, there are a number of options with broad and national reach, such as Edutopia, that will help you showcase the accomplishments and approaches of your students, classroom, team, or school.

For those of you who would love to share your work but don't necessarily love the idea of writing about it, presenting at local or national conferences can be equally fulfilling. As they have experimented with personalized learning environments, many teachers we work with have taken the leap to present at state-level conferences, such as Vermont's Dynamic Landscapes and the Middle Grades Collaborative's annual conference. They've shared their work regionally with the New England League of Middle Schools. And they have showcased it on the national stage at the Deeper Learning conference and the Association for Middle Level Education conference, among other venues.

Whether you're part of a team or teaching solo, sharing your work requires you to reflect more formally on what is working and what might be improved. It further invites you to consider what your next steps are in innovating. The presence of an audience of peers compels you to entertain questions and make critical connections that you might not have considered on your own. Finally, you typically receive feedback that can be validating at a time when you just might be feeling out on a limb!

Study Your—and Your Students'—Work

Studying your teaching is another great way to keep up momentum and help sustain your work. Action research, which is inquiry conducted by and for the person taking the action, can be a great match for innovative educators. A central purpose of action research is to assist the researchers (in this case, teachers) in improving or refining their actions (in this case, teaching). The iterative and cyclical process of taking action, collecting and analyzing data, and reporting results, action research is powered by the teachers' own relevant, personally meaningful focus. As such, in just the same way as student-directed projects, engagement is all but guaranteed.[5]

Vermont teachers have employed action research in lots of ways as they've tried to personalize learning. And they report great results, particularly when treating students' perspectives as important sources of data. Kim Scott, a teacher at Main Street Middle School, wanted to increase the reading engagement and success of students in her classroom. She was interested in how greater personalization might contribute to that objective. Kim hoped to increase student buy-in and willingness to read, and to promote individual self-awareness around reading abilities. Through a series of student surveys, she used scales, multiple-choice questions, and other methods to assess students' interest in reading improvement (e.g., I would love to improve my reading skills); students' self-awareness (e.g., which activities help you become a better reader?), and students' preferences (e.g., I prefer to read when . . .). After trying various strategies and soliciting further student input, Kim's biggest takeaways regarding literacy tools were that gamification and interaction helped but that the most powerful approaches for her students included personal choice, immediacy of feedback, close readings, and modeling. And more to the point, the action research served as a structure for her to reflect systematically on her practice and maintain forward momentum.

Shelburne Community School teachers Kelly Spreen and Lauren Goracy also embraced action research as they explored the role of personal choice in physical education classes. As PE and special educators respectively, Spreen and Goracy collected student data to determine how choice in wellness activities affected student engagement. At the end of their research Spreen noted, "Personal choice and personalized learning has completely changed the culture of middle school PE at our school. At any given time, you can look around and see full engagement and this is something that would not happen during a traditional, full-class game setting."[6] By conducting action research, as well as co-teaching, these two teachers leveraged the built-in structure provided by focused inquiry to analyze their teaching with each other.

Partner with Students

We've shared a number of ways that teachers partner with students in teaching and learning. Partnering with them in matters of school change can be equally, if not more, rewarding. Shelburne Community School teacher Sam Nelson, for instance, lunches with representative groups of students once a week as a way for them to offer feedback on curriculum. It can also be a great reminder that you're not alone in striving to improve the schooling experience for young adolescents. Whether you're in a self-contained classroom or part of an interdisciplinary or grade-level team, your own students can serve as a source of partnership and sustenance.

You may recall from earlier chapters that PLPs weren't always a huge hit with students in the beginning of the transition to personalized learning in

Vermont. With an at-times too heavy emphasis on goal-setting and too little opportunity for meaningful and engaging learning, the PLP alone didn't offer the kind of flexible pathways we know are critical to personalization. Jana Fabri-Sbardellati, a teacher at Hunt Middle School in Burlington, reflected on this challenge:

> My colleagues and I had been struggling to see where the engagement lies for the learners. It all sounded so good to us when initially presented by our administrators, that PLPs would allow us to personalize learning for *all* students. However, forcing students to fill in the boxes we've created for them, based on goals that may or may not have meaning for the students, add to that having an inconsistent time set aside for these pursuits, and this has been a recipe for disaster. Instead of what I envisioned, PLP time is met with groans from the students, and teachers for that matter.[7]

Inviting students to become part of the solution, and in particular, in the co-creation of the PLP itself, has proven highly effective at a number of schools. Crossett Brook Middle School's Brainado and Shelburne Community School's Personal Interest Projects, described in earlier chapters, both resulted from bringing students into the conversation about improving learning. Similarly, the PLP (re)Design Project has become an annual opportunity for teachers and students across schools to convene and leverage design thinking as a strategy to create effective, relevant and meaningful PLPs.[8]

Assume New Leadership Roles

As you get deeper into the work of innovating, you may find yourself drawn into new roles and positions. You'll want to consider if and how these roles can serve to sustain positive momentum for the change you're helping to create while also supporting your personal invigoration for this work. We've observed several roles emerge in relation to the personalization movement in Vermont schools. For instance, the creation of new building- or district-level positions intended to support personalized and proficiency-based learning has become increasingly common. The reallocation of FTE's is one way schools are managing this change despite tight budgets. Some positions use a teacher-coaching model, helping other educators to understand and adapt their pedagogy to integrate personalization in their classrooms. Lamoille South Supervisory Union, for example, created the position of proficiency-based learning and technology integration coach for this purpose. Other new roles serve students more directly, such as the personalized learning and multiple pathways coordinator, which was created at Lamoille Union High School as a way to oversee students' personal learning plans and coordinate multiple pathway learning experiences. Still other roles enable teachers to remain in their classrooms while providing essential leadership in school change efforts.

If your school is fortunate to use a model of distributed governance, joining the teacher leadership committee can be a powerful way to provide important input at a schoolwide level while fostering your sense of professional efficacy. Guiding new teachers can keep you similarly on track, working as a cooperating teacher with pre-service teachers or serving as a mentor to new teachers. Each of these opportunities has led to considerable success when educators noticed the emerging opportunities to overcome bureaucratic obstacles, align with system mandates, and inform the thinking of teaching colleagues and administrators. In these ways, collaborative and distributed leadership can break the familiar cycle of initiative fatigue and create a way for teachers to be heard and participate meaningfully in school and district change efforts.

Build Personal and Collective Efficacy

Earlier we explored the basics of personal efficacy for young adolescents. Through the example of several students, we saw how meaningful work can contribute to a strong sense of efficaciousness. It's equally important to consider the role of teacher efficacy in a change process. Although few teachers may have expected it at the outset of their journey, many do report feeling efficacious as they transition to personalized learning. Moments of professional efficacy on the part of teachers can be rare and hard won, yet feeling efficacious as a teacher is critical to success. Notice or create opportunities to witness the very real and important changes you're making in students' experience with school. Survey them to inform your work, but also to hear their testimony to your work.

Further, as you look to sustain innovation, collaborating with colleagues around a common goal can establish a shared purpose and generate collective efficacy across your team, department, or school faculty. In the field of education, the term collective efficacy refers to "the judgments of teachers in a school that the faculty as a whole can organize and execute the courses of action required to have a positive effect on students."[9] Collective efficacy is a powerful influencer with potentially dramatic payoffs for you and your students alike. In schools where teachers believe in their combined ability to affect student outcomes, students achieve at higher levels.[10]

As we reflect on the many teachers we know who are working together to personalize learning, this makes a lot of sense. It's easy to imagine the strong sense of collective efficacy generated by educators at Crossett Brook Middle School as they engaged in Brainado, by the teachers at Shelburne Middle School as they collaborated on revising the school's Personal Interest Projects, and by the Burke Town School faculty as they committed to a multi-year plan to ensure that every student experienced a successful personalized, self-directed, and community-based project in their eighth-grade year.

While this is not a new idea—over the past few decades we have seen this repeatedly tested and proven in schools—collective efficacy is one of the best forces we have for cultivating change in schools and positive outcomes for students.[11] In fact, educational researchers Jenni Donohoo, John Hattie, and Rachel Eells found that "collective teacher efficacy is greater than three times more powerful and predictive of student achievement than socioeconomic status. It is more than double the effect of prior achievement and more than triple the effect of home environment and parental involvement."[12] What's more, collective efficacy is a social resource that is renewed, rather than depleted, by its use. Evidence of impact reinforces the collective behavior and motivation.

Plan and Establish Milestones

So how can educators build personal and collective efficacy like this in their school communities? Creating structures for teacher collaboration, promoting teacher leadership and decision-making, and even simply educating staff about collective efficacy are a few effective ways.[13] Highlighting evidence of impact is another. We think about this in terms of establishing milestones. In earlier chapters, we've described the use of milestones, such as the PLP conference, as a strategy for maintaining momentum for precisely this reason. Observable moments like the conference can remind you of the impact you're making and help sustain you through some of the tougher moments of school change. A complex change agenda like personalization requires some fundamental connections to be appreciated before people can make meaning of the separate parts. This can be done through these deep but manageable milestones. It's also more consistent with what we know about how people learn, stay motivated, and embrace change, rather than expecting people to be satisfied by waiting until year three to see how it might all come together. That's not rewarding, enjoyable or sustainable; that's change that neglects the human element. It's rational but not inspiring.

Successful schools help teachers identify—personally and collectively—meaningful reasons for making change. Together teachers can create a process that is invigorating, rather than exhausting, to find the sweet spot in the converging interests of teachers, students, and families. The work is propelled forward when teachers notice even their hardest-to-reach students exhibiting an excitement for coming to school, a drive to dig deeper into learning, and an appreciation not just for the learning itself, but for the teacher's willingness to take the risk to make it happen. By planning change strategically and collaboratively, seeking sustenance from the work as it unfolds, and intentionally building a support system, many of the teachers we know have sustained bold change for years, far longer and more intensively than they imagined possible. Fabri-Sbardellati from Hunt Middle School reflected:

> One of the reasons I chose to teach at the middle level is because this is when students start to ask some of those bigger questions about the world and their place in it. Their interests and passions start to take shape, and while they are still very present-centered, they can start to have meaningful discussions about what their future could look like. With the right structures in place—adequate time for a small advisory group, sacred time set aside each week for Personalized Learning check-ins, flexible curriculum that allows for the integration of personalized learning, a faculty member dedicated to connecting students with the right resources, etc.—our conversations can turn from, "How do we get them to dot all the i's and cross all the t's in these prescribed boxes?" to, "How can we help them envision a path forward that harnesses their passions and strengths, then help them document this journey?" If that's our focus, I predict engagement for students *and* adults will increase exponentially.[14]

IN CLOSING

The shift to personalized learning environments is described by many of our teachers as the hardest work they've done in their careers. It calls upon their best abilities as creative thinkers and researchers, designers and iterators, planners and collaborators, and, each in their own way, leaders. All of this on top of everything else it takes to be a middle school teacher. Yet they keep working at it, pushing themselves to try new things, find new solutions, and perhaps most painful of all, giving up once-favorite practices they've discovered never really worked. These teachers persevere in the hard work of change because they are inspired by the promise that personalized learning holds for their students. They find deep and personal meaning in the work. They've discovered collective meaning as well, and the collective joy that comes with it. They engage in new learning and take uncomfortable risks because they believe it will make a meaningful difference for their students and their schools, and in so doing, make the world a better place. In short, these teachers are engaged learners.

This book is about handing off the hopes realized and lessons learned by those who want every young adolescent to be an engaged learner, to have that most human of experiences. Not just when they're grown up, or when they reach the next stage of their education. But now and every day. Each student's encounter with engagement may ebb and flow just as it does for us as educators. But in high-functioning, personalized learning environments, and even as those environments develop, students experience engagement in ways they won't forget. They'll forever appreciate the power of knowing and sharing who they are, of charting their own course, and acknowledging their progress along the way. We hope this book inspires you to pursue personalized learning with your own students and prepares you to know each of them well, help them craft their pathway, and celebrate with them all the remarkable ways they grow.

NOTES

Introduction

1. Robert Balfanz, *Putting Middle Grades Students on the Graduation Path* (Westerville: National Middle School Association, 2009).

2. Steven Netcoh, "Balancing Freedom and Limitations: A Case Study of Choice Provision in a Personalized Learning Class," *Teaching and Teacher Education* 66 (2017): 383–392, https://doi.org/10.1016/j.tate.2017.05.010; Susan Patrick, Maria Worthen, Dale Frost, and Susan Gentz, *Promising State Policies for Personalized Learning* (Vienna: International Association for K–12 Online Learning, 2016), www.inacol.org/wp-content/uploads/2016/05/iNACOL-Promising-State-Policies-for-Personalized-Learning.pdf.

3. "Individualized Learning Plans across the U.S.," Office of Disability Employment Policy, https://www.dol.gov/odep/ilp/map/.

4. Patrick, Worthen, Frost, and Gentz, *Promising State Policies for Personalized Learning*, 12.

5. Frances Workman, Christopher Thomas, and Jackson Berman, *Vermont's Post-Secondary Education Enrollment* (Burlington: The Vermont Legislative Research Service, 2016), https://www.uvm.edu/~vlrs/Education/VT%20Higher%20Ed%20Enrollment.pdf.

6. John Fischer, *Act 77, Education Quality Standards, and the Transformation of Vermont Learning* (Barre: Vermont Agency of Education, 2015), http://legislature.vermont.gov/assets/Documents/2016/WorkGroups/House%20Education/Teaching%20Innovation/W~John%20Fischer~Powerpoint%20-%20Act%2077,%20Education%20Quality%20Standards%20and%20the%20Transformation%20of%20Vermont%20Learning~2-3-2015.pdf.

7. "Personalized Learning," Vermont Agency of Education, http://education.vermont.gov/student-learning/personalized-learning.

8. P. Gayle Andrews, ed., *Research to Guide Practice in Middle Grades Education* (Westerville: Association for Middle Level Education, 2013).

9. Michael Fullan and Joanne Quinn, *Coherence: The Right Drivers in Action for Schools, Districts, and Systems* (Thousand Oaks: Corwin, 2015); Roger D. Goddard, Wayne K. Hoy, and Anita Woolfolk Hoy, "Collective Efficacy Beliefs: Theoretical Developments, Empirical Evidence, and Future Directions," *Educational Researcher* 33, no. 3 (2004): 4, http://journals.sagepub.com/doi/10.3102/0013189X033003003; Jenni Donohoo, John Hattie, and Rachel Eells, "The Power of Collective Efficacy," *Educational Leadership* 75, no. 6

(2018): 40–44, http://www.ascd.org/publications/educational-leadership/mar18/vol75/num06/The-Power-of-Collective-Efficacy.aspx.

10. Darling-Hammond, L., Hyler, M. E., Gardner, M. (2017). *Effective Teacher Professional Development*. Palo Alto, CA: Learning Policy Institute.

11. Netcoh, "Balancing Freedom and Limitations"; Steven Netcoh and Penny A. Bishop, "Personalized Learning in the Middle Grades: A Case Study of One Team's Successes and Challenges," *Middle Grades Research Journal* 11, no. 2 (2017): 33–48; Jessica DeMink-Carthew, Mark W. Olofson, Life LeGeros, Steven Netcoh, and Susan Hennessey, "An Analysis of Approaches to Goal-Setting in Middle Grades Personalized Learning Environments," *Research in Middle Level Education Online* 40, no. 10 (2017): 1–11, https://doi.org/10.1080/19404476.2017.1392689; John M. Downes, Penny A. Bishop, and James F. Nagle, "Tapping the Experts in Effective Practices: Students as Educators in Middle Grades Professional Development," *Middle School Journal*, 48, no. 4 (2017): 27–35, https://doi.org/10.1080/00940771.2017.1343057.

12. Mark W. Olofson, John M. Downes, Carmen Petrick Smith, Life LeGeros, Penny A. Bishop, "An Instrument to Measure Teacher Practices to Support Personalized Learning in the Middle Grades," *Research in Middle Level Education Online* 41, no. 7 (2018): 1–21, https://doi.org/10.1080/19404476.2018.1493858; Mark W. Olofson, John M. Downes, Penny A. Bishop, and Carmen Petrick Smith, "Can PD Move the Needle on Personalized Pedagogical Practices? Evidence from the Middle Grades" (paper presented at the annual meeting for the American Educational Research Association, New York, New York, April 13–17, 2018); Penny Bishop, John Downes, Steven Netcoh, Jessica DeMink-Carthew, Katy Farber, Life LeGeros, and Tricia Stokes, "Middle Grades Teachers' Dispositions in Personalized Learning Environments," in *Preparing Middle Level Educators for 21st Century Schools: Enduring Beliefs, Changing Times, Evolving Practices*, eds. Penny B. Howell et al. (Charlotte: Information Age Publishing, Inc., 2018), 229–254; Katy Farber, John M. Downes, and Penny A. Bishop, "Teacher Roles in Emerging Middle Grades Personalized Learning Environments" (paper presented at the annual meeting for the American Educational Research Association, New York, New York, April 13–17, 2018).

13. Steven Netcoh, Mark W. Olofson, John M. Downes, and Penny A. Bishop, "Professional Learning with Action Research in Innovative Middle Schools," *Middle School Journal* 48, no. 3 (2017): 25–33; John M. Downes, Penny A. Bishop, Meredith Swallow, Mark Olofson, and Susan Hennessey, "Collaborative Action Research for Middle Grades Improvement," *Educational Action Research* 24, no. 2 (2016): 194–215, https://doi.org/10.1080/09650792.2015.1058169.

14. Katy Farber and Penny Bishop, "Service Learning in the Middle Grades: Learning by Doing and Caring," *Research in Middle Level Education Online* 41, no. 2 (2018): 1–15, https://doi.org/10.1080/19404476.2017.1415600; Life LeGeros, Steven Netcoh, Penny Bishop, John Downes, and Mark W. Olofson, "Genius Hour as an Anchor Experience for Implementing Personalized Learning in a Vermont Middle School" (paper presented at the annual meeting for the American Educational Research Association, New York, New York, April 13–17, 2018). Ryan Becker and Penny Bishop, "'Think Bigger about

Science': Using Twitter for Learning in the Middle Grades," *Middle School Journal* 47, no. 3 (2016): 4–16.

15. John M. Downes and Penny Bishop, "Educators Engage Digital Natives and Learn from Their Experiences with Technology," *Middle School Journal* 43, no. 5 (2012): 6–15; Meredith Swallow, "The Year-Two Decline: Exploring the Incremental Experiences of a 1:1 Technology Initiative," *Journal of Research on Technology in Education* 47, no. 2 (2015): 122–137, https://doi.org/10.1080/15391523.2015.999641; John M. Downes and Penny A. Bishop, "The Intersection between 1:1 Laptop Implementation and the Characteristics of Effective Middle Level Schools," *Research in Middle Level Education Online* 38, no. 7 (2015): 1–16, https://doi.org/10.1080/19404476.2015.11462120.

16. "A Snapshot of K–12 Competency Education State Policy Across the United States," International Association for K–12 Online Learning, https://www.inacol.org/wp-content/uploads/2016/04/2016-Snapshot-of-CBE-State-Policy_timestamp.pdf.

17. Penny Bishop, John Downes, and James Nagle, "How Personal Learning is Working in Vermont," *Educational Leadership* 74, no. 6 (2017), http://www.ascd.org/publications/educational-leadership/mar17/vol74/num06/How-Personal-Learning-Is-Working-in-Vermont.aspx.

18. James Nagle and Don Taylor, "Using a Personal Learning Framework to Transform Middle Grades Teaching Practice," *Middle Grades Research Journal* 11, no. 1 (2017): 85–100. Bishop, Downes, and Nagle, "How Personal Learning is Working in Vermont."

19. Bruce Dixon and Susan Einhorn, *The Right to Learn: Identifying Precedents for Sustainable Change* (Anytime Anywhere Learning Foundation, ideasLAB, and Maine Center for Digital Learning, 2011), https://thebigsummit.files.wordpress.com/2011/05/right-to-learn-big-summit-whitepaper1.pdf.

Chapter 1

1. Rashawn Ray, Lynne Sacks, and Janet Twyman. *Equity and Personalized Learning: A Research Review* (Washington, DC: Council of Chief State School Officers, 2017), https://www.ccsso.org/sites/default/files/2017-12/Advancing%20Equity%20through%20Personalized%20Learning—A%20Research%20Overview_0.pdf

2. Benjamin Herold. "The Case Against Personalized Learning," *Education Week*, August 11, 2017, https://www.edweek.org/ew/articles/2017/11/08/the-cases-against-personalized-learning.html.

3. *Early Progress: Interim Research on Personalized Learning* (Seattle: Bill & Melinda Gates Foundation, 2014), http://k12education.gatesfoundation.org/wp-content/uploads/2015/06/Early-Progress-on-Personalized-Learning-Full-Report.pdf.

4. *Early Progress: Interim Research on Personalized Learning* (Seattle: Bill & Melinda Gates Foundation, 2014), http://k12education.gatesfoundation.org/wp-content/uploads/2015/06/Early-Progress-on-Personalized-Learning-Full-Report.pdf.

5. John F. Pane, Elizabeth D. Steiner, Matthew D. Baird, and Laura S. Hamilton, *Continued Progress: Promising Evidence on Personalized Learning* (Santa Monica: Rand Corporation, 2015), https://www.rand.org/pubs/research_reports/RR1365.html.

6. "Personalized Learning," The Glossary of Education Reform, https://www.edglossary .org/personalized-learning/; Pane, Steiner, Baird, & Hamilton, *Continued Progress*.

7. Barbara Bray and Kathleen McClaskey, *Make Learning Personal: The What, Who, WOW, Where, and Why* (Thousand Oaks: Corwin, 2015).

8. Bray and McClaskey, *Make Learning Personal*.

9. Allison Zmuda, Greg Curtis, and Diane Ullman, *Learning Personalized: The Evolution of the Contemporary Classroom* (San Francisco: Jossey-Bass, 2015).

10. World Economic Forum, *The Future of Jobs: Employment, Skills and Workforce Strategy for the Fourth Industrial Revolution* (Geneva: World Economic Forum, 2016), http://www3 .weforum.org/docs/WEF_Future_of_Jobs.pdf.

11. Bray and McClaskey, *Make Learning Personal*.

12. Andrea Sykes, Cynthia Decker, Michelle Verbrugge, and Katrina Ryan, *Personalized Learning Progress: Case Studies of Four Race to the Top–District Grantees' Early Implementation* (Washington, DC: District Reform Support Network, 2014); Benjamin Herold, "Facebook's Zuckerberg to Bet Big on Personalized Learning," *Education Week*, March 7, 2016, https://www.edweek.org/ew/articles/2016/03/07/facebooks-zuckerberg-to-bet-big-on-personalized.html.

13. Pane, Steiner, Baird, & Hamilton, *Continued Progress*.

14. Heather Roberts-Mahoney, Alexander J. Means, and Mark J. Garrison, "Netflixing Human Capital Development: Personalized Learning Technology and the Corporatization of K–12 Education," *Journal of Education Policy* 31, no. 4 (2016): 405-420.

15. Benjamin Riley, "Personalization vs. How People Learn," *Educational Leadership* 74, no. 6 (2017): 68–72.

16. OECD, *Students, Computers and Learning: Making the Connection* (Paris: OECD Publishing, 2015), http://dx.doi.org/10.1787/9789264239555-en.

17. Barbara Means, Yukie Toyama, Robert Murphy, and Marianne Baki, "The Effectiveness of Online and Blended Learning: A Meta-Analysis of the Empirical Literature," *Teachers College Record* 115, no. 3 (2013): 1–47.

18. Ibid; James L. Woodworth, et al., *Online Charter School Study 2015* (Stanford, CA: Center for Research on Education Outcomes, 2015), https://credo.stanford.edu/pdfs/Online CharterStudyFinal2015.pdf.

19. Saro Mohammed, "Understanding What Doesn't Work in Personalized Learning," *Brown Center Chalkboard*, November 3, 2017, https://www.brookings.edu/blog/brown-center-chalkboard/2017/11/03/understanding-what-doesnt-work-in-personalized-learning/.

20. Vicky Rideout, *The Common Sense Census: Media Use by Tweens and Teens* (San Francisco: Common Sense, 2015), https://www.commonsensemedia.org/sites/default/files/ uploads/research/census_researchreport.pdf.

21. John M. Downes and Penny Bishop, "Educators Engage Digital Natives and Learn from Their Experiences with Technology," *Middle School Journal* 43, no. 5 (2012): 6–15.

22. Chris Stevenson and Penny Bishop, "Curriculum That is Relevant, Challenging, Integrative, and Exploratory," in *This We Believe in Action: Implementing Successful Middle Level Schools*, 2nd ed., ed. Thomas O. Erb (Westerville: National Middle School Association,

2012), 29–46; Steven Netcoh and Penny A. Bishop, "Personalized Learning in the Middle Grades: A Case Study of One Team's Successes and Challenges," *Middle Grades Research Journal* 11, no. 2 (2017): 33–48.

23. Jacquelynne S. Eccles and Carol Midgely, "Stage-Environment Fit: Developmentally Appropriate Classrooms for Young Adolescents," in *Research on Motivation in Education*, vol 3., eds. Carole Ames and Russell Ames (San Diego: Academic Press, Inc., 1989), 139–186.

24. National Middle School Association, *This We Believe: Successful Schools for Young Adolescents* (Westerville, OH, 2010). Rose L. Colby, *Competency-Based Education: A New Architecture for K–12 Schooling* (Cambridge: Harvard Education Press, 2017), 102.

25. National Middle School Association, *This We Believe*.

26. Chris Sturgis and Katherine Casey, *Designing for Equity: Leveraging Competency-Based Education to Ensure All Students Succeed*, (Vienna: International Association for K–12 Online Learning, 2018), https://www.inacol.org/wp-content/uploads/2018/03/CompetencyWorks-DesigningForEquity.pdf; Ray, Sacks, and Twyman, *Equity and Personalized Learning*.

27. Penny Bishop, John Downes, and James Nagle, "How Personal Learning is Working in Vermont," *Educational Leadership* 74, no. 6 (2017), http://www.ascd.org/publications/educational-leadership/mar17/vol74/num06/How-Personal-Learning-Is-Working-in-Vermont.aspx.

28. Ray, Sacks, and Twyman, *Equity and Personalized Learning*, 8.

29. "Personal Learning Plan," The Glossary of Education Reform, https://www.edglossary.org/personal-learning-plan/.

30. Susan Patrick, Maria Worthen, Dale Frost, and Susan Gentz, *Promising State Policies for Personalized Learning* (Vienna: International Association for K–12 Online Learning, 2016), www.inacol.org/wp-content/uploads/2016/05/iNACOL-Promising-State-Policies-for-Personalized-Learning.pdf; Hanover Research, *Best Practices in Personalized Learning Environments (Grades 4–9)* (Washington, DC: Hanover Research, 2012), https://www.hanoverresearch.com/media/Best-Practices-in-Personalized-Learning-Environments.pdf.

31. Eric Toshalis and Michael J. Nakkula, *Motivation, Engagement, and Student Voice.* (Boston: Jobs for the Future, 2012), https://studentsatthecenterhub.org/wp-content/uploads/2012/04/Motivation-Engagement-Student-Voice-Students-at-the-Center-1.pdf.

32. John Downes, Steven Netcoh, Katy Farber, Scott Thompson, Penny Bishop, and Jessica DeMink-Carthew, "Pathways to Personalization in Middle Schools" (paper presented at the annual meeting for the American Educational Research Association, San Antonio, Texas, April 27–May 1, 2017).

33. Will Richardson, "Preparing Students to Learn without Us," *Educational Leadership* 69, no. 5 (2012): 22–26, http://www.ascd.org/publications/educational-leadership/feb12/vol69/num05/Preparing-Students-to-Learn-Without-Us.aspx.

34. James Rickabaugh, "The Importance of Competency-Based Learning in a Personalized Learning Environment," July 15, 2013, www.competencyworks.org/reflections/the-importance-of-competency-based-learning-in-a-personalized-learning-environment.

35. James F. Nagle and Don Taylor, "Using a Personal Learning Framework to Transform Middle Grades Teacher Practice," *Middle Grades Research Journal*, 11, no. 1 (2017): 85–100.

36. Nellie Mae Education Foundation, *Putting Students at the Center: A Reference Guide* (Quincy: Nellie Mae Education Foundation, 2014), http://studentsatthecenterhub.org/wp-content/legacyimg/NMEF_sclrframeweb.pdf.

37. "Personalized Learning," The Glossary of Education Reform, https://www.edglossary.org/personalized-learning/.

38. For a list of experimental studies supporting this finding, visit: http://www.udlcenter.org/research/researchevidence/checkpoint7_1.

39. "Stages of PLE, v5," Make Learning Personal, http://kathleenmcclaskey.com/stages-of-personalized-learning-enviroments/.

40. "Stages of PLE, v5," Make Learning Personal, http://kathleenmcclaskey.com/stages-of-personalized-learning-enviroments/.

41. Bray and McClaskey, "Building Personalized Learning Environments," https://www.advanc-ed.org/source/building-personalized-learning-environments.

Chapter 2

1. William Damon, Jenni Menon, and Kendall Cotton Bronk, "The Development of Purpose During Adolescence," *Applied Developmental Science* 7, no. 3 (2003): 121.

2. National Middle School Association, *This We Believe: Successful Schools for Young Adolescents* (Westerville, OH, 2010).

3. Erik Erikson, *Identity: Youth and Crisis* (New York: W. W. Norton & Company, Inc., 1968); Jane Loevinger, *Ego Development* (San Francisco: Jossey-Bass, 1976).

4. Damon, Menon, and Cotton Bronk, "The Development of Purpose During Adolescence."

5. William Damon, *The Path to Purpose* (New York: Free Press, 2009).

6. Damon, Menon, and Cotton Bronk, "The Development of Purpose During Adolescence," 120.

7. Damon, Menon, and Cotton Bronk, "The Development of Purpose During Adolescence."

8. Kathleen Cushman and Wendy Baron, "The Art and Science of Developing Student Agency," New Teacher Center, May 30, 2017, https://newteachercenter.org/blog/2017/05/30/art-science-developing-student-agency/.

9. Eric Toshalis and Michael J. Nakkula, *Motivation, Engagement, and Student Voice.* (Boston: Jobs for the Future, 2012), 2, https://studentsatthecenterhub.org/wp-content/uploads/2012/04/Motivation-Engagement-Student-Voice-Students-at-the-Center-1.pdf.

10. Cushman and Baron, "The Art and Science of Developing Student Agency."

11. Erikson, *Identity: Youth and Crisis*; Tija Ragelienė, "Links of Adolescents Identity Development and Relationship with Peers: A Systematic Literature Review," *Journal of Canadian Academy of Child and Adolescent Psychiatry* 25, no. 2 (2016): 97–105.

12. Laurence Steinberg, *Adolescence*, 8th ed. (New York: McGraw-Hill, 2008).

13. Sarah Brody Shulkind and Jack Foote, "Creating a Culture of Connectedness through Middle School Advisory Programs," *Middle School Journal* 41, no. 1 (2009): 20–27, https://doi.org/10.1080/00940771.2009.11461700.

14. John J. Wallace, "Effects of Interdisciplinary Teaching Team Configuration upon the Social Bonding of Middle School Students" *Research in Middle Level Education Online* 30, no. 5 (2007): 1–18, https://doi.org/10.1080/19404476.2007.11462038.

15. Annette M. La Greca and Hannah Moore Harrison, "Adolescent Peer Relations, Friendships, and Romantic Relationships: Do They Predict Social Anxiety and Depression?" *Journal of Clinical Child and Adolescent Psychology* 34, no. 1 (2005): 49–61, doi: 10.1207/s15374424jccp3401_5; Rachel Yeung and Bonnie Leadbeater, "Adults Make a Difference: The Protective Effects of Parent and Teacher Emotional Support on Emotional and Behavioral Problems of Peer-Victimized Adolescents," *Journal of Community Psychology* 38, no. 1 (2010): 80–98, https://doi.org/10.1002/jcop.20353.

16. Chris Stevenson, *Teaching Ten to Fourteen Year Olds*, 3rd ed. (Boston: Allyn & Bacon, 2002).

17. World Economic Forum, *The Future of Jobs: Employment, Skills and Workforce Strategy for the Fourth Industrial Revolution* (Geneva: World Economic Forum, 2016), http://www3.weforum.org/docs/WEF_Future_of_Jobs.pdf.

18. Yigal Rosen, Steve Ferrara, and Maryam Mosharraf, eds., *Handbook of Research on Technology Tools for Real-World Skill Development* (Hershey: Information Science Reference, 2016).

19. Resiliency Initiatives. (2011). Embracing a strength-based perspective and practice in education. *The California School Psychologist*, 9, 1–24.

20. "Geography of Self," http://lumsvt.wixsite.com/self.

21. See https://www.un.org/sustainabledevelopment/development-agenda/.

22. cafelottivt "Come take a look of the @eastburkeschool's art show while its still here!" Instagram, March 28, 2018. https://www.instagram.com/p/Bg3siDinJUM/?utm_source=ig_web_share_sheet.

23. David T. Conley, *A New Era for Educational Assessment* (Boston: Jobs for the Future, 2014), https://studentsatthecenterhub.org/wp-content/uploads/2014/09/A-New-Era-for-Educational-Assessment-092414_0-2.pdf.

24. Emily Rinkema, "Proficiency, Personalization, and a Cocktail Napkin: Or, How PBL Became PPBL," CVU Learns: One School's Journey to Standards Based Learning, May 10, 2018, http://cvulearnsblog.blogspot.com/.

25. A. W. Bendig, "The Reliability of Letter Grades," *Educational and Psychological Measurement* 13, no. 2 (1953): 311-321, https://doi.org/10.1177%2F001316445301300215; Jessica Lahey, "Letter Grades Deserve an F," *The Atlantic*, March 12, 2014, https://www.theatlantic.com/education/archive/2014/03/letter-grades-deserve-an-f/284372/; Curt M. Adams et al., *An Examination of the Oklahoma State Department of Education's A-F Report Card* (Norman: The Oklahoma Center for Education Policy and The Center for Educational Research and Evaluation, 2013), https://okea.org/assets/files/A-F%20Study.pdf.

26. Steven Netcoh, "Balancing Freedom and Limitations: A Case Study of Choice Provision in a Personalized Learning Class," *Teaching and Teacher Education* 66 (2017): 383–392, https://doi.org/10.1016/j.tate.2017.05.010.

27. Vermont Agency of Education, *Personalized Learning Plan Critical Elements* (Barre: Vermont Agency of Education, 2017), http://education.vermont.gov/sites/aoe/files/documents/edu-plp-critical-elements.pdf.

28. Vermont Agency of Education, *Personalized Learning Plan*.

Chapter 3

1. Jacquelynne S. Eccles et al., "Development during Adolescence: The Impact of Stage Environment Fit on Young Adolescents' Experiences in Schools and in Families," *American Psychologist* 48, no. 2 (1993): 90–101.

2. Jacquelynne S. Eccles, "The Development of Children Ages 6 to 14," *The Future of Children* 9, no. 2 (1999): 40–41, DOI: 10.2307/1602703.

3. Eccles, "The Development of Children," 40–41.

4. Eccles, "The Development of Children," 40.

5. Penny A. Bishop and Susanna W. Pflaum, "Middle School Students' Perceptions of Social Dimensions as Influencers of Academic Engagement," *Research in Middle Level Education Online* 29, no. 1 (2005): 10, https://doi.org/10.1080/19404476.2005.11462025.

6. Kenneth L. Brighton, *Coming of Age: The Education and Development of Young Adolescents* (Westerville: National Middle School Association, 2007); Lisa M. Raphael and Meghan Burke, "Academic, Social, and Emotional Needs in a Middle Grades Reform Initiative," *Research in Middle Level Education Online* 35, no. 6 (2012): 1–13, https://doi.org/10.1080/19404476.2012.11462089.

7. Laura Shubilla and Chris Sturgis, *The Learning Edge: Supporting Student Success in a Competency-Based Learning Environment* (Vienna: International Association for K-12 Online Learning, 2012), 8, https://www.inacol.org/wp-content/uploads/2015/02/the-learning-edge.pdf.

8. World Economic Forum, *New Vision for Education: Fostering Social and Emotional Learning through Technology* (Geneva: World Economic Forum, 2016), http://www3.weforum.org/docs/WEF_New_Vision_for_Education.pdf.

9. Shubilla and Sturgis, *The Learning Edge*, 16.

10. Penny Bishop and Garet Allen-Malley, *The Power of Two: Partner Teams in Action* (Westerville: National Middle School Association, 2004); Susan J. Boyer and Penny A. Bishop, "Young Adolescent Voices: Students' Perceptions of Interdisciplinary Teaming," *Research in Middle Level Education Online* 28, no. 1 (2004): 1–19; Katrien Vangrieken, Filip Dochy, Elisabeth Raes, and Eva Kyndt, "Teacher Collaboration: A Systematic Review," *Educational Research Review* 15 (2015): 17–40. https://doi.org/10.1016/j.edurev.2015.04.002.

11. "Stages of PLE, v5," Make Learning Personal, http://kathleenmcclaskey.com/stages-of-personalized-learning-enviroments/.

12. Howard Kirschenbaum and Valerie Land Henderson, eds., *The Carl Rogers Reader* (New York: Houghton Mifflin, 1989), 321.

13. Malcolm Knowles, *Self-Directed Learning: A Guide for Learners and Teachers* (New York: Cambridge Books, 1975).

14. Terrie E. Moffitt et al., "A Gradient of Childhood Self-Control Predicts Health, Wealth, and Public Safety," *Proceedings of the National Academy of Sciences of the United States of America* 108, no. 7 (2011): 2693–2698, https://doi.org/10.1073/pnas.1010076108.

15. Moffitt et al., "A Gradient of Childhood Self-Control."

16. "Executive Function & Self-Regulation," Center on the Developing Child, https://developingchild.harvard.edu/science/key-concepts/executive-function.

17. Adele Diamond and Daphne S. Ling, "Conclusions about Interventions, Programs, and Approaches for Improving Executive Functions That Appear Justified and Those That, Despite Much Hype, Do Not," *Developmental Cognitive Neuroscience* 18 (2016): 34–48, https://doi.org/10.1016/j.dcn.2015.11.005.

18. "Executive Function Activities for Adolescents," Center on the Developing Child, https://www.neurodevelop.com/File/20e0d315-6f74-45f9-b8ff-4be7e8ce4b96.

19. "What is SEL?" The Collaborative for Academic, Social, and Emotional Learning (CASEL), https://casel.org/what-is-sel/.

20. Rebecca D. Taylor, Joseph A. Durlak, Eva Oberle, Roger P. Weissberg, "Promoting Positive Youth Development Through School-Based Social and Emotional Learning Interventions: A Meta-Analysis of Follow-Up Effects," *Child Development* 88, no. 4 (2017): 1156–1171, https://doi.org/10.1111/cdev.12864.

21. "What is SEL?" CASEL, https://casel.org/what-is-sel/.

22. "What is SEL?" CASEL.

23. National Middle School Association, *This We Believe: Successful Schools for Young Adolescents* (Westerville, OH, 2010).

24. Elizabeth G. Cohen, Rachel A. Lotan, Beth A. Scarloss, and Adele R. Arellano, "Complex Instruction: Equity in Cooperative Learning Classrooms," *Theory into Practice* 38, no. 2 (1999): 80–86, https://doi.org/10.1080/00405849909543836.

25. Cohen, Lotan, Scarloss, and Arellano, "Complex Instruction."

26. Buck Institute for Education, http://bie.org.

27. "The Grade 6 World at Rumney," http://56rumney.blogspot.com/search?q=all+school+meeting; Katy Farber, "iLead: A Model for Service Learning and Leadership," Innovation: Education, February 13, 2017, http://tiie.w3.uvm.edu/blog/ilead-a-model-for-yearlong-service-learning-and-leadership/#.WuHPFSPMzOT.

28. Susan Hennessey, "What Vermont Students Really Think about Personal Learning Plans," Innovation: Education, September 14, 2016, http://tiie.w3.uvm.edu/blog/designing-plps-with-students/.

29. Life LeGeros, "Use a Student Leadership Team for Feedback on PLPs," Innovation: Education, June 26, 2017, http://tiie.w3.uvm.edu/blog/use-a-student-leadership-team-for-feedback-on-plps/#.W1OD1S2ZPOR.

30. John M. Downes, "From Teacher-Exclusive Planning to Teacher-Student Planning: The Promise of Partnering in a Connected World," in *Middle Grades Curriculum: Voices and Visions of the Self-Enhancing School*, eds. Kathleen Roney and Richard P. Lipka (Charlotte: Information Age Publishing, 2013), 253–270.

31. Jean Rudduck, "Student Voice, Student Engagement, and School Reform," in *International Handbook of Student Experience in Elementary and Secondary Schools*, eds. Dennis Thiessen and Alison Cook-Sather (Dordrecht: Springer, 2007), 587–610.

32. Rudduck, "Student Voice, Student Engagement, and School Reform," 598.

33. "Transferable Skills." Great Schools Partnership, https://www.greatschoolspartnership
.org/transferableskills/.

34. "Transferable Skills: Sample Graduation Proficiencies and Performance Indicators," Vermont Agency of Education, http://education.vermont.gov/sites/aoe/files/documents/
edu-proficiency-based-education-transferrable-skills-sample-graduation-proficiencies
.pdf (for expanded rubrics of all five transferable skills, see http://education.vermont
.gov/student-learning/proficiency-based-learning/transferable-skills).

35. BRSU PLP Continuum K8, https://docs.google.com/document/d/1X2hQvNJ3Rljt9GjHl
mbA_PHlkfCd3VN8vHUE_MRd9i0/edit.

36. "Transferable Skills: Sample Graduation Proficiencies and Performance Indicators,"
Vermont Agency of Education.

37. Steven B. Mertens, Nancy Flowers, Vincent A. Anfara Jr., and Micki M. Caskey, "Common Planning Time," *Middle School Journal* 41, no. 5 (2010): 50–57, https://doi.org/10
.1080/00940771.2010.11461741.

38. Christopher M. Cook and Shawn A. Faulkner, "The Use of Common Planning Time:
A Case Study of Two Kentucky Schools to Watch," *Research in Middle Level Education
Online* 34, no. 2 (2010): 1–12, https://doi.org/10.1080/19404476.2010.11462075; Nancy
Flowers, Steven B, Mertens, and Peter F. Mulhall, "What Makes Interdisciplinary Teams
Effective?" *Middle School Journal* 31, no. 4 (2000): 53–56, https://doi.org/10.1080/009407
71.2000.11494640; Mertens, Flowers, Anfara Jr., and Caskey, "Common Planning Time."

39. Mertens, Flowers, Anfara Jr., and Caskey, "Common Planning Time."

40. Larry G. Daniel, *Research Summary: Flexible Scheduling* (Westerville: National Middle
School Association, 2007), http://www.amle.org/portals/0/pdf/research_summaries/
Flexible_Scheduling.pdf.

41. Daniel, *"Research Summary: Flexible Scheduling."*

42. John M. Downes and Penny A. Bishop, "The Intersection between 1:1 Laptop Implementation and the Characteristics of Effective Middle Level Schools," *Research in
Middle Level Education Online* 38, no. 7 (2015): 1–16, https://doi.org/10.1080/19404476
.2015.11462120.

43. Common Sense Media, https://commonsensemedia.org.

44. TouchCast, https://touchcast.com.

45. Protean, https://www.protean.me/.

46. Seesaw, https://web.seesaw.me.

47. Weebly, https://Weebly.com; Wix, wix.com.

48. VoiceThread, https://voicethread.com.

Chapter 4

1. Sandra K. M. Tsang, Eadaoin K. P. Hui, and Bella C. M. Law, "Positive Identity as a Positive Youth Development Construct: A Conceptual Review," *The Scientific World Journal*
2012, Article ID 529691 (2012): 1–8, http://dx.doi.org/10.1100/2012/529691.

2. Erik Erikson, *Identity: Youth and Crisis* (New York: W. W. Norton & Company, Inc., 1968); Micki M. Caskey and Vincent A. Anfara Jr., *Research Summary: Young Adolescents' Developmental Characteristics* (Westerville: National Middle School Association, 2007), https://pdxscholar.library.pdx.edu/cgi/viewcontent.cgi?article=1009&context=ci_fac.

3. Harold D. Grotevant, "Adolescent Development in Family Contexts," in *Handbook of Child Psychology: Volume 3: Social, Emotional, and Personality Development*, 5th ed., eds. Nancy Eisenberg and William Damon (Hoboken: John Wiley & Sons, Inc., 1998), 1097–1149.

4. Peter C. Scales, "Characteristics of Young Adolescents," in *This We Believe: Keys to Educating Young Adolescents* (Westerville: National Middle School Association, 2010), 63–62.

5. Tsang, Hui, and Law, "Positive Identity as a Positive Youth Development Construct."

6. Chris Stevenson, *Teaching Ten to Fourteen Year Olds*, 3rd ed. (Boston: Allyn & Bacon, 2002), 128.

7. Phillip C. Schlechty, *Engaging Students: The Next Level of Working on the Work*, 2nd ed. (San Francisco: John Wiley & Sons, Inc., 2011).

8. "Learner Profiles," The Institute for Personalized Learning, http://institute4pl.org/index.php/our-model/core-components/learner-profiles/.

9. "Learner Profiles."

10. Next Generation Learning Challenges, *Personalized Learning Plans and Learner Profiles* (Washington, DC: EDUCAUSE, 2016), https://library.educause.edu/~/media/files/library/2016/1/ngt1601-pdf.

11. Barbara Bray and Kathleen McClaskey, "A Step-by-Step Guide to Personalize Learning," *Learning and Leading with Technology* 40, no. 7 (2013): 12–19, https://files.eric.ed.gov/fulltext/EJ1015153.pdf; "About Universal Design for Learning," Center for Applied Special Technology (CAST), http://www.cast.org/our-work/about-udl.html#.WuHfwyPMzOQ.

12. "Vermont Personalized Learning Plan: Conceptual Framework Narrative for Students," Vermont Agency of Education, http://education.vermont.gov/sites/aoe/files/documents/edu-personalized-learning-conceptual-framework-students.pdf.

13. "Geography of Self," http://lumsvt.wixsite.com/self.

14. Craig Roland, Digital Storytelling in the Classroom. *SchoolArts* 105, no. 7 (2006): 26.

15. Cynthia Reyes and Kathleen Brinegar, "Lessons Learned: Using the Literacy Histories of Education Students to Foster Empathy," *Teaching and Teacher Education* 59 (2016): 327–337, https://doi.org/10.1016/j.tate.2016.06.014.

16. Cynthia Reyes and Bill Clark, "Exploring Writing through the Digital Story with English Language Learners: A Collaborative Approach," in *Creating Collaborative Learning Communities to Improve English Learner Instruction: College Faculty, School Teachers, and Pre-service Teachers Learning Together in the 21st Century*, ed. James Nagle (Charlotte: Information Age Publishing, 2013) 43–60; Cynthia Reyes, "'This I Believe:' Addressing Cultural Competency with the Digital Narratives of Middle Grades English Language Learners," in *Transforming Learning Environments: Strategies to Shape the Next Generation*, ed. Fayneese Miller (Bingley, Emerald Group Publishing Limited, 2012), 171–191.

17. Reyes, "'This I Believe:' Addressing Cultural Competency."

18. "Geography of Self," http://lumsvt.wixsite.com/self.

19. Identity Project: Who am I now?, https://docs.google.com/document/d/15YJ8bmyX5iso fjASX75VlfEw0Fh03RHxH7pEhEzrsCw/edit.

20. Team Summit: Personal Learning Page, Community Page, https://docs.google.com/document/d/1jeqM1dVVSzjCov3FLIhHGysLpmIzp_aph8ICUXaNQUk/edit.

21. http://blogs.oregonstate.edu/fyeuhds/files/2013/09/Identity-Board-Sample-2013.pdf.

22. "A Kids' Guide to Canada, If I Really Knew You (The Cultural Iceberg)," https://akgt canada.com/if-i-really-knew-you/.

23. Audrey Homan, "How Can Students Teach Educators about Social Identity?" Innovation: Education, February 26, 2018, http://tiie.w3.uvm.edu/blog/how-can-students-teach-educators-about-social-identity/#more-14988.

24. Emily Hoyler, "'Who Are We as West Rutland?'" Innovation: Education, May 23, 2018, http://tiie.w3.uvm.edu/blog/who-are-we-as-west-rutland/#.Ww4UdVMvzOQ.

25. "Vermont Personalized Learning Plan: Conceptual Framework Narrative for Students," Vermont Agency of Education, http://education.vermont.gov/sites/aoe/files/documents/edu-personalized-learning-conceptual-framework-students.pdf.

26. Rachel Mark, "I Is for Identity," Innovation: Education, September 2, 2015, https://tiie .w3.uvm.edu/blog/tech-rich-ways-students-can-explore-identity/#.W1OSeS2ZPOR.

Chapter 5

1. "Schlechty Center on Engagement," Schlechty Center, https://www.rcsdk12.org/cms/lib/NY01001156/Centricity/Domain/1053/sc_pdf_engagement.pdf.

2. "Schlechty Center on Engagement," Schlechty Center.

3. Jacquelynne S. Eccles, "The Development of Children Ages 6 to 14," *The Future of Children* 9, no. 2 (1999): 30–44, http://www.jstor.org/stable/1602703.

4. Elaine M. Allensworth and John Q. Easton, *The On-Track Indicator as a Predictor of High School Graduation* (Chicago: Consortium on Chicago School Research, 2005), https://consortium.uchicago.edu/sites/default/files/publications/p78.pdf. Robert Balfanz, *Putting Middle Grades Students on the Graduation Path* (Westerville: National Middle School Association, 2009).

5. Phillip Schlechty, *Shaking up the Schoolhouse: How to Support and Sustain Educational Innovation* (San Francisco: Jossey-Bass, 2001), 10.

6. Edward Brazee, "Curriculum for Whom?" in *What Current Research Says to the Middle Level Practitioner*, ed. Judith L. Irvin (Columbus: National Middle School Association, 1997), 187.

7. Common Core Standards, http://www.corestandards.org/; Next Generation Science Standards, http://www.nextgenscience.org/; National Core Arts Standards, https://www .nationalartsstandards.org/.

8. David A. Sousa, "Brain-Friendly Learning for Teachers," *Educational Leadership* 66 (Online June 2009), http://www.ascd.org/publications/educational_leadership/summer09/vol66/num09/Brain-Friendly_Learning_for_Teachers.aspx.

9. "Stages of PLE, v5," Make Learning Personal, http://kathleenmcclaskey.com/stages-of-personalized-learning-enviroments/.

10. Katy Farber, John M. Downes, and Penny A. Bishop, "Teacher Roles in Emerging Middle Grades Personalized Learning Environments" (paper presented at the annual meeting for the American Educational Research Association, New York, New York, April 13–17, 2018).

11. "Schlechty Center on Engagement," Schlechty Center, https://www.rcsdk12.org/cms/lib/NY01001156/Centricity/Domain/1053/sc_pdf_engagement.pdf.

12. "What Are Flexible Pathways?" Vermont Agency of Education, April 19, 2017, http://education.vermont.gov/sites/aoe/files/documents/edu-plp-what-are-flexible-pathways.pdf.

13. Schlechty, *Shaking up the Schoolhouse*, 9.

14. National Middle School Association, *This We Believe: Keys to Educating Young Adolescents* (Westerville: National Middle School Association, 2010).

15. Penny A. Bishop and Susanna W. Pflaum, "Student Perceptions of Action, Relevance, and Pace," *Middle School Journal* 36, no. 4 (2005): 4–12.

16. John M. Downes and Penny Bishop, "Educators Engage Digital Natives and Learn from Their Experiences with Technology," *Middle School Journal* 43, no. 5 (2012): 6–15

17. Katy Farber and Penny Bishop, "Service Learning in the Middle Grades: Learning by Doing and Caring," *Research in Middle Level Education Online* 41, no. 2 (2018): 1–15, https://doi.org/10.1080/19404476.2017.1415600.

18. Chris Stevenson and Penny Bishop, "Curriculum That Is Fair, Relevant, Challenging, Integrative, and Exploratory."

19. "What is PBL?" Buck Institute for Education, http://www.bie.org/about/what_pbl.

20. "The Framework for High Quality Project Based Learning," High Quality Project Based Learning, https://hqpbl.org.

21. John Larmer and John R. Mergendoller, "Gold Standard PBL: Essential Project Design Elements," PBL Blog, April 21, 2015, http://www.bie.org/blog/gold_standard_pbl_essential_project_design_elements.

22. "Our Model," KID Consortium, http://kidsconsortiumarchives.com/learningservice.php.

23. Cathryn Berger Kaye, *The Complete Guide to Service Learning: Proven, Practical Ways to Engage Students in Civic Responsibility, Academic Curriculum, & Social Action*, 2nd ed. (Minneapolis: Free Spirit Publishing Inc., 2010).

24. Katy Farber, *Real and Relevant: A Guide for Service and Project-Based Learning*, 2nd ed. (Lanham: Rowman & Littlefield, 2017).

25. Farber, *Real and Relevant*.

26. Created by Katy Farber, Rachel Mark, and Jeanie Phillips.

27. "Stages of PLE, v5," Make Learning Personal, http://kathleenmcclaskey.com/stages-of-personalized-learning-enviroments/.

28. For more on learning how to write driving questions, see Buck Institute for Education's Driving Question Tubric at https://www.bie.org/object/document/driving_question_tubric.

29. James A. Beane. "Curriculum Integration and the Disciplines of Knowledge," *The Phi Delta Kappan* 76, no. 8 (1995): 616.

30. James A. Beane, *A Middle School Curriculum: From Rhetoric to Reality*, 2nd ed. (Columbus: National Middle School Association, 1993).

31. For more about the Alpha Team, see: Sue Kuntz, *The Story of Alpha: A Multiage, Student-Centered Team, 33 Years and Counting* (Columbus: National Middle School Association, 2005).

32. Dot-voting is one of many ways to manage classroom decision making. See http://dotmocracy.org.

33. Jeanie Phillips, "How to Plan a Service Learning Project in 5 Stages," Innovation: Education, June 20, 2018, http://tiie.w3.uvm.edu/blog/how-to-plan-a-service-learning-project/#.W1SBpy2ZPOQ.

34. "Stages of PLE, v5," Make Learning Personal, http://kathleenmcclaskey.com/stages-of-personalized-learning-enviroments/.

35. See https://www.un.org/sustainabledevelopment/development-agenda/.

36. Emily Hoyler, "How to Tell your PBL Story," Innovation: Education, November 13, 2017, https://tiie.w3.uvm.edu/blog/how-to-tell-your-pbl-story/#.W1IWui2ZPOS.

37. LaunchPad, https://launchpad.savilabs.org/; Padlet, https://padlet.com/.

38. Emily Hoyler, "4 Times to Connect Students with an Authentic Audience," Innovation: Education, March 15, 2018, https://tiie.w3.uvm.edu/blog/4-times-to-connect-students-with-an-authentic-audience/#.W1VMBC2ZPO.

39. Jeanie Phillips, "How to Build a Better (Student-Made) Chicken Coop," Innovation: Education, March 6, 2018. http://tiie.w3.uvm.edu/blog/student-made-chicken-coops/#.W1VLNS2ZPOR.

Chapter 6

1. Pedro Noguera, Linda Darling-Hammond, and Diane Friedlaender, *Equal Opportunity for Deeper Learning* (Boston: Jobs for the Future, 2015), https://jfforg-prod-prime.s3.amazonaws.com/media/documents/Equal-Opportunity-for-Deeper-Learning-Executive-Summary-092315.pdf.

2. Diane Friedlaender et al., *Student-Centered Schools: Closing the Opportunity Gap (Research Brief)* (Stanford: Stanford Center for Opportunity Policy in Education, 2014), https://edpolicy.stanford.edu/sites/default/files/scope-pub-student-centered-research-brief.pdf.

3. Lev Vygotsky, *Mind in Society* (Cambridge: Harvard University Press, 1978); David Wood, Jerome S. Bruner, and Gail Ross, "The Role of Tutoring in Problem Solving," *Journal of Child Psychology and Psychiatry* 17, no. 2 (1976): 89–100, https://doi.org/10.1111/j.1469-7610.1976.tb00381.x; "Scaffolding," The Glossary of Education Reform, https://www.edglossary.org/scaffolding/.

4. Vygotsky, *Mind in Society*.

5. Andrianes Pinantoan, "Instructional Scaffolding: A Definitive Guide," informED, March 20, 2013, https://www.opencolleges.edu.au/informed/teacher-resources/scaffolding-in-education-a-definitive-guide/.

6. Andrew Miller, "Planning for PBL Implementation," Edutopia, January 18, 2018, https://www.edutopia.org/article/planning-pbl-implementation.

7. Carol Ann Tomlinson, "What Is Differentiated Instruction?" Reading Rockets, http://www.readingrockets.org/article/what-differentiated-instruction.

8. "What is Blended Learning?" Christensen Institute, https://www.christenseninstitute.org/blended-learning/.

9. "What is Blended Learning?" iNACOL, https://www.inacol.org/news/what-is-blended-learning/.

10. Susan Hennessey, "Assessment in Proficiency-Based Classrooms," Innovation: Education, December 4, 2016, https://tiie.w3.uvm.edu/blog/shifting-assessment-in-proficiency-based-classrooms/#.W1TPBC2ZPOS.

11. "The UDL Guidelines," Center for Applied Special Technology (CAST), http://udlguidelines.cast.org/?utm_medium=web&utm_campaign=none&utm_source=udlcenter&utm_content=site-banner.

12. Thomas Guskey, "Formative Classroom Assessment and Benjamin S. Bloom: Theory, Research and Implications" (paper presented at the annual meeting for the American Educational Research Association, Montréal, Canada, April 11–15, 2005).

13. Jennifer Gonzalez, "Using Playlists to Differentiate Instruction," Cult of Pedagogy, September 4, 2016, https://www.cultofpedagogy.com/student-playlists-differentiation/.

14. Tom Vander Ark, "The Perks of Personalized Pathways & Playlists," Getting Smart, November 10, 2015, http://www.gettingsmart.com/2015/11/the-perks-of-personalized-pathways-playlists/.

15. Susan Hennessey, "Personalize Learning with Open Educational Resources," Innovation: Education, December 9, 2015, http://tiie.w3.uvm.edu/blog/open-educational-resources/#.W1SnNi2ZPOQ.

16. Noah Hurlburt, "Independent Student Playlists - Remixed," https://docs.google.com/document/d/11y_3_APLMtHjydL_W2DtfZ94MyTOGUgGg2v4cHXXMho/edit.

17. Explore the HyperDocs and Student Centered Learning Google+ Community at https://plus.google.com/u/0/communities/114380077074592058394.

18. Susan Hennessey, "Managing Time in Blended Classrooms," Innovation: Education, March 11, 2016, https://tiie.w3.uvm.edu/blog/managing-time-in-blended-classrooms/#.W1SHDi2ZPOR.

19. Katy Farber, "6 Ways Teachers Are Using Padlet," Innovation: Education, February 28, 2018, http://tiie.w3.uvm.edu/blog/ways-teachers-are-using-padlet/#.W1SM7y2ZPOR.

20. Life LeGeros, "Revolutionize Student Research with Padlet," Innovation: Education, June 6, 2016, http://tiie.w3.uvm.edu/blog/student-research-with-padlet/#.W1U_7C2ZPOR.

21. Karl M. Kapp, *The Gamification of Learning and Instruction: Game-based Methods and Strategies for Training and Education* (San Francisco: Pfeiffer, 2012).

22. Chris Bologna, "Let's Play Education: Telling the Story of My Learning Lab," Tarrant Institute Learning Lab, http://tiie.w3.uvm.edu/learninglab/2018/03/20/lets-play-education/.

23. Joseph Luft, *Group Processes: An Introduction to Group Dynamics*, 2nd ed. (Palo Alto: National Press Books, 1970).

24. Life LeGeros, "What Are the Benefits of Taking Genius Hour School-Wide?" Innovation: Education, May 18, 2017, https://tiie.w3.uvm.edu/blog/taking-genius-hour-school-wide/#.W4AdiRpKg_U.

25. You can learn more about Brainado at this great Padlet: https://padlet.com/lifelegeros/7e3i7rf381n8.

26. Jeanie Phillips and Rachel Mark, "Sharing Your School's Passion Projects," Innovation: Education, February 2, 2018, http://tiie.w3.uvm.edu/blog/passion-projects/#.W1SBJS2ZPOQ.

27. Diana Rendina, "Defining Makerspaces: What the Research Says," Renovated Learning, April 2, 2015, http://renovatedlearning.com/2015/04/02/defining-makerspaces-part-1/.

28. Laura Fleming, "What Constitutes 'MAKING'?" Worlds of Learning, October 26, 2016, https://worlds-of-learning.com/2016/10/26/what-constitutes-making/.

29. "A WAPL Recap," The Library as Incubator Project, May 13, 2012, http://www.libraryasincubatorproject.org/?p=4594.

30. Edward P. Clapp, Jessica Ross, Jennifer O. Ryan, and Shari Tishman, *Maker-Centered Learning: Empowering Young People to Shape Their Worlds* (San Francisco: Jossey-Bass, 2017).

31. To learn more about EMMA, visit http://www.minimakerbus.org.

32. Lucie deLaBruere and Life LeGeros, "The Maker Movement and Transferable Skills," Innovation: Education, October 3, 2017, https://tiie.w3.uvm.edu/blog/making-as-evidence-of-transferable-skills/#.W4WVlC2ZPOR.

33. DeLaBruere and LeGeros, "The Maker Movement."

34. Lucie deLaBruere and Life LeGeros, "The Maker Movement and Transferable Skills," Innovation: Education, October 5, 2017, https://tiie.w3.uvm.edu/blog/making-as-evidence-of-problem-solving/.

Chapter 7

1. David Elkind, "Egocentrism in Adolescence," *Child Development* 38, No. 4 (1967), 1025-1034, DOI: 10.2307/1127100.

2. "What is Proficiency-Based Learning?" Vermont Agency of Education, http://education.vermont.gov/sites/aoe/files/documents/edu-proficiency-based-education-what-is-proficiency-based-learning.pdf.

3. Ibid.

4. David T. Conley, *A New Era for Educational Assessment* (Boston: Jobs for the Future, 2014), https://studentsatthecenterhub.org/wp-content/uploads/2014/09/A-New-Era-for-Educational-Assessment-092414_0-2.pdf.

5. "Standards-Based," The Glossary of Education Reform, https://www.edglossary.org/standards-based/.

6. "Habits of Work Grading and Reporting," Great Schools Partnership, https://www.greatschoolspartnership.org/proficiency-based-learning/grading-reporting/habits-work-grading-reporting/.

7. "What is Proficiency-Based Grading?" New England Secondary Schools Consortium, 2, https://www.newenglandssc.org/wp-content/uploads/2015/12/NESSC_I_Want_to_Know_More_No12.pdf.

8. Ken B. O'Connor, *How to Grade for Learning: Linking Grades to Standards*, 2nd ed. (Thousand Oaks: Corwin Press, 2002).

9. Matt Townsley, "What is the Difference between Standards-Based Grading (or Reporting) and Competency-Based Education?" CompetencyWorks, November 11, 2014, https://www.competencyworks.org/analysis/what-is-the-difference-between-standards-based-grading/.

10. Life LeGeros, "4 Ways to Begin Using Scales for Assessment," Innovation: Education, October 19, 2016, https://tiie.w3.uvm.edu/blog/scales-for-assessment/#.W4KXGRpKg_U.

11. Life LeGeros, "The Crucial Role of Practice in a Proficiency-Based Environment," Innovation: Education, March 3, 2017, https://tiie.w3.uvm.edu/blog/practice-for-proficiency/#.W4BLLhpKg_U.

12. National Middle School Association, *This We Believe: Successful Schools for Young Adolescents* (Westerville, OH, 2010).

13. Paul Black and Dylan Wiliam, "Inside the Black Box: Raising Standards Through Classroom Assessment," *Phi Delta Kappa* 80, no. 2 (1998): 2, http://faa-training.measuredprogress.org/documents/10157/15652/InsideBlackBox.pdf; Karee E. Dunn and Sean W. Mulvenon, "A Critical Review of Research on Formative Assessment: The Limited Scientific Evidence of the Impact of Formative Assessment in Education," *Practical Assessment, Research & Evaluation* 14, no. 7 (2009), 3, http://www.pareonline.net/pdf/v14n7.pdf.

14. https://www.youtube.com/watch?time_continue=3&v=EJV0ro-BsiY.

15. Robert J. Marzano, "The Art and Science of Teaching / When Students Track Their Progress," *Health and Learning* 67, no. 4 (December 2009/January 2010), 86–87, http://www.ascd.org/publications/educational-leadership/dec09/vol67/num04/When-Students-Track-Their-Progress.aspx.

16. Marzano, "The Art and Science of Teaching.

17. Neal McIntyre and Rachel Mark, "4 Key Concepts for Families about Proficiency-Based Reporting," Innovation: Education, January 24, 2018, https://tiie.w3.uvm.edu/blog/4-key-concepts-families-proficiency-based-reporting/#.W4BNzxpKg_U.

18. Chris Sturgis, "Harvard and Wellesley and Tufts, Oh My! (And Did I Mention MIT and Babson?)," Competency Works, https://www.competencyworks.org/k-12-higher-education/harvard-and-wellesley-and-tufts-oh-my-and-did-i-mention-mit-and-babson/.

19. Erika Blauth and Sarah Hadjian, *How Selective Colleges and Universities Evaluate Proficiency-Based High School Transcripts: Insights for Students and Schools* (Boston: New England Board of Higher Education, 2016), http://www.nebhe.org/info/pdf/policy/Policy_Spotlight_How_Colleges_Evaluate_PB_HS_Transcripts_April_2017.pdf.

20. Pedro Noguera, Linda Darling-Hammond, and Diane Friedlaender, *Equal Opportunity for Deeper Learning* (Boston: Jobs for the Future, 2015), https://jfforg-prod-prime.s3.amazonaws.com/media/documents/Equal-Opportunity-for-Deeper-Learning-Executive-Summary-092315.pdf.

21. Rachel Mark, "Why Host a Whole-School Exhibition?" Innovation: Education, April 6, 2018, https://tiie.w3.uvm.edu/blog/why-host-a-whole-school-exhibition-of-work/#.W4AfyRpKg_U.

22. Katy Farber, "Culminating Events for Project-Based Learning," Innovation: Education, January 11, 2017, http://tiie.w3.uvm.edu/blog/culminating-events-for-project-based-learning/#.W1PFUi2ZPOQ.

23. Rachel Mark, "Why Host a Whole-School Exhibition?"

24. Rachel Mark, "When Students Share Their Work, It Deepens the Learning," Innovation: Education, April 20, 2018, http://tiie.w3.uvm.edu/blog/deeper-learning-exhibition/#.W1S2ZC2ZPOR.

25. Rachel Mark, "Why Host a Whole-School Exhibition?"

Chapter 8

1. Ken Bergstrom, "Attending to the Rhythm of Early Adolescence: Five Basics of Personal Efficacy," in *Living and Learning in the Middle Grades: The Dance Continues*, ed. Ken Bergstrom, Penny Bishop, and Judy Carr (Westerville: National Middle School Association, 2001), 7–15.

2. Susan Combee, "The Relationship Between Administrative Support and Teacher Efficacy in the Professional Life of Special Education Teachers" (PhD diss., Virginia Commonwealth University, 2014), https://scholarscompass.vcu.edu/cgi/viewcontent.cgi?article=4474&context=etd; Lu Minghui, Hao Lei, Chen Xiaomeng, and Miloň Potměšilc, "Teacher Efficacy, Work Engagement, and Social Support Among Chinese Special Education School Teachers," *Frontiers in Psychology*, 9 (2018): 1–8, https://doi.org/10.3389/fpsyg.2018.00648.

3. Madiha Shah, "The Importance and Benefits of Teacher Collegiality in Schools – A Literature Review," *Procedia - Social and Behavioral Sciences* 46 (2012): 1242-1246, https://doi.org/10.1016/j.sbspro.2012.05.282.

4. Donald Hackmann, James Kenworthy, and Sharon Nibbelink, "Student Empowerment through Student-Led Conferences," *Middle School Journal* 30, no. 1 (1998): 35–39, https://doi.org/10.1080/00940771.1998.11494561; National Middle School Association, *This We Believe: Keys to Educating Young Adolescents* (Westerville: National Middle School Association, 2010); Epstein, J. (2007). Connections count. Improving family and community involvement in secondary schools. *Principal Leadership, 8*(2), 16–22.

5. Donald G. Hackman, "Student-Led Conferences at the Middle Level," *ERIC Digest*, EDO-PS-97-19 (1997), 1, https://www.researchgate.net/profile/Donald_Hackmann/publication/237349516_Student-Led_Conferences_at_the_Middle_Level/links/5441670f0cf2e6f0c0f61d09/Student-Led-Conferences-at-the-Middle-Level.pdf.

6. Cheri Tuinstra and Diana Hiatt-Michael, "Student-Led Parent Conferences in Middle Schools," *School Community Journal* 14, no. 1 (2004): 59–80.

7. Tuinstra and Hiatt-Michael, "Student-Led Parent Conferences in Middle Schools."

8. Donald G. Hackman, "Student-Led Conferences at the Middle Level"; Lynn Le Countryman and Merrie Schroeder, "When Students Lead Parent-Teacher Conferences," *Educational Leadership* 53, no. 7 (1996): 64–68.

9. John A. Borba and Cherise M. Olvera, "Student-Led Parent-Teacher Conferences" *The Clearing House* 74, no. 6 (2001): 333–336, https://www.jstor.org/stable/30192115.

10. Audrey Homan, "Student-Led Conferences and Engagement in PLPs," Innovation: Education, February 10, 2016, http://tiie.w3.uvm.edu/blog/student-led-conferences-and-engagement-in-plps/#.Wud89CPMzOR.

11. Homan, "Student-Led Conferences and Engagement."

12. Tuinstra and Hiatt-Michael, "Student-Led Parent Conferences in Middle Schools."

13. Homan, "Student-Led Conferences and Engagement in PLPs."

14. Homan, "Student-Led Conferences and Engagement in PLPs."

15. Homan, "Student-Led Conferences and Engagement in PLPs."

16. Jessica DeMink-Carthew, Mark W. Olofson, Life LeGeros, Steven Netcoh, and Susan Hennessey, "An Analysis of Approaches to Goal-Setting in Middle Grades Personalized Learning Environments," *Research in Middle Level Education Online* 40, no. 10 (2017): 1–11, https://doi.org/10.1080/19404476.2017.1392689.

17. Life LeGeros, "The Rise of the Project-Based PLP," Innovation: Education, January 12, 2018, https://tiie.w3.uvm.edu/blog/the-rise-of-the-project-based-plp/#.W4LpVJNKjq0.

18. Phillip Schlechty, *Shaking up the Schoolhouse: How to Support and Sustain Educational Innovation* (San Francisco: Jossey-Bass, 2001), 9.

19. "What is WOOP?" Character LAB, https://www.characterlab.org/woop/; George T. Doran, "There's a S.M.A.R.T. Way to Write Management's Goals and Objectives," *Management Review* 70, no. 11 (1981): 35–36.

20. Life LeGeros, "What Makes for Good Goal-Setting in a PLP?" Innovation: Education, November 18, 2015, http://tiie.w3.uvm.edu/blog/what-makes-for-good-goal-setting-in-a-plp/#.W1e_QC2ZPOS.

21. LeGeros, "The Rise of the Project-Based PLP."

22. LeGeros, "The Rise of the Project-Based PLP."

23. "Growth and Reflection," PLP Pathways, https://sites.google.com/site/plppathways/growth-and-reflection#TOC-Setting-Goals.

24. LeGeros, "What makes for good goal-setting in a PLP?"

25. You can download a digital version of the planning table from our website at www.learninginthemiddle.org.

Chapter 9

1. Douglas B. Reeves, *Transforming Professional Development into Student Results* (Alexandria: ASCD, 2010).

2. Kevin Hunt, "Our Work is Worth It!" PLP Pathways Blog, February 10, 2018, http://plppathways.blogspot.com/2018/02/our-work-is-worth-it.html.

3. PLP Pathways, http://www.plppathways.org.

4. VT Flexible Pathways Collaborative, http://collaborativeteam.blogspot.com/.

5. Richard Sagor, *Guiding School Improvement with Action Research* (Alexandria: Association for Supervision and Curriculum Development, 2000).

6. Life LeGeros, "Phys Ed 2.0: More Learning, Less Suffering," Innovation: Education, May 30, 2018, https://tiie.w3.uvm.edu/blog/personalizing-p-e/#.W4BmlxpKg_U.

7. Jana Fabri-Sbardellati, "Oh, the Challenges! Oh, the Possibilities!" VT Flexible Pathways Collaborative, April 19, 2018, http://collaborativeteam.blogspot.com/2018/04/oh-challenges-oh-possibilities.html.

8. Susan Hennessey, "(Re)Designing PLPs with Students," Innovation: Education, September 16, 2016, http://tiie.w3.uvm.edu/blog/designing-plps-with-students/#.W0Dw8COZPOQ.

9. Roger D. Goddard, Wayne K. Hoy, and Anita Woolfolk Hoy, "Collective Efficacy Beliefs: Theoretical Developments, Empirical Evidence, and Future Directions," *Educational Researcher* 33, no. 3 (2004): 4, http://journals.sagepub.com/doi/10.3102/0013189X033003003.

10. Albert Bandura, "Perceived Self-Efficacy in Cognitive Development and Functioning," *Educational Psychologist* 28, no. 2 (1993), 117–148, https://doi.org/10.1207/s15326985ep2802_3.

11. Curt M. Adams and Patrick B. Forsyth, "Proximate Sources of Collective Teacher Efficacy," *Journal of Educational Administration* 44, no. 6 (2006): 625–642.

12. Jenni Donohoo, John Hattie, and Rachel Eells, "The Power of Collective Efficacy," *Educational Leadership* 75, no. 6 (2018): 40–44, http://www.ascd.org/publications/educational-leadership/mar18/vol75/num06/The-Power-of-Collective-Efficacy.aspx.

13. Jennifer Donohoo, "Collective Efficacy: Together We Can Make a Difference," CORWINconnect, April 7, 2016, http://corwin-connect.com/2016/04/collective-efficacy-together-we-can-make-a-difference/.

14. Fabri-Sbardellati, "Oh the Challenges! Oh the Possibilities!"

ABOUT THE AUTHORS

PENNY A. BISHOP is Professor of Middle Level Education at the University of Vermont, where she conducts research on schooling for young adolescents and teaches future middle grades educators. She is co-author of several books and more than fifty articles on effective middle grades practice. Dr. Bishop has served as principal investigator on numerous grants, including as founding director of the Tarrant Institute for Innovative Education, bringing over $13 million dollars to Vermont schools to improve the learning and lives of middle grades students. A former middle school teacher, Dr. Bishop has served as chair of the American Educational Research Association's special interest group on Middle Level Education Research; as chair of the Association for Middle Level Education's Research Advisory Board; and as a Sir Ian Axford Public Policy Fellow to the New Zealand Ministry of Education, providing research on schooling policies for young adolescents in that country. She is the recipient of The John H. Lounsbury Award for Distinguished Achievement in Middle Level Education, the highest award given by the AMLE.

JOHN M. DOWNES is director of the Tarrant Institute for Innovative Education at the University of Vermont. Since joining UVM, Dr. Downes has led the development the Institute's model of collaborative school change and teacher-directed professional development, which has now served middle grades faculties in more than sixty schools. He has led several grants and evaluations, published more than twenty articles and chapters, and delivered dozens of state and national presentations on topics including technology integration, young adolescents' post-secondary aspirations, teachers and students partnering in school change and professional development, and their experiences as they shift to personalized learning environments. His fifteen years at the university builds upon ten years in a middle school helping its teachers and leaders design and implement more engaging learning for students with technology, curriculum integration, teaming, and collaborative teacher learning.

KATY FARBER is professional development coordinator at the University of Vermont's Tarrant Institute for Innovative Education. She currently conducts research about adolescent education and partners with schools to help them personalize learning, engage students, and participate in action research. She is the author of three books about education: *Why Great Teachers Quit and How We Can Stop the Exodus* (Corwin Press, 2010); *Change the World with Service Learning* (Rowman & Littlefield, 2011); *Real and Relevant: A Guide to Service and Project-Based Learning*, 2nd edition (Rowman & Littlefield, 2017); and several chapters and articles. Recent publications can be found in *Current Issues in Middle Level Education; Exploring the Impact of the Dissertation in Practice*; and *The Handbook of Research in Middle Level Education*. Dr. Farber was a classroom teacher for seventeen years and regularly presents at state and national conferences.

INDEX